Alice & Zoroku 3

story & art by TETSUYA IMAI

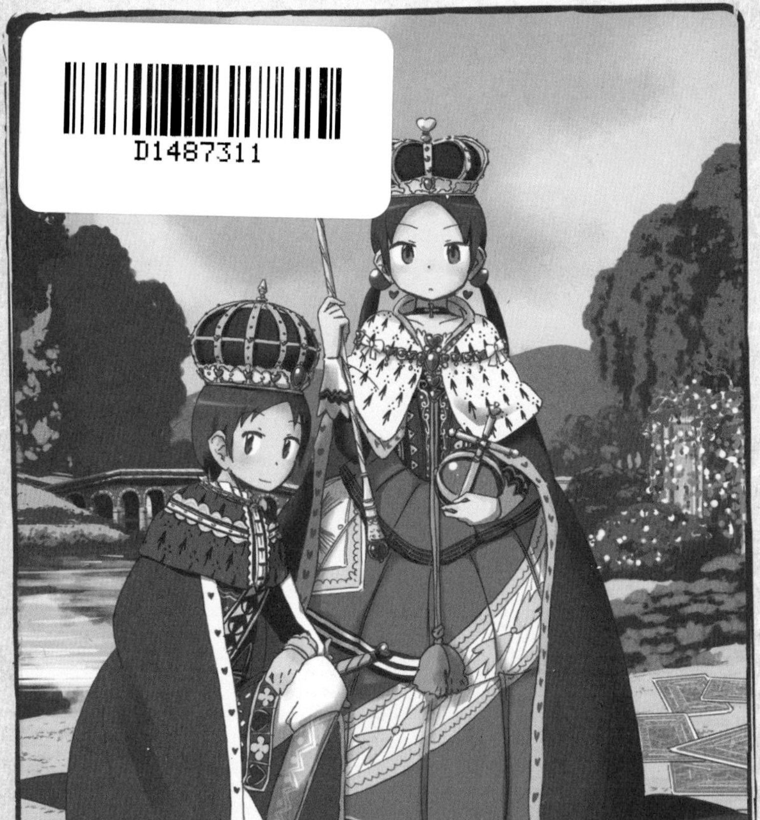

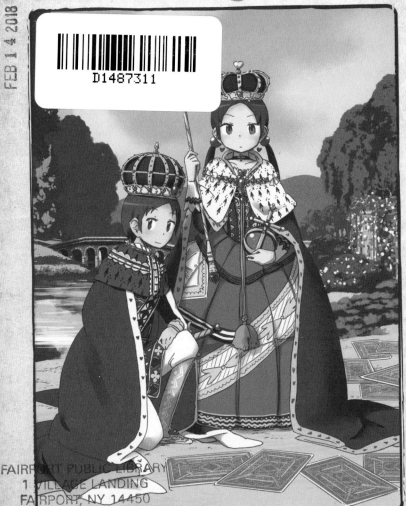

First came ten soldiers carrying clubs; these were all shaped like the three gardeners, oblong and flat, with their hands and feet at the corners: next the ten courtiers; these were ornamented all over with diamonds, and walked two and two, as the soldiers did. After these came the royal children; there were ten of them, and the little dears came jumping merrily along hand in hand, in couples: they were all ornamented with hearts. Next came the guests, mostly Kings and Queens, and among them Alice recognized the White Rabbit: it was talking in a hurried nervous manner, smiling at everything that was said, and went by without noticing her. Then followed the Knave of Hearts, carrying the King's crown on a crimson velvet cushion; and, last of all this grand procession, came the King and Queen of Hearts.

Alice's Adventures in Wonderland,
Chapter 8   —Lewis Carroll

The queen turned crimson

with fury, and, after glaring at

her for a moment like a wild

beast, began screaming,

"Off with her head!"

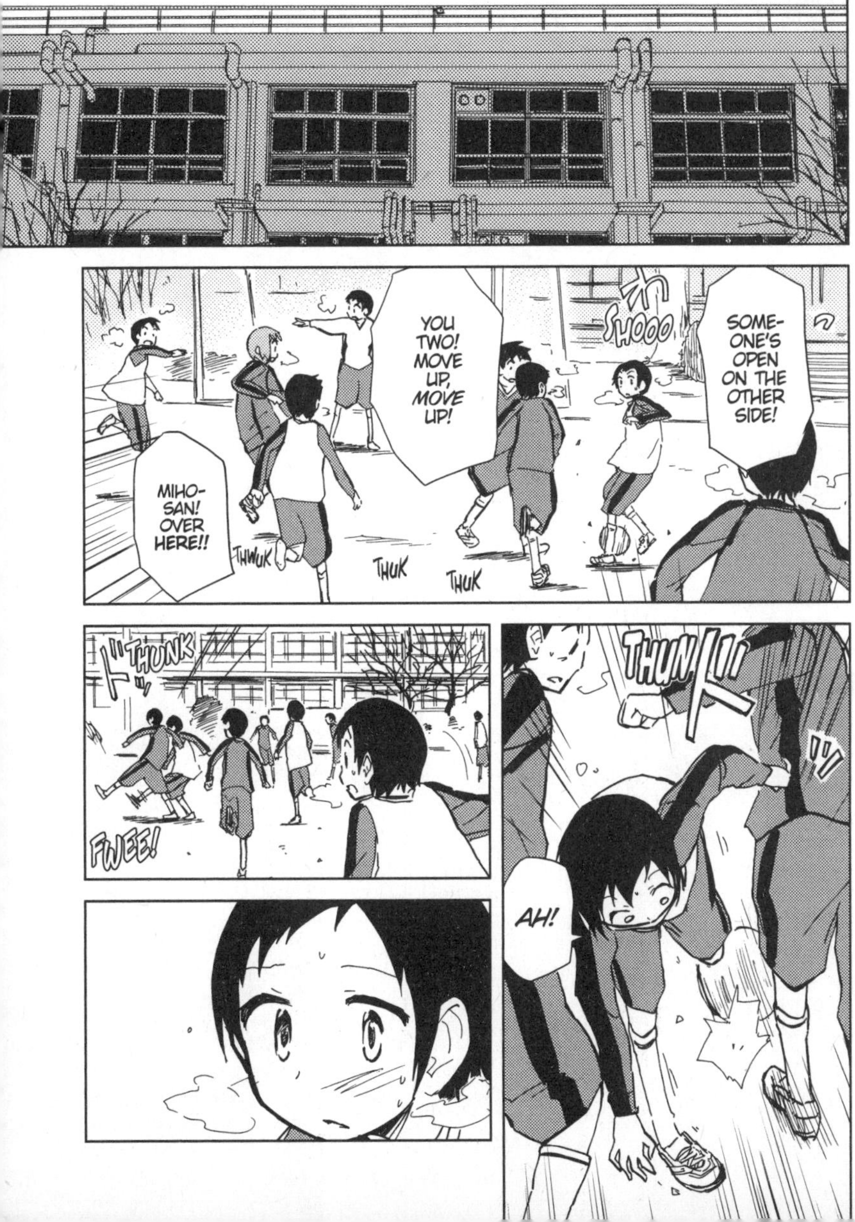
SOME-ONE'S OPEN ON THE OTHER SIDE!
SHOOO
YOU TWO! MOVE UP, MOVE UP!
MIHO-SAN! OVER HERE!!
THUK
THUK
THWUK
THUNK!!
AH!
THUNK
FWEE!

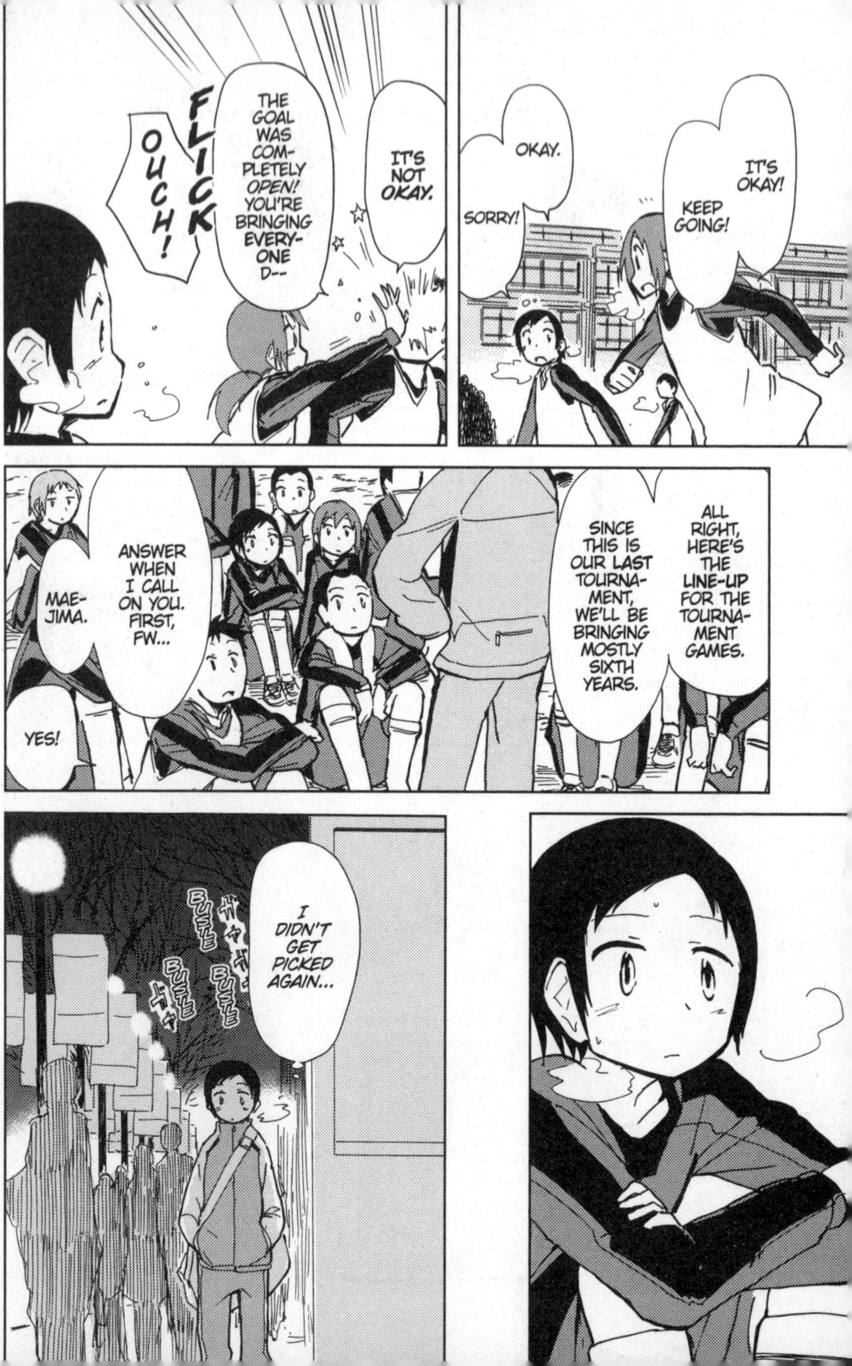
IT'S OKAY!
KEEP GOING!
OKAY.
SORRY!
IT'S NOT OKAY.
THE GOAL WAS COMPLETELY OPEN! YOU'RE BRINGING EVERYONE D--
FLICK
OUCH!
ALL RIGHT, HERE'S THE LINE-UP FOR THE TOURNAMENT GAMES.
SINCE THIS IS OUR LAST TOURNAMENT, WE'LL BE BRINGING MOSTLY SIXTH YEARS.
ANSWER WHEN I CALL ON YOU. FIRST, FW...
MAEJIMA.
YES!
I DIDN'T GET PICKED AGAIN...
BUSTLE
BUSTLE
BUSTLE

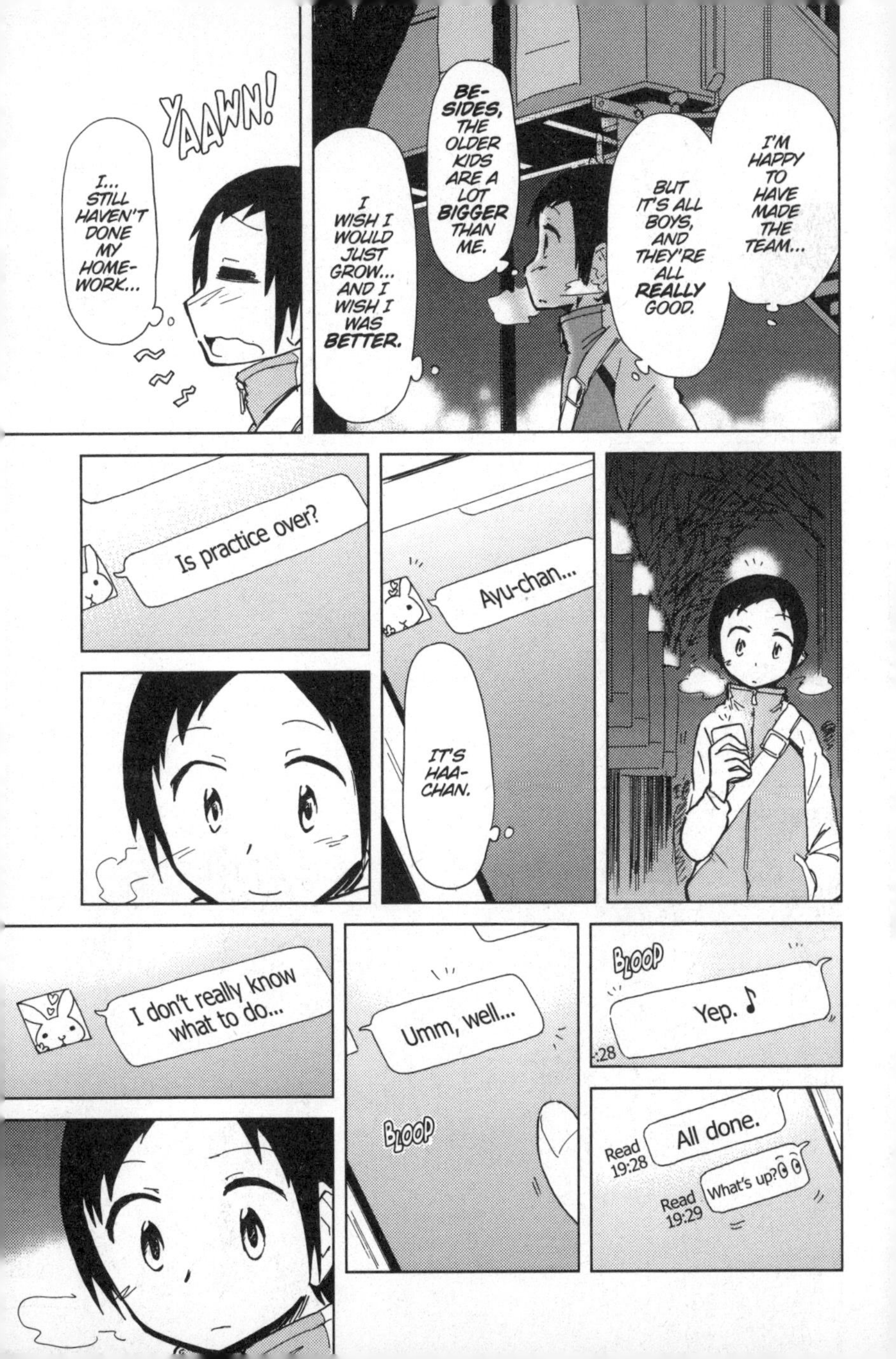

I'M HAPPY TO HAVE MADE THE TEAM...
BUT IT'S ALL BOYS, AND THEY'RE ALL REALLY GOOD.
BESIDES, THE OLDER KIDS ARE A LOT BIGGER THAN ME.
I WISH I WOULD JUST GROW... AND I WISH I WAS BETTER.
YAAWN!
I... STILL HAVEN'T DONE MY HOMEWORK...
Ayu-chan...
IT'S HAA-CHAN.
Is practice over?
BLOOP
Yep. ♪
:28
Read 19:28
All done.
Read 19:29
What's up?
Umm, well...
BLOOP
I don't really know what to do...

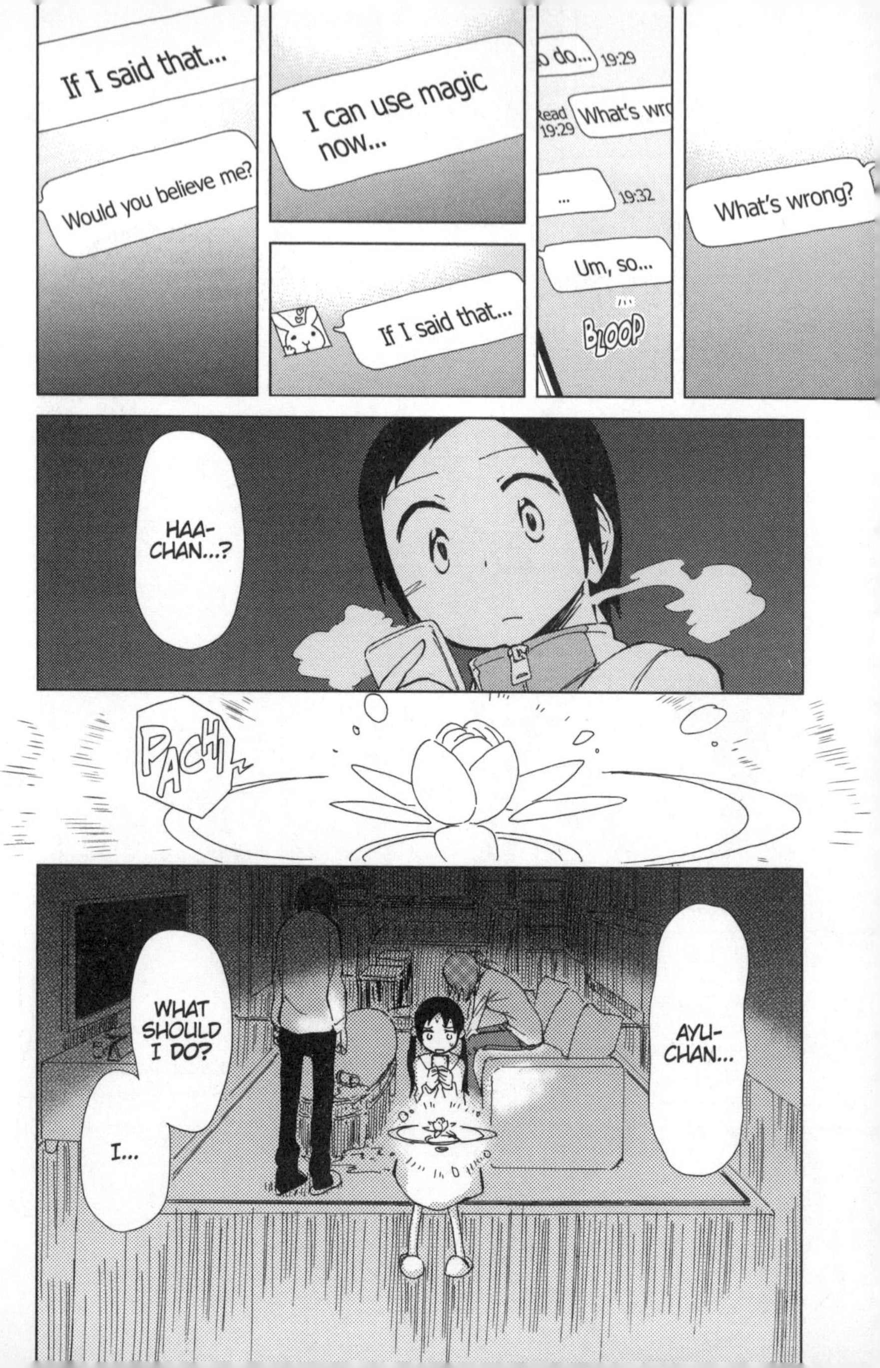

What's wrong?
o do... 19:29
Read 19:29
What's wro
... 19:32
Um, so...
BLOOP
I can use magic now...
If I said that...
If I said that...
Would you believe me?
HAA-CHAN...?
PACHI
AYU-CHAN...
WHAT SHOULD I DO?
I...

Chapter.9
The Queen of Boredom

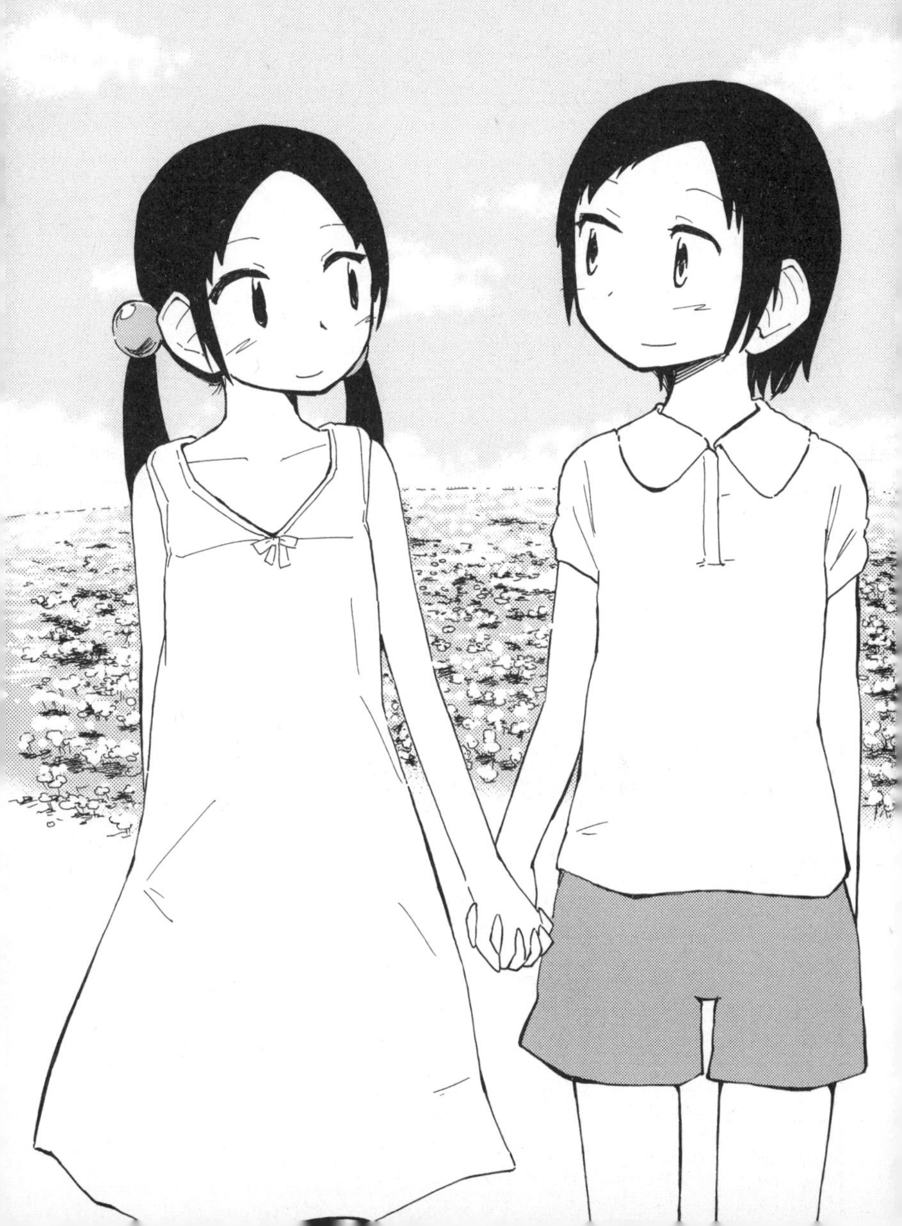

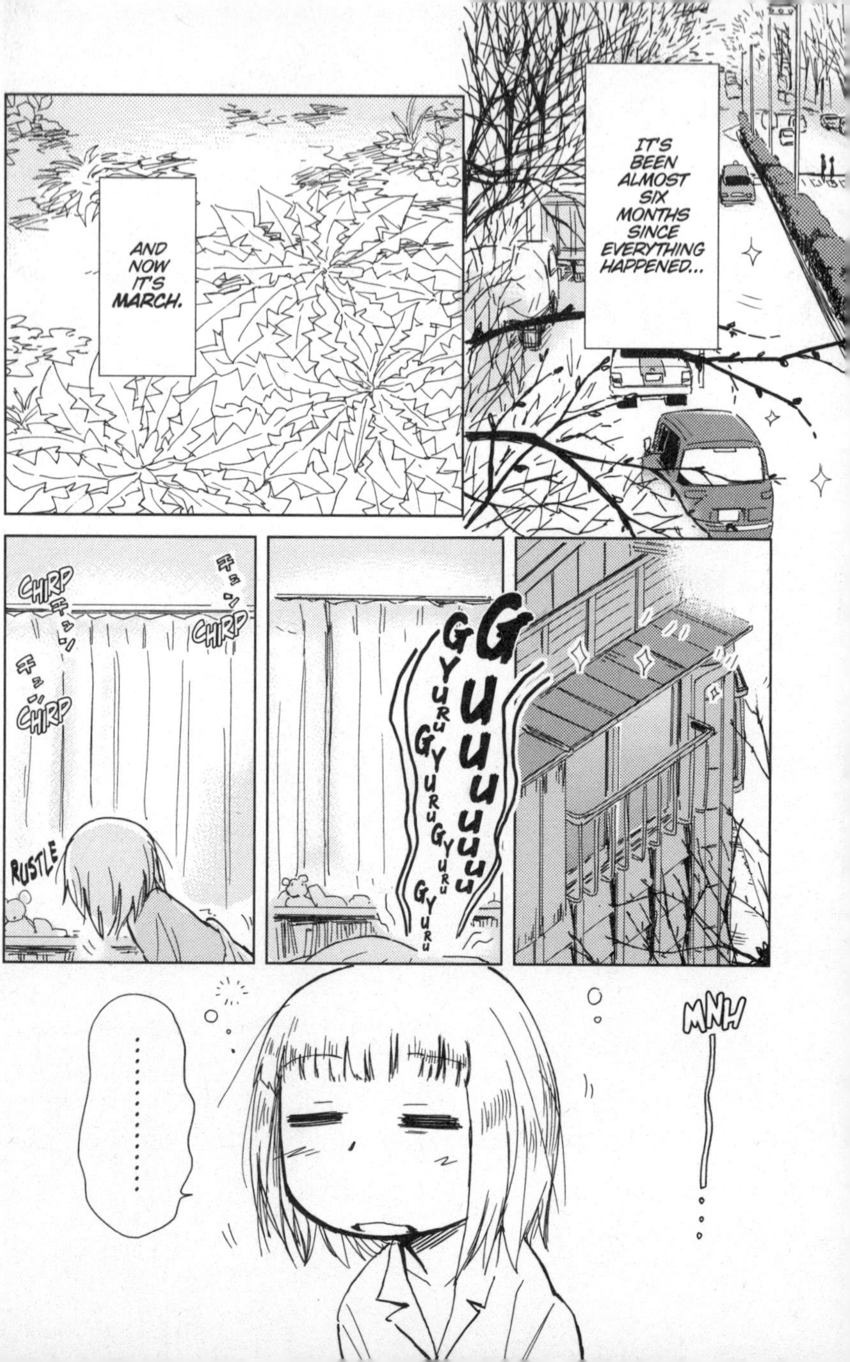
IT'S BEEN ALMOST SIX MONTHS SINCE EVERYTHING HAPPENED...
AND NOW IT'S MARCH.
GGUUUUUUU
GYURU GYURU GYURU GYURU
CHIRP
CHIRP
CHIRP
RUSTLE
MNH—...
......

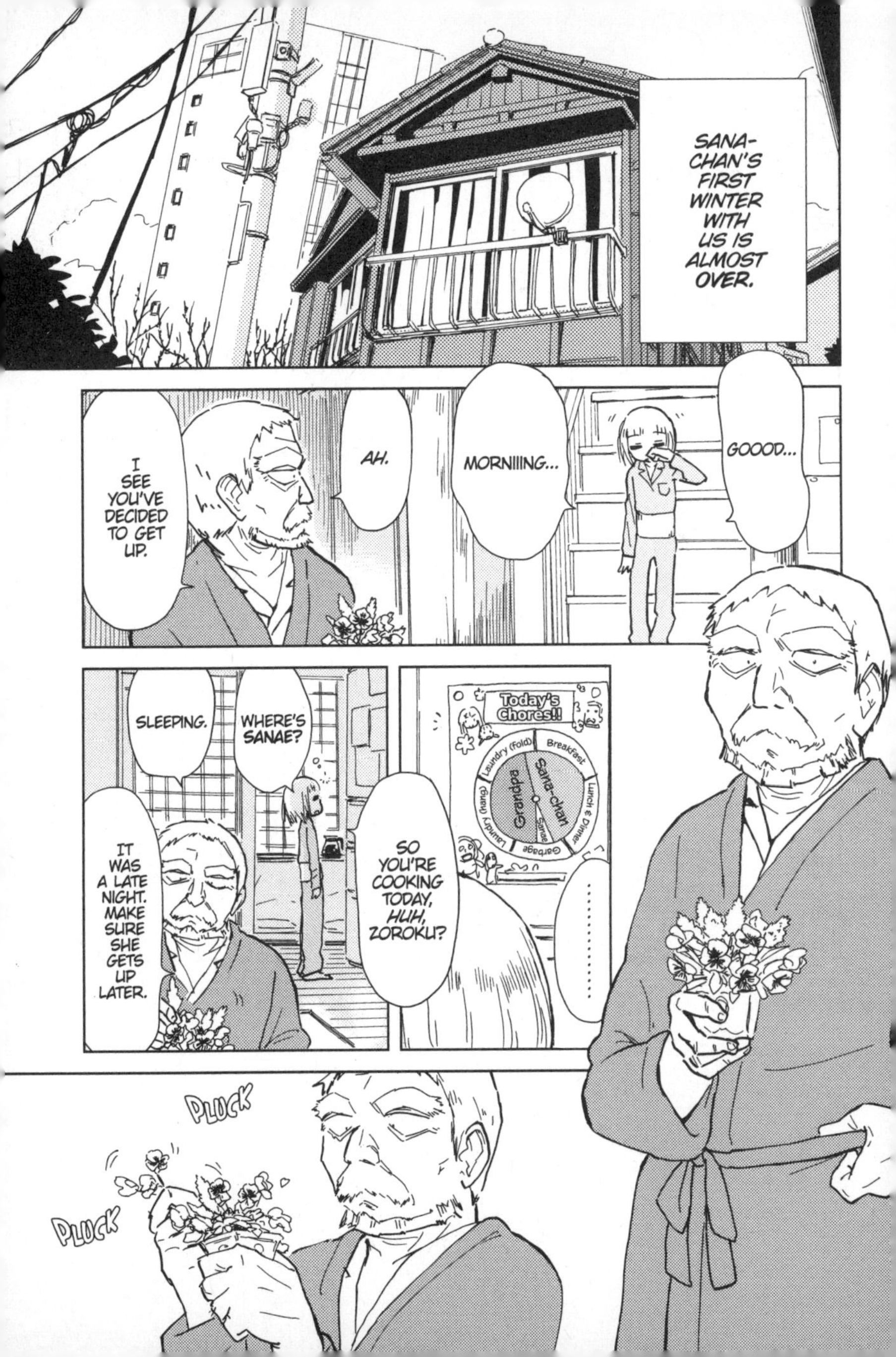
SANA-CHAN'S FIRST WINTER WITH US IS ALMOST OVER.
GOOOD...
MORNIIING...
AH.
I SEE YOU'VE DECIDED TO GET UP.
Today's Chores!!
Breakfast
Lunch & Dinner
Garbage
Laundry (hang)
Laundry (fold)
Sana-chan
Sanae
Grandpa
......
SO YOU'RE COOKING TODAY, HUH, ZOROKU?
WHERE'S SANAE?
SLEEPING.
IT WAS A LATE NIGHT. MAKE SURE SHE GETS UP LATER.
PLUCK
PLUCK

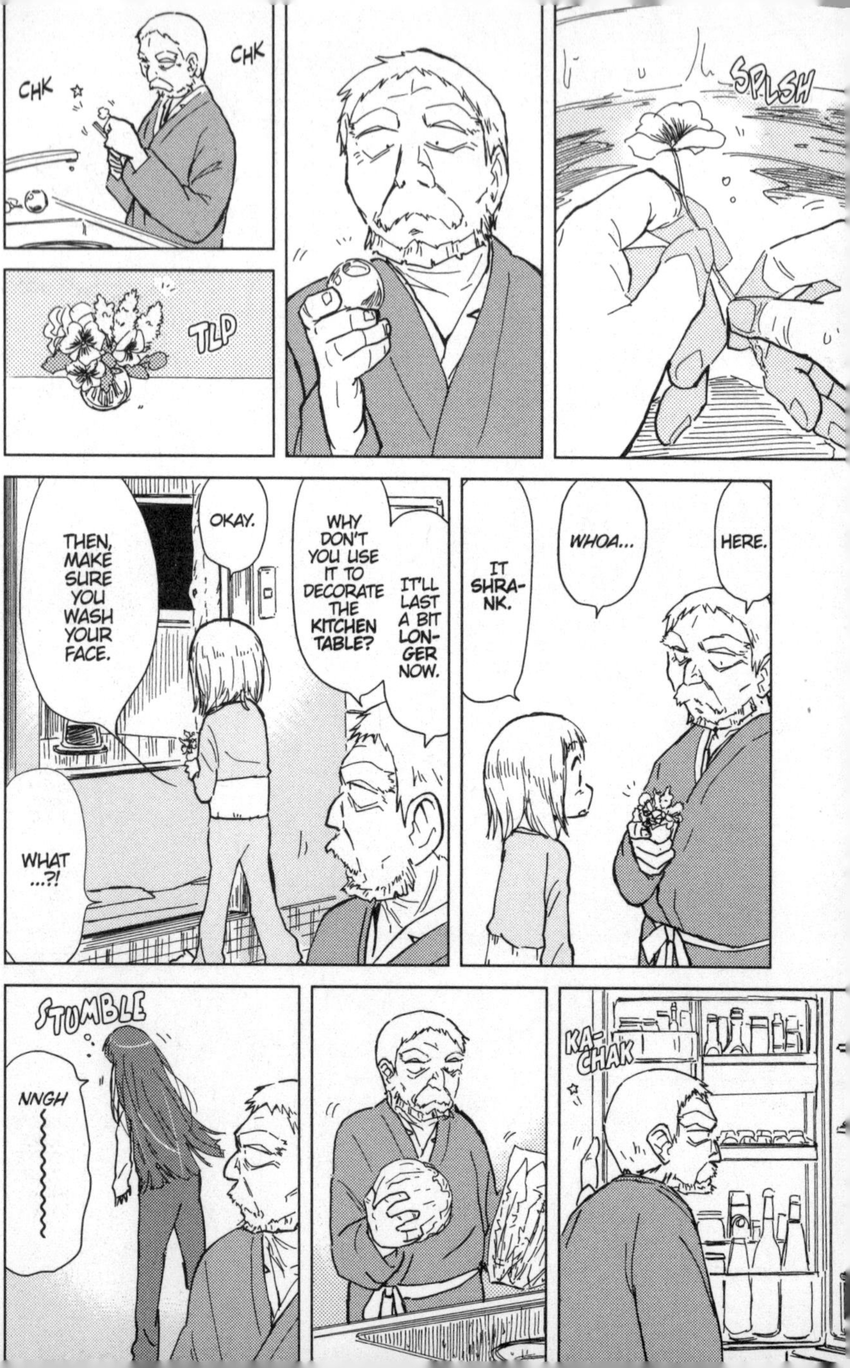
SPLSH
CHK
CHK
TLP
HERE.
WHOA...
IT SHRA-NK.
IT'LL LAST A BIT LONGER NOW.
WHY DON'T YOU USE IT TO DECORATE THE KITCHEN TABLE?
OKAY.
THEN, MAKE SURE YOU WASH YOUR FACE.
WHAT ...?!
KA-CHAK
STUMBLE
NNGH

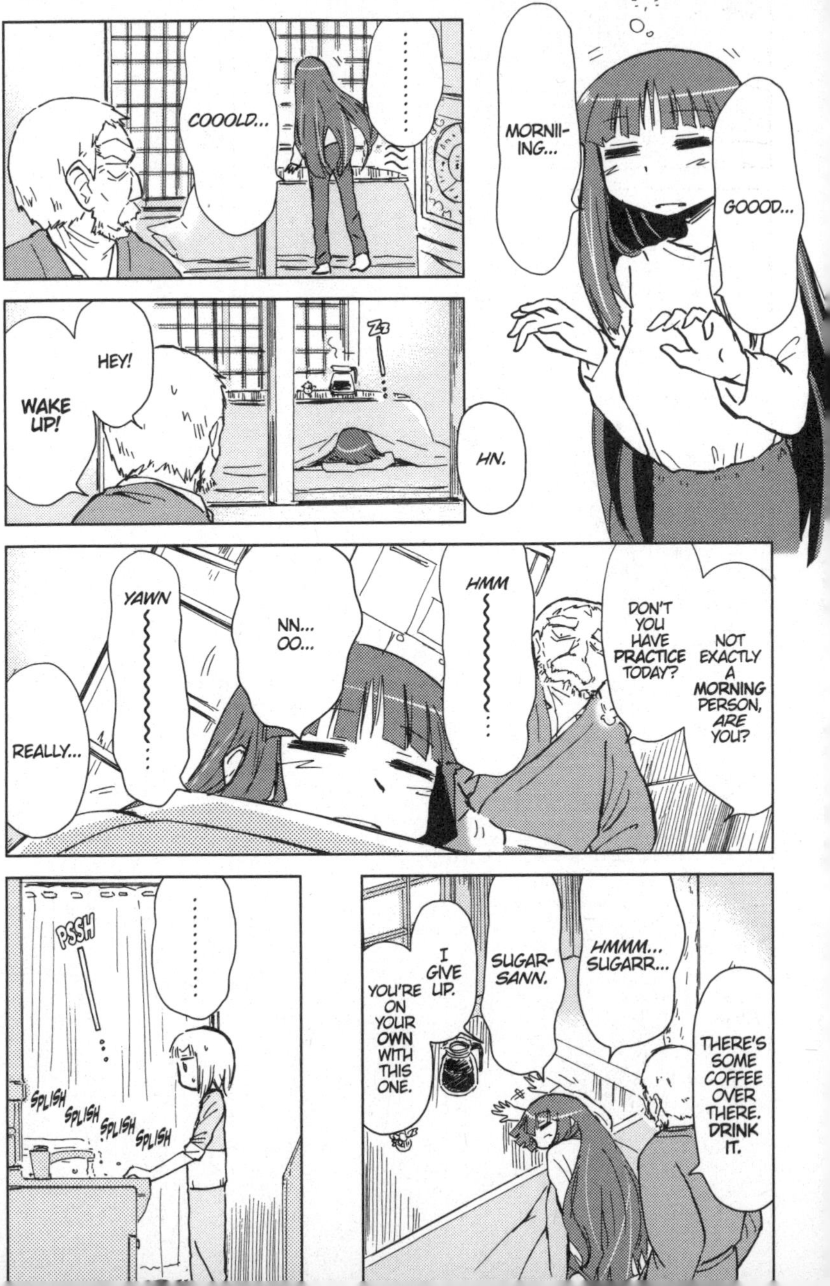
GOOOD...
MORNIIING...
HN.
......
COOOLD...
HEY!
WAKE UP!
NOT EXACTLY A MORNING PERSON, ARE YOU?
DON'T YOU HAVE PRACTICE TODAY?
HMM
NN... OO...
YAWN
REALLY...
THERE'S SOME COFFEE OVER THERE. DRINK IT.
HMMM... SUGARR...
SUGAR-SANN.
I GIVE UP.
YOU'RE ON YOUR OWN WITH THIS ONE.
......
PSSH
SPLISH SPLISH SPLISH SPLISH

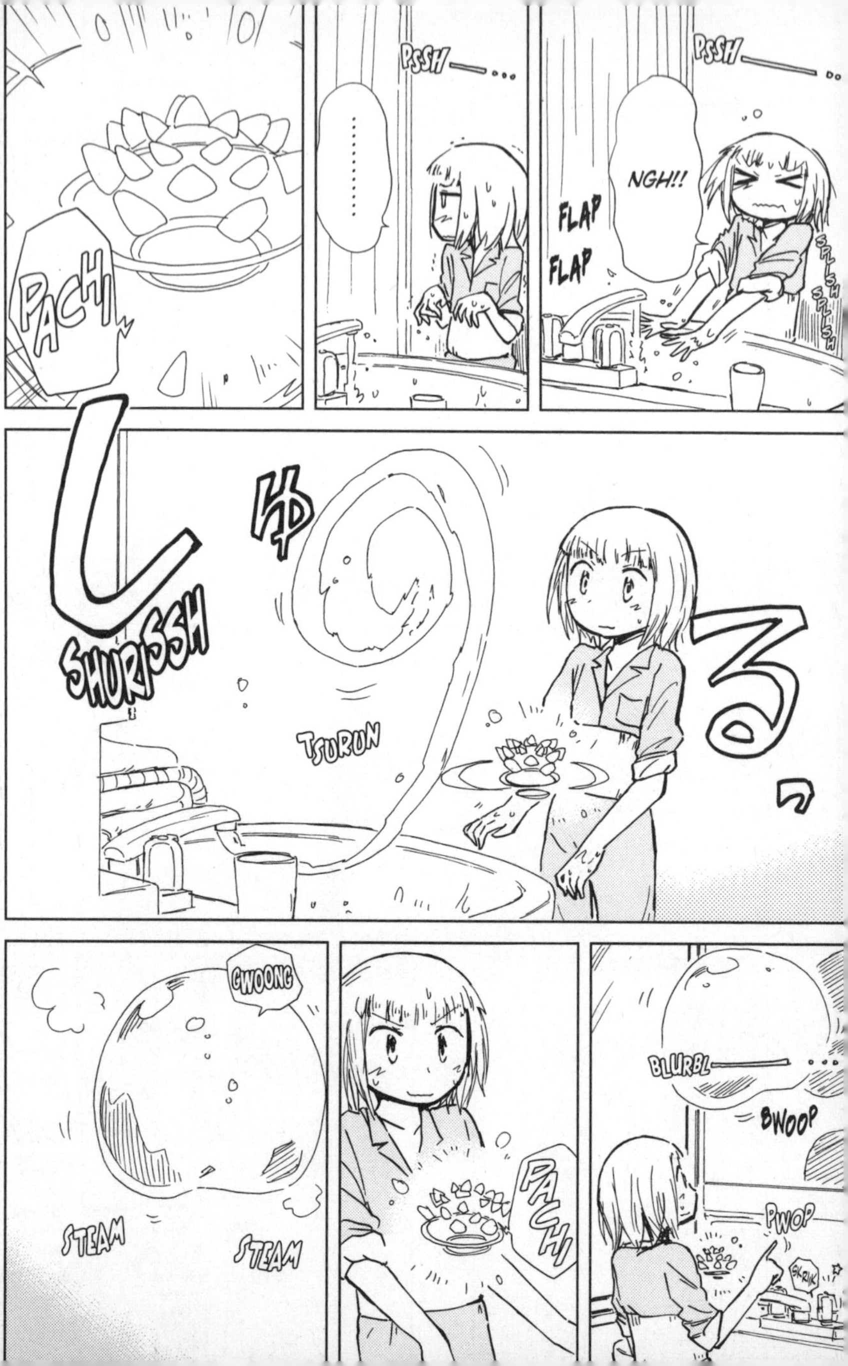
PSSH——...
NGH!!
FLAP
FLAP
SPLISH
SPLISH
PSSH——...
……
PACHI
しゅるっ
SHURISSH
TSURUN
BLURBL——...
BWOOP
PWOP
SKRIK
PACHI
GWOONG
STEAM
STEAM

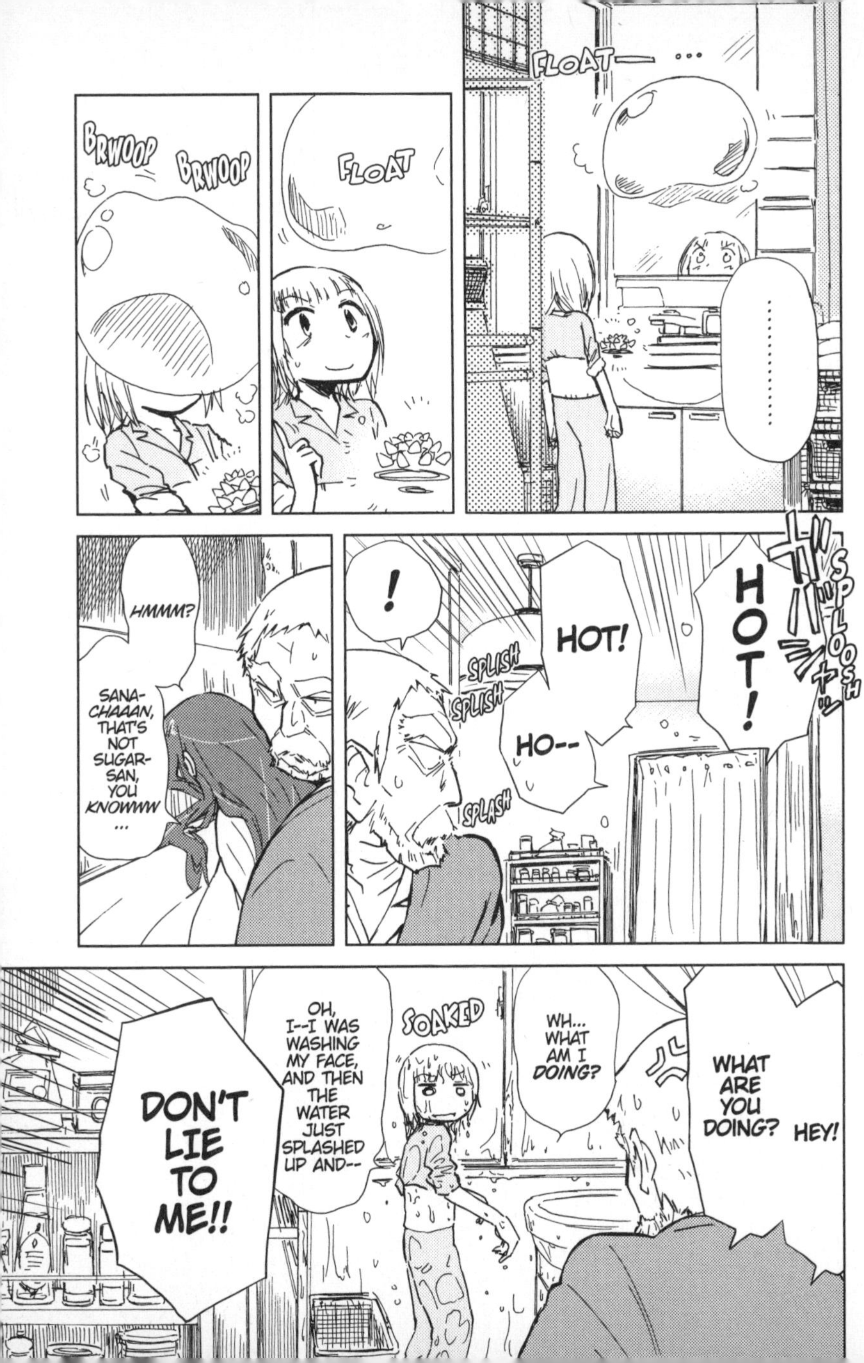
FLOAT—
...
......
FLOAT
BRWOOP
BRWOOP
SPLOOSH
HOT!
HOT!
!
SPLISH
SPLISH
HO--
SPLASH
HMMM?
SANA-CHAAAN, THAT'S NOT SUGAR-SAN, YOU KNOWWW...
HEY!
WHAT ARE YOU DOING?
WH... WHAT AM I DOING?
SOAKED
OH, I--I WAS WASHING MY FACE, AND THEN THE WATER JUST SPLASHED UP AND--
DON'T LIE TO ME!!

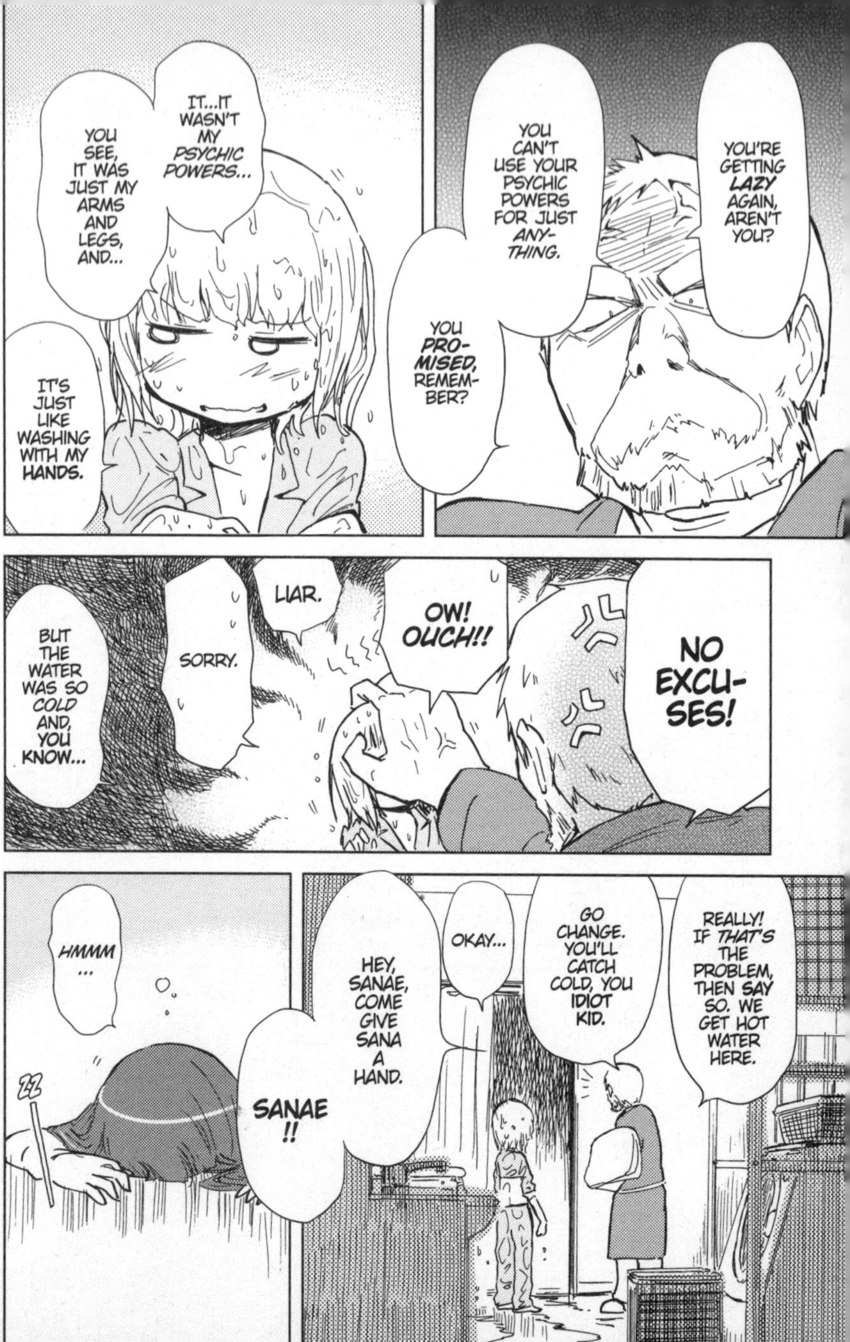
YOU'RE GETTING LAZY AGAIN, AREN'T YOU?
YOU CAN'T USE YOUR PSYCHIC POWERS FOR JUST ANYTHING.
YOU PROMISED, REMEMBER?
IT...IT WASN'T MY PSYCHIC POWERS...
YOU SEE, IT WAS JUST MY ARMS AND LEGS, AND...
IT'S JUST LIKE WASHING WITH MY HANDS.
NO EXCUSES!
OW! OUCH!!
LIAR.
SORRY.
BUT THE WATER WAS SO COLD AND, YOU KNOW...
REALLY! IF THAT'S THE PROBLEM, THEN SAY SO. WE GET HOT WATER HERE.
GO CHANGE. YOU'LL CATCH COLD, YOU IDIOT KID.
OKAY...
HEY, SANAE, COME GIVE SANA A HAND.
SANAE!!
HMMM...
ZZ

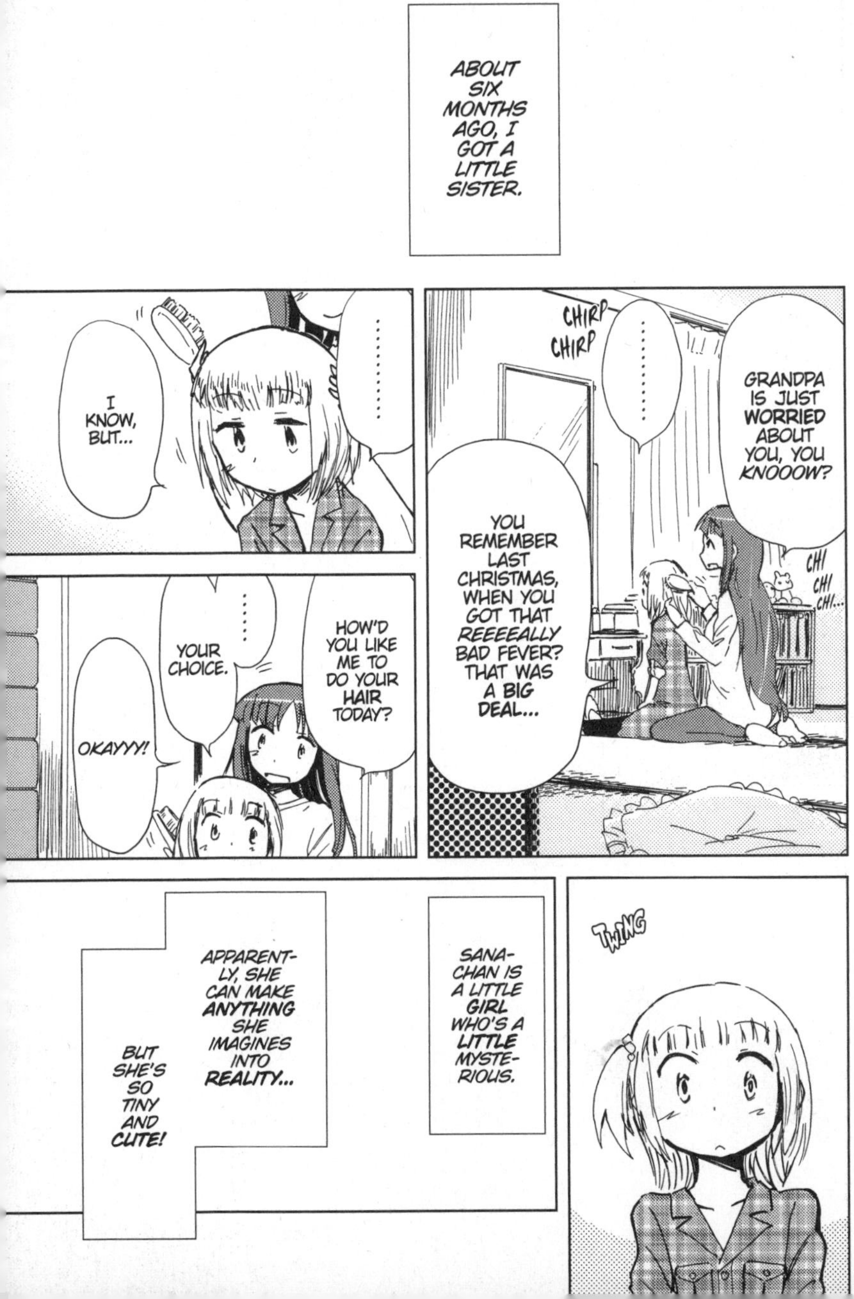
ABOUT SIX MONTHS AGO, I GOT A LITTLE SISTER.
GRANDPA IS JUST WORRIED ABOUT YOU, YOU KNOOOW?
......
CHIRP CHIRP
CHI CHI CHI...
YOU REMEMBER LAST CHRISTMAS, WHEN YOU GOT THAT REEEEALLY BAD FEVER? THAT WAS A BIG DEAL...
......
I KNOW, BUT...
HOW'D YOU LIKE ME TO DO YOUR HAIR TODAY?
......
YOUR CHOICE.
OKAYYY!
TWING
SANA-CHAN IS A LITTLE GIRL WHO'S A LITTLE MYSTERIOUS.
APPARENTLY, SHE CAN MAKE ANYTHING SHE IMAGINES INTO REALITY...
BUT SHE'S SO TINY AND CUTE!

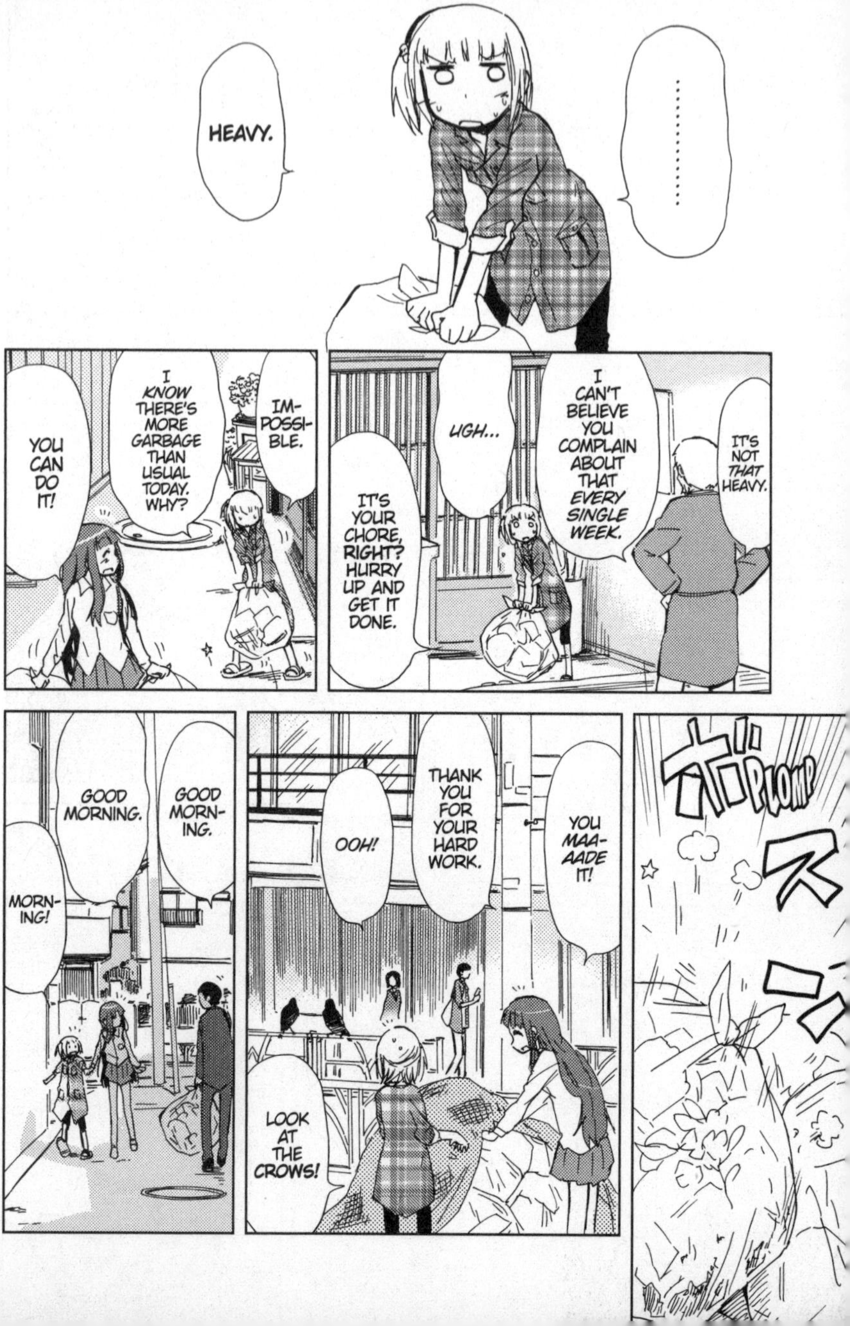

......
HEAVY.
IT'S NOT THAT HEAVY.
I CAN'T BELIEVE YOU COMPLAIN ABOUT THAT EVERY SINGLE WEEK.
UGH...
IT'S YOUR CHORE, RIGHT? HURRY UP AND GET IT DONE.
IM-POSSI-BLE.
I KNOW THERE'S MORE GARBAGE THAN USUAL TODAY. WHY?
YOU CAN DO IT!
PLOMP
YOU MAAAADE IT!
THANK YOU FOR YOUR HARD WORK.
OOH!
LOOK AT THE CROWS!
GOOD MORN-ING.
GOOD MORNING.
MORN-ING!

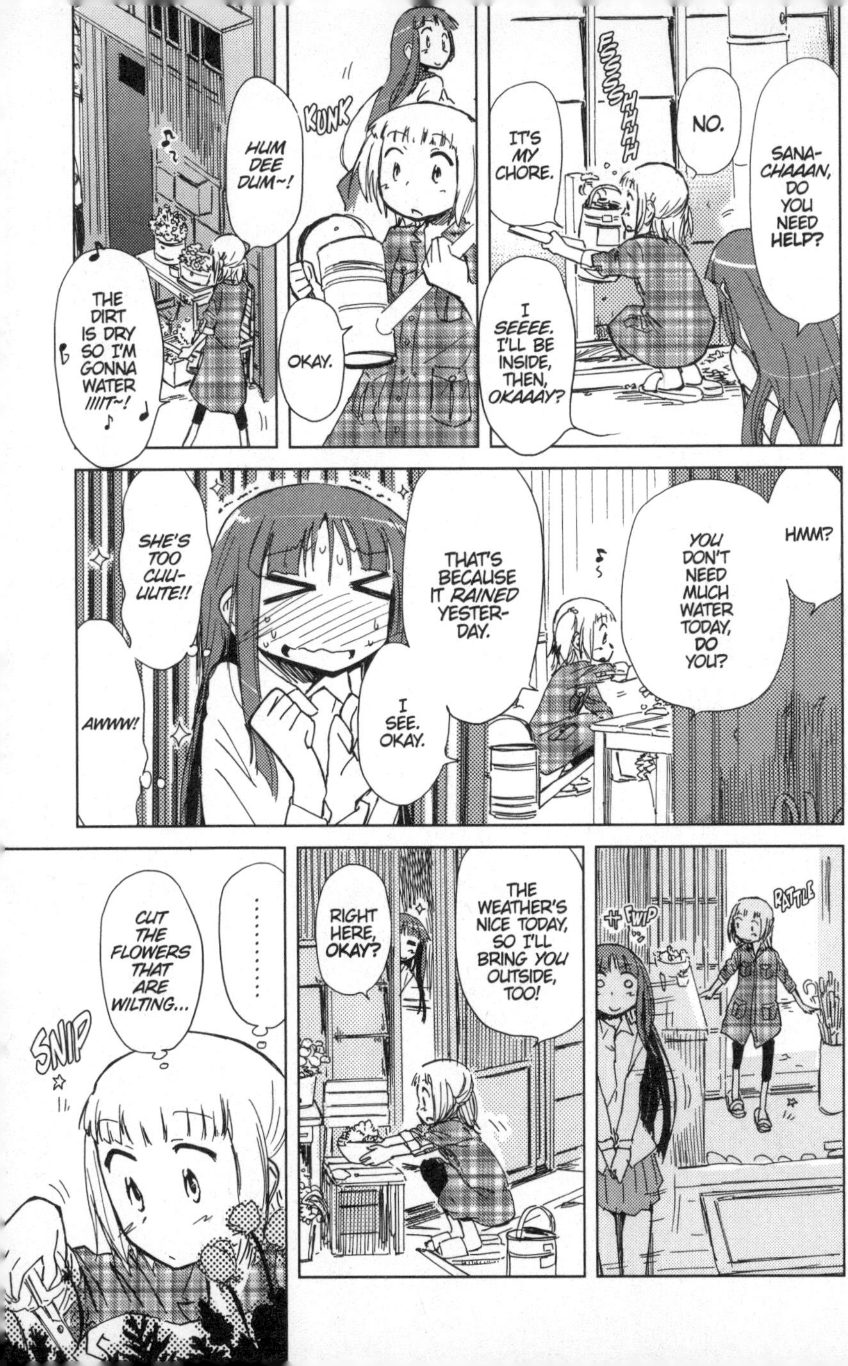
SANA-CHAAAN, DO YOU NEED HELP?
NO.
FSSSHHHH
IT'S MY CHORE.
I SEEEE. I'LL BE INSIDE, THEN, OKAAAY?
KUNK
OKAY.
HUM DEE DUM~!
THE DIRT IS DRY SO I'M GONNA WATER IIIIIT~!
HMM?
YOU DON'T NEED MUCH WATER TODAY, DO YOU?
THAT'S BECAUSE IT RAINED YESTER-DAY.
I SEE. OKAY.
SHE'S TOO CUUUUTE!!
AWWW!
RATTLE
FWIP
THE WEATHER'S NICE TODAY, SO I'LL BRING YOU OUTSIDE, TOO!
RIGHT HERE, OKAY?
......
CUT THE FLOWERS THAT ARE WILTING...
SNIP

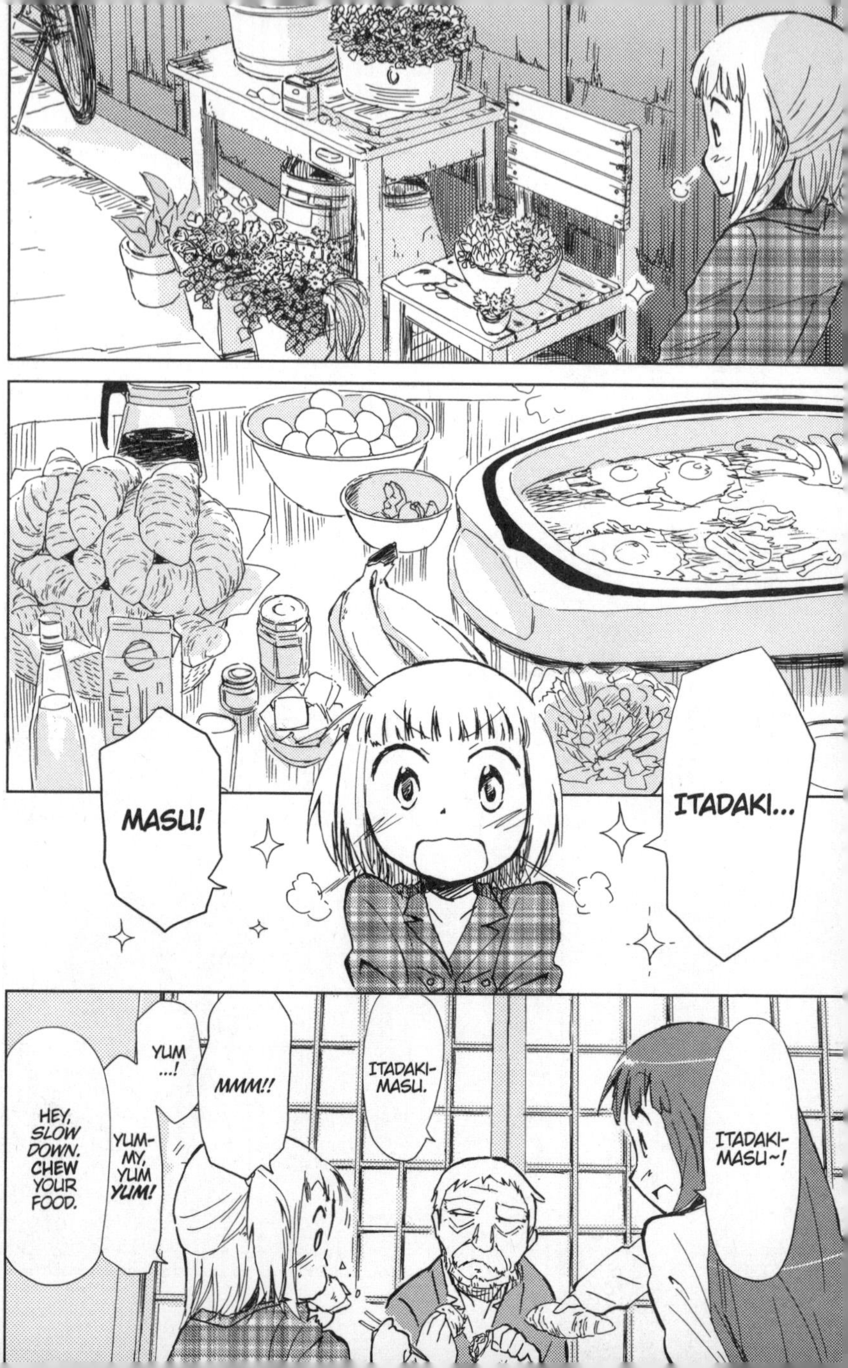
ITADAKI...
MASU!
ITADAKI-MASU~!
ITADAKI-MASU.
MMM!!
YUM ...!
YUM-MY, YUM YUM!
HEY, SLOW DOWN. CHEW YOUR FOOD.

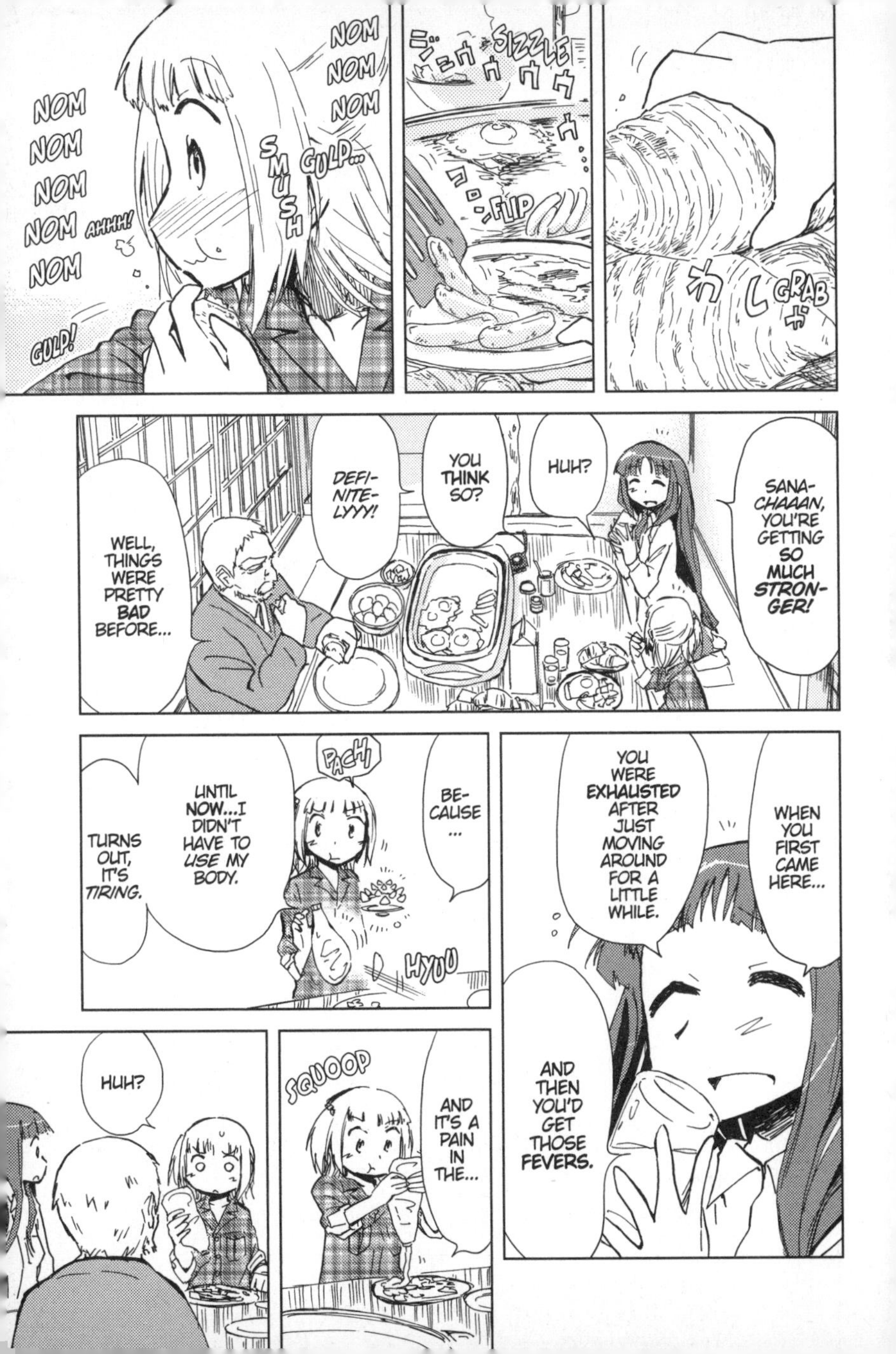
GRAB
SIZZLE
FLIP
NOM NOM NOM
SMUSH
GULP...
NOM NOM NOM NOM NOM
AHHH!
GULP!
SANA-CHAAAN, YOU'RE GETTING SO MUCH STRONGER!
HUH?
YOU THINK SO?
DEFINITELYYY!
WELL, THINGS WERE PRETTY BAD BEFORE...
WHEN YOU FIRST CAME HERE...
YOU WERE EXHAUSTED AFTER JUST MOVING AROUND FOR A LITTLE WHILE.
AND THEN YOU'D GET THOSE FEVERS.
BECAUSE...
PACHI
UNTIL NOW...I DIDN'T HAVE TO USE MY BODY.
TURNS OUT, IT'S TIRING.
HYUU
SQUOOP
AND IT'S A PAIN IN THE...
HUH?

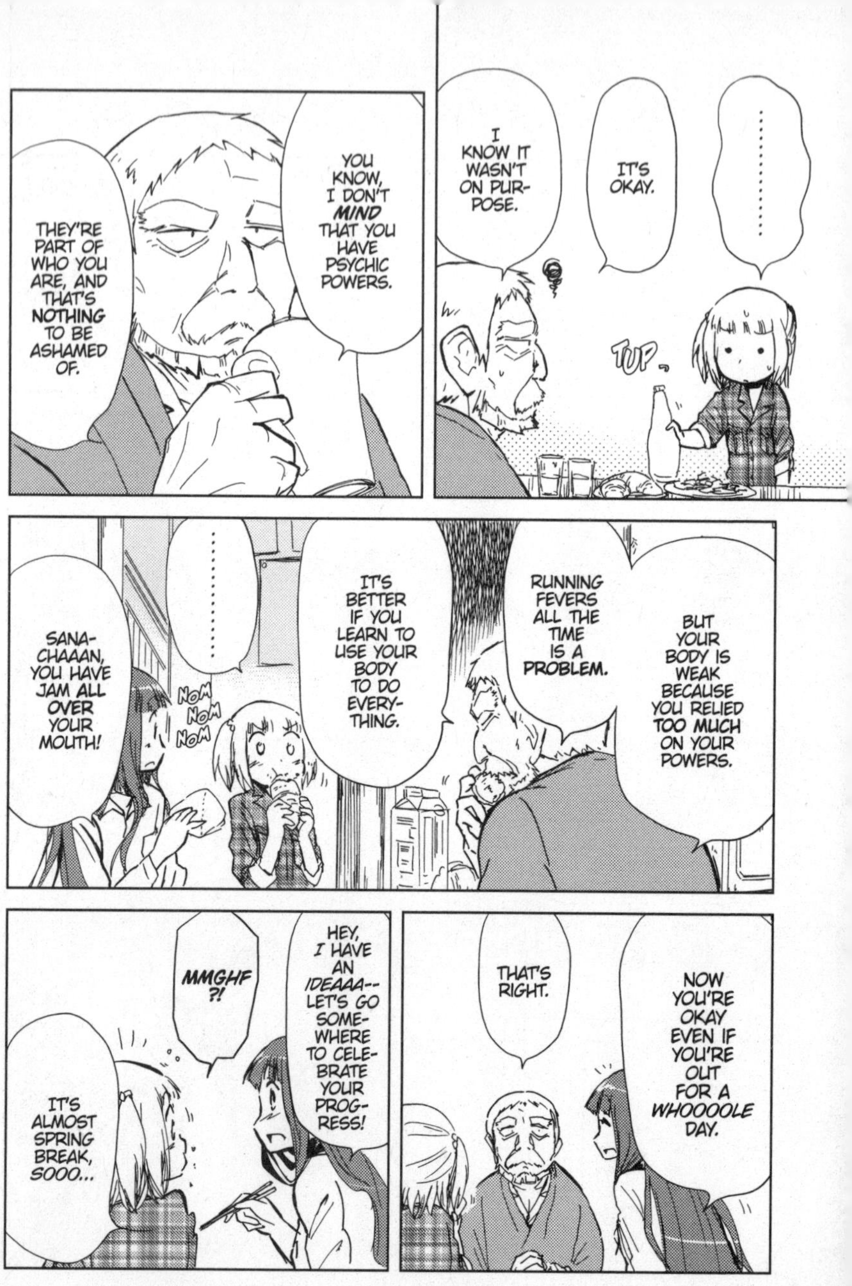
......
IT'S OKAY.
I KNOW IT WASN'T ON PURPOSE.
TUP
YOU KNOW, I DON'T MIND THAT YOU HAVE PSYCHIC POWERS.
THEY'RE PART OF WHO YOU ARE, AND THAT'S NOTHING TO BE ASHAMED OF.
BUT YOUR BODY IS WEAK BECAUSE YOU RELIED TOO MUCH ON YOUR POWERS.
RUNNING FEVERS ALL THE TIME IS A PROBLEM.
IT'S BETTER IF YOU LEARN TO USE YOUR BODY TO DO EVERY-THING.
......
NOM NOM NOM
SANA-CHAAAN, YOU HAVE JAM ALL OVER YOUR MOUTH!
NOW YOU'RE OKAY EVEN IF YOU'RE OUT FOR A WHOOOOLE DAY.
THAT'S RIGHT.
HEY, I HAVE AN IDEAAA-- LET'S GO SOME-WHERE TO CELE-BRATE YOUR PROG-RESS!
MMGHF ?!
IT'S ALMOST SPRING BREAK, SOOO...

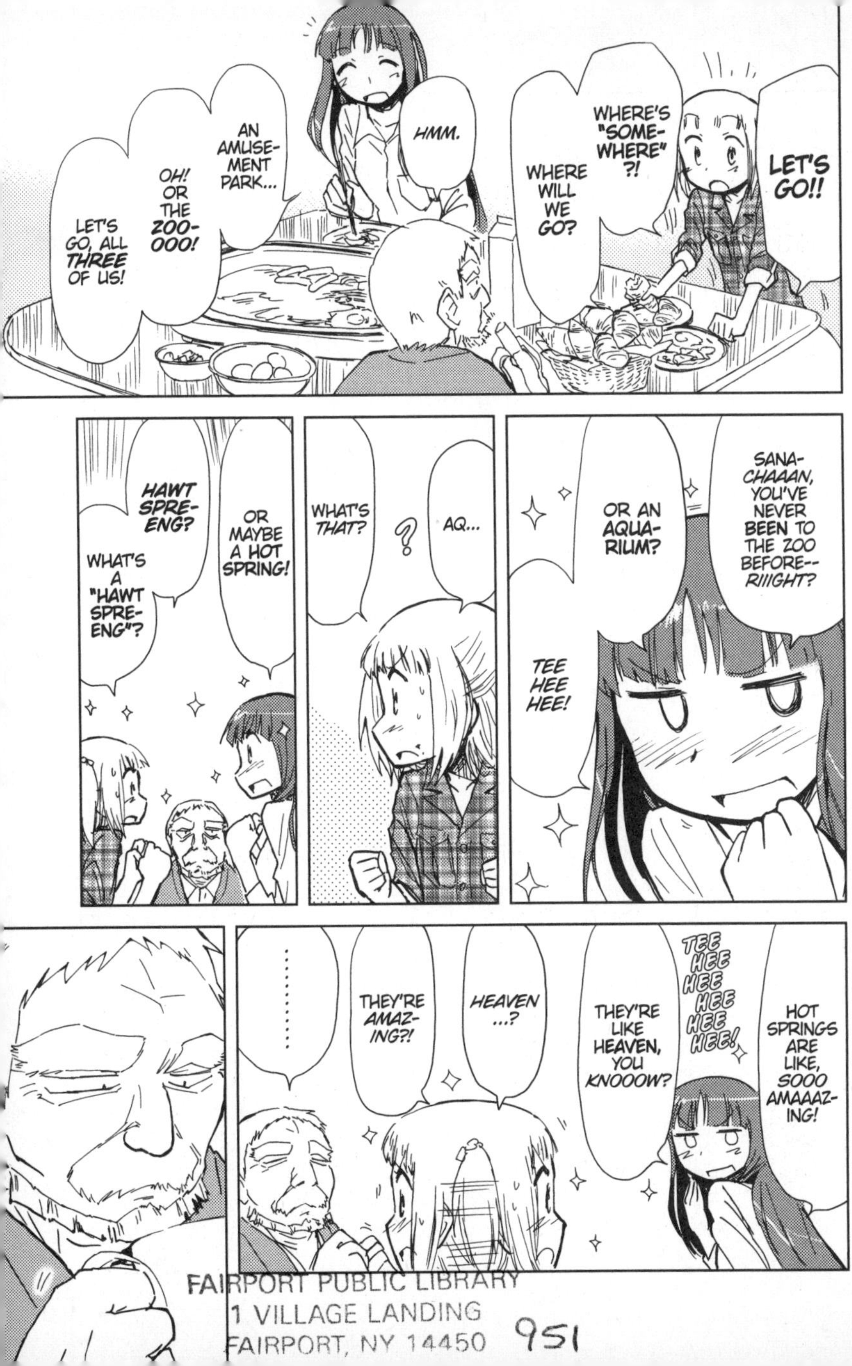
LET'S GO!!
WHERE'S "SOME-WHERE"?!
WHERE WILL WE GO?
HMM.
AN AMUSE-MENT PARK...
OH! OR THE ZOO-OOO!
LET'S GO, ALL THREE OF US!
SANA-CHAAAN, YOU'VE NEVER BEEN TO THE ZOO BEFORE--RIIIGHT?
OR AN AQUA-RIUM?
TEE HEE HEE!
AQ...
?
WHAT'S THAT?
OR MAYBE A HOT SPRING!
HAWT SPRE-ENG?
WHAT'S A "HAWT SPRE-ENG"?
HOT SPRINGS ARE LIKE, SOOO AMAAAZ-ING!
TEE HEE HEE HEE HEE HEE!
THEY'RE LIKE HEAVEN, YOU KNOOOW?
HEAVEN ...?
THEY'RE AMAZ-ING?!
......

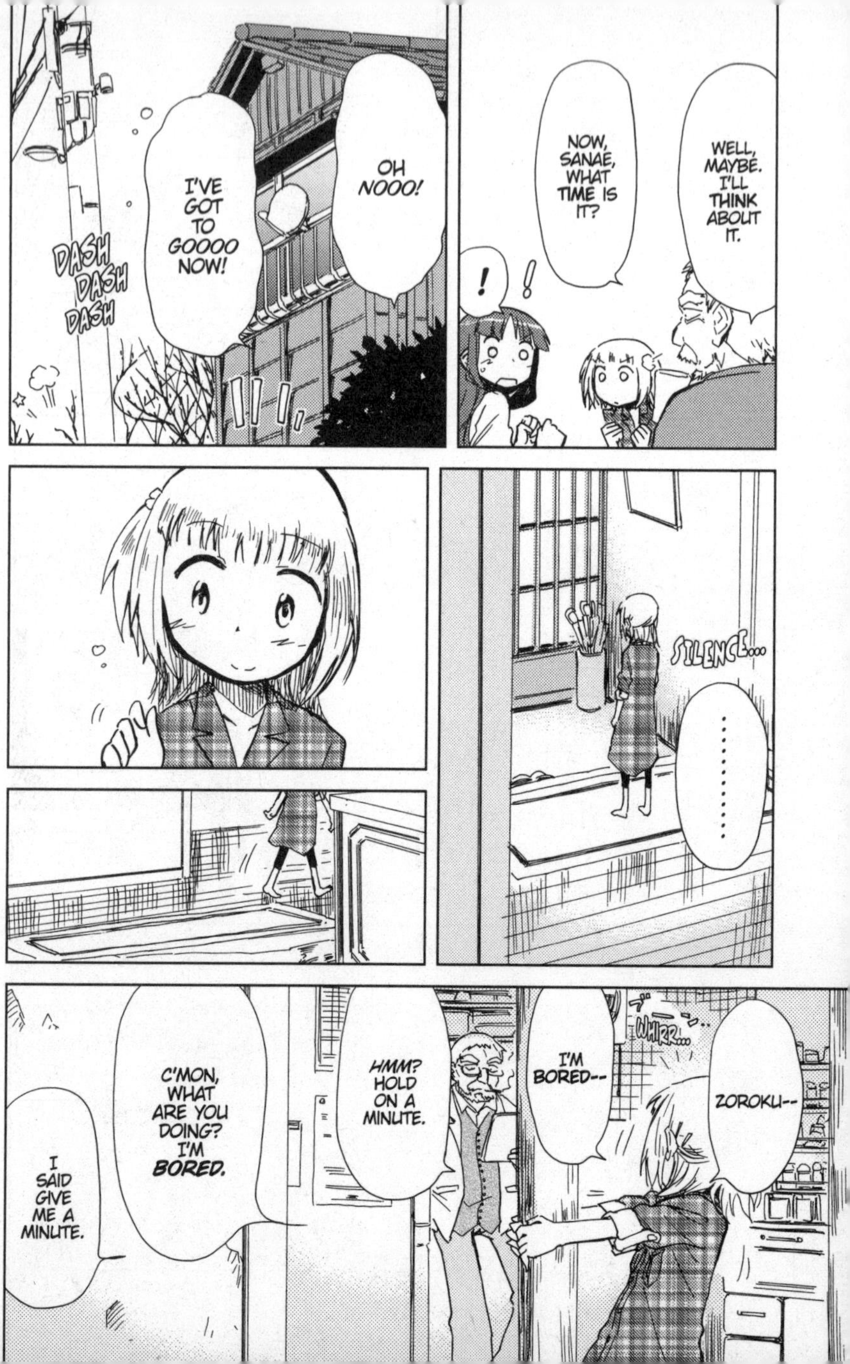
WELL, MAYBE. I'LL THINK ABOUT IT.
NOW, SANAE, WHAT TIME IS IT?
!
!
OH NOOO!
I'VE GOT TO GOOOO NOW!
DASH DASH DASH
SILENCE...
....
ZOROKU--
WHIRR...
I'M BORED--
HMM? HOLD ON A MINUTE.
C'MON, WHAT ARE YOU DOING? I'M BORED.
I SAID GIVE ME A MINUTE.

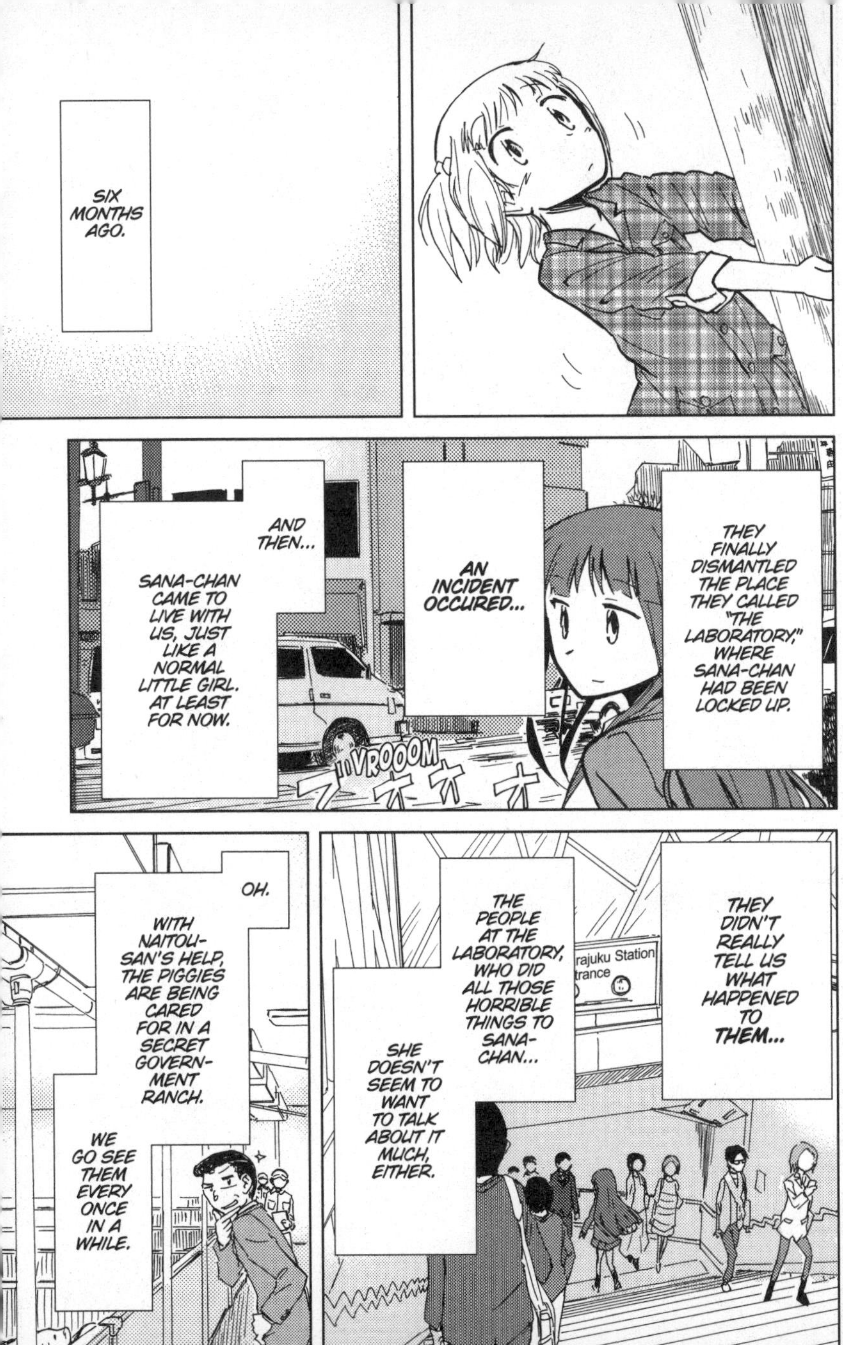
SIX MONTHS AGO.
THEY FINALLY DISMANTLED THE PLACE THEY CALLED "THE LABORATORY," WHERE SANA-CHAN HAD BEEN LOCKED UP.
AN INCIDENT OCCURED...
AND THEN...
SANA-CHAN CAME TO LIVE WITH US, JUST LIKE A NORMAL LITTLE GIRL. AT LEAST FOR NOW.
VROOOM
THEY DIDN'T REALLY TELL US WHAT HAPPENED TO THEM...
THE PEOPLE AT THE LABORATORY, WHO DID ALL THOSE HORRIBLE THINGS TO SANA-CHAN...
SHE DOESN'T SEEM TO WANT TO TALK ABOUT IT MUCH, EITHER.
OH.
WITH NAITOU-SAN'S HELP, THE PIGGIES ARE BEING CARED FOR IN A SECRET GOVERN-MENT RANCH.
WE GO SEE THEM EVERY ONCE IN A WHILE.

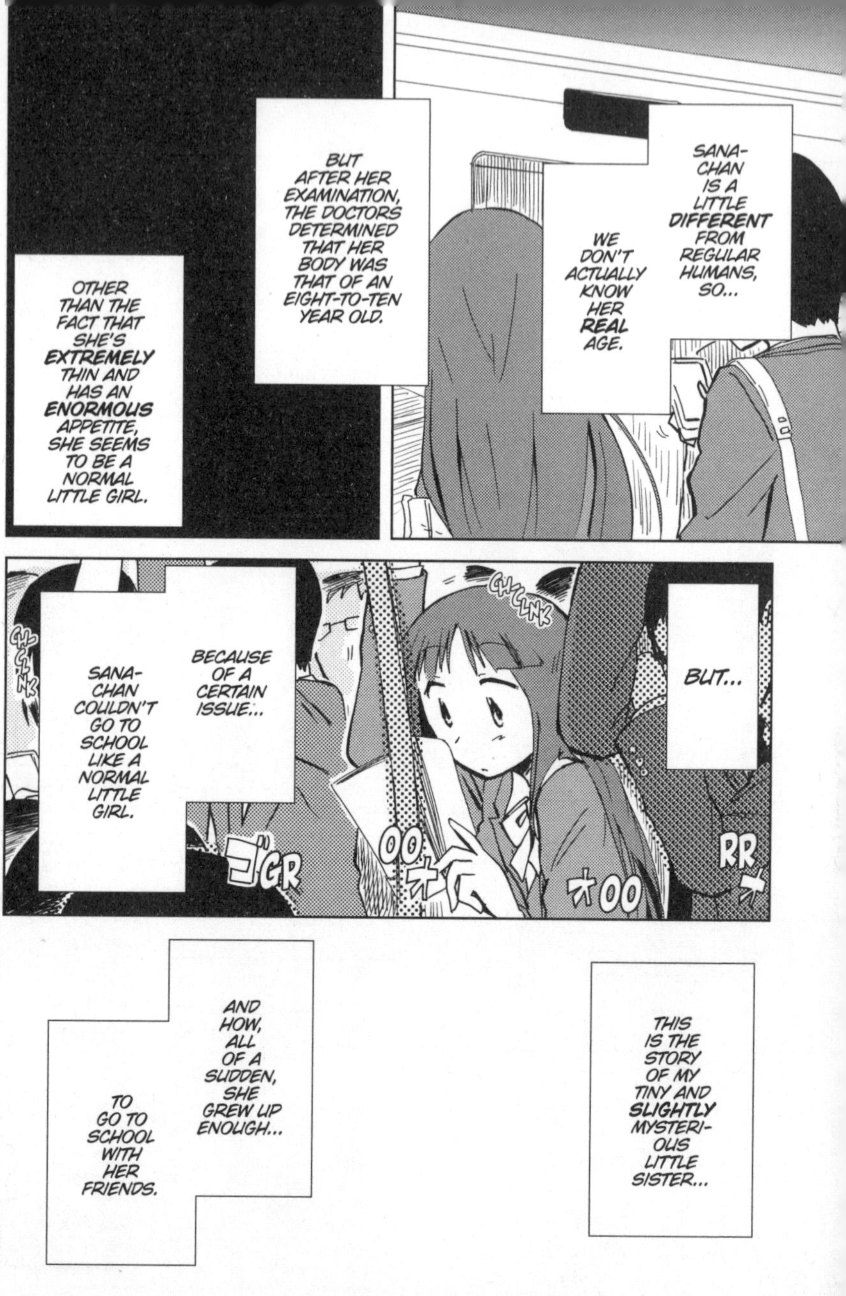
SANA-CHAN IS A LITTLE **DIFFERENT** FROM REGULAR HUMANS, SO...
WE DON'T ACTUALLY KNOW HER **REAL** AGE.
BUT AFTER HER EXAMINATION, THE DOCTORS DETERMINED THAT HER BODY WAS THAT OF AN EIGHT-TO-TEN YEAR OLD.
OTHER THAN THE FACT THAT SHE'S **EXTREMELY** THIN AND HAS AN **ENORMOUS** APPETITE, SHE SEEMS TO BE A NORMAL LITTLE GIRL.
BUT...
RR
OO
CHCLNK
OO
BECAUSE OF A CERTAIN ISSUE...
SANA-CHAN COULDN'T GO TO SCHOOL LIKE A NORMAL LITTLE GIRL.
GR
CHCLNK
THIS IS THE STORY OF MY TINY AND **SLIGHTLY** MYSTERIOUS LITTLE SISTER...
AND HOW, ALL OF A SUDDEN, SHE GREW UP ENOUGH...
TO GO TO SCHOOL WITH HER FRIENDS.

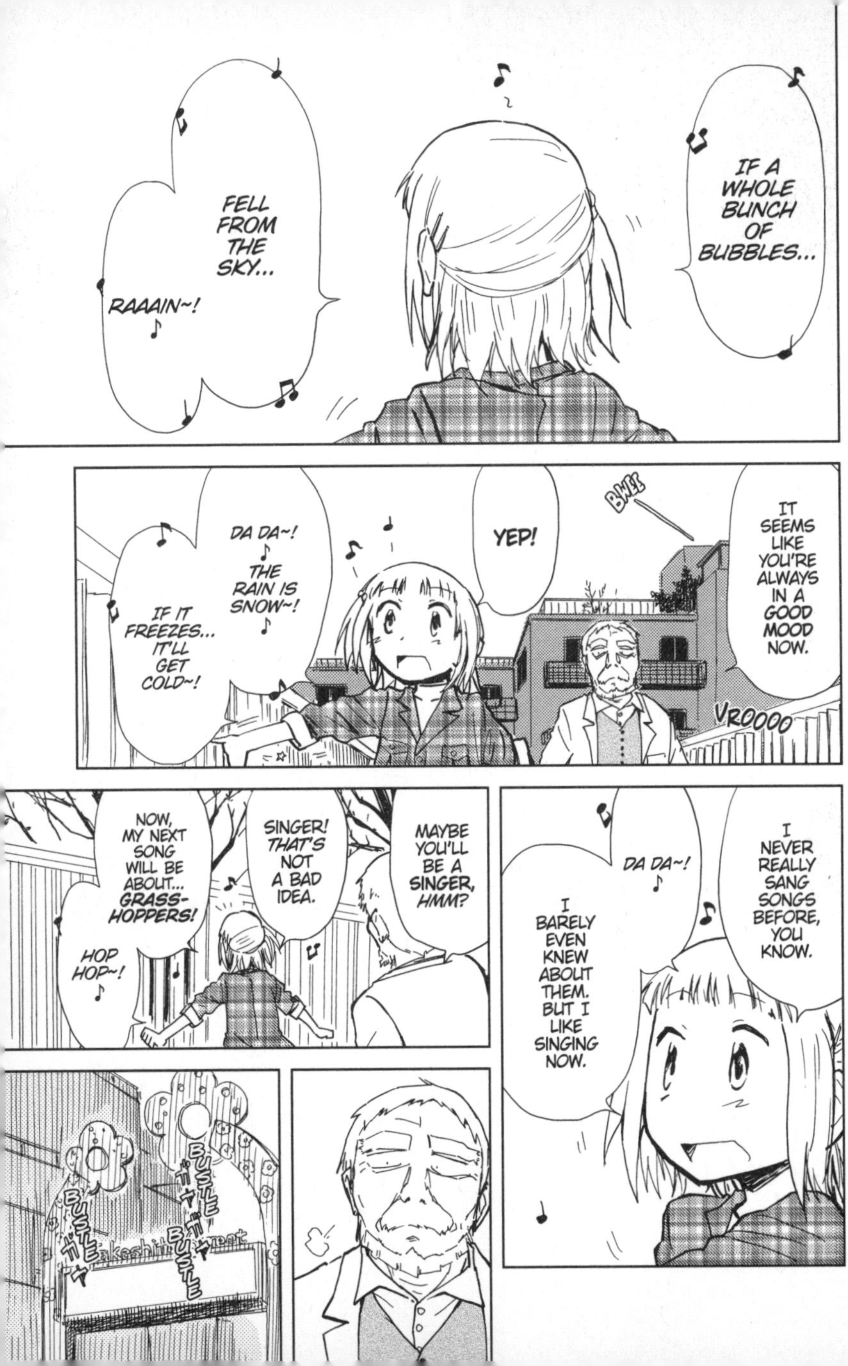
IF A WHOLE BUNCH OF BUBBLES...
FELL FROM THE SKY...
RAAAIN~! ♪
BWEE
IT SEEMS LIKE YOU'RE ALWAYS IN A GOOD MOOD NOW.
VROOOO
YEP!
DA DA~! ♪ THE RAIN IS SNOW~! ♪
IF IT FREEZES... IT'LL GET COLD~!
I NEVER REALLY SANG SONGS BEFORE, YOU KNOW.
DA DA~! ♪
I BARELY EVEN KNEW ABOUT THEM. BUT I LIKE SINGING NOW.
MAYBE YOU'LL BE A SINGER, HMM?
SINGER! THAT'S NOT A BAD IDEA.
NOW, MY NEXT SONG WILL BE ABOUT... GRASSHOPPERS!
HOP HOP~! ♪
BUSTLE
BUSTLE
BUSTLE
BUSTLE

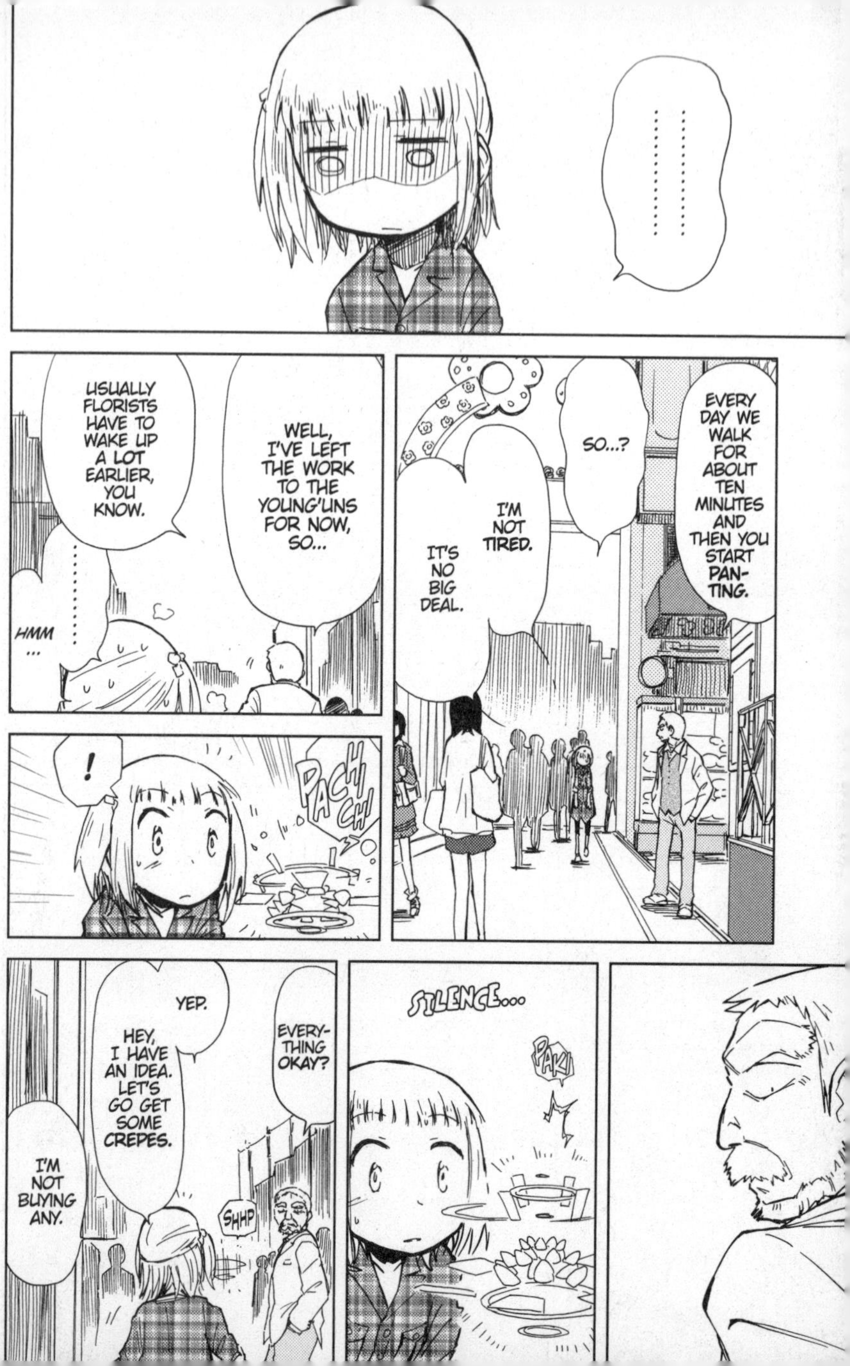
……
EVERY DAY WE WALK FOR ABOUT TEN MINUTES AND THEN YOU START PAN-TING.
SO...?
I'M NOT TIRED.
IT'S NO BIG DEAL.
WELL, I'VE LEFT THE WORK TO THE YOUNG'UNS FOR NOW, SO...
USUALLY FLORISTS HAVE TO WAKE UP A LOT EARLIER, YOU KNOW.
……
HMM ...
!
PACHI CH
SILENCE...
PAKI
EVERY-THING OKAY?
YEP.
HEY, I HAVE AN IDEA. LET'S GO GET SOME CREPES.
I'M NOT BUYING ANY.
SHHP

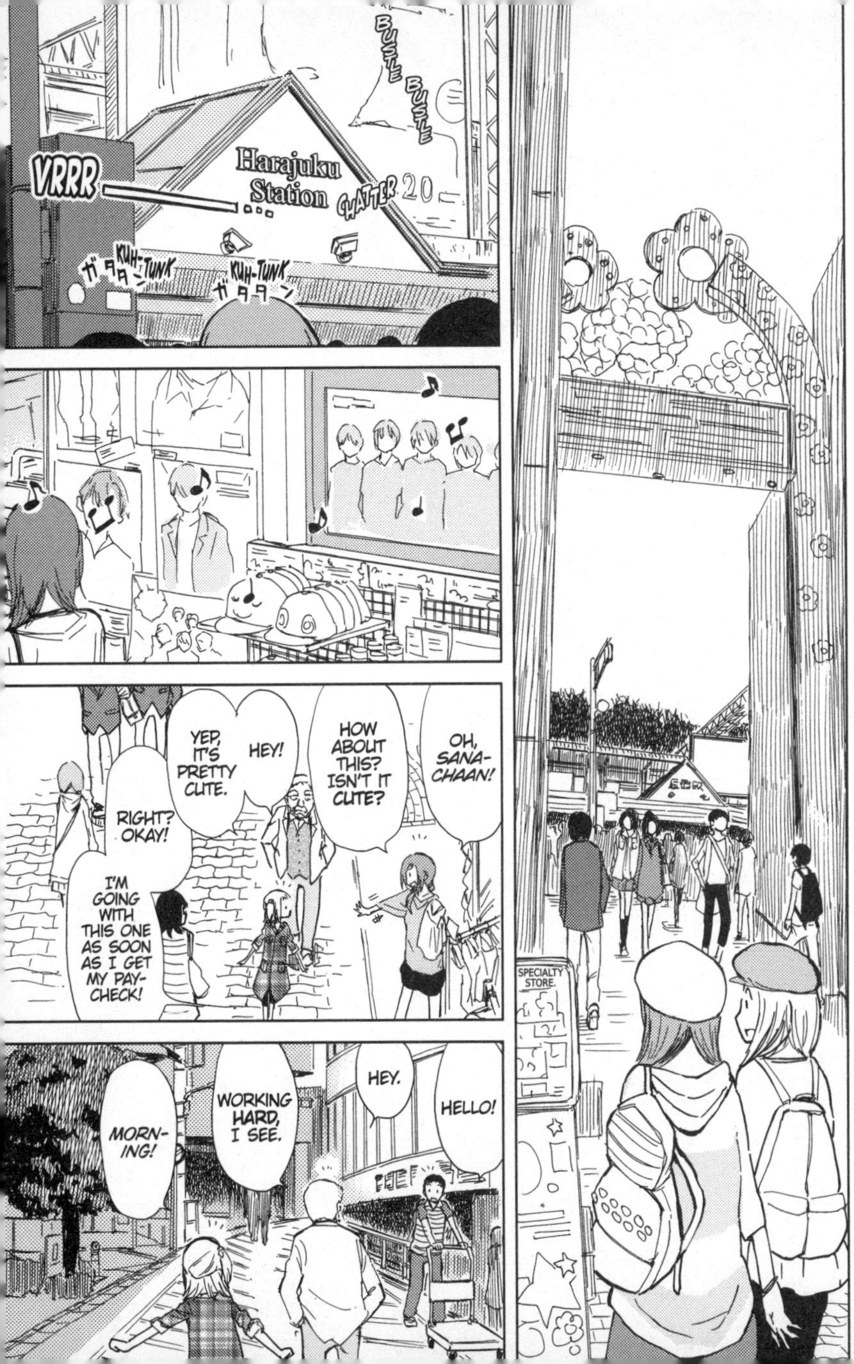
SPECIALTY STORE.
BUSTLE BUSTLE
Harajuku Station
CHATTER
VRRR
KUH-TUNK
KUH-TUNK
OH, SANA-CHAAN!
HOW ABOUT THIS? ISN'T IT CUTE?
HEY!
YEP, IT'S PRETTY CUTE.
RIGHT? OKAY!
I'M GOING WITH THIS ONE AS SOON AS I GET MY PAY-CHECK!
HELLO!
HEY.
WORKING HARD, I SEE.
MORN-ING!

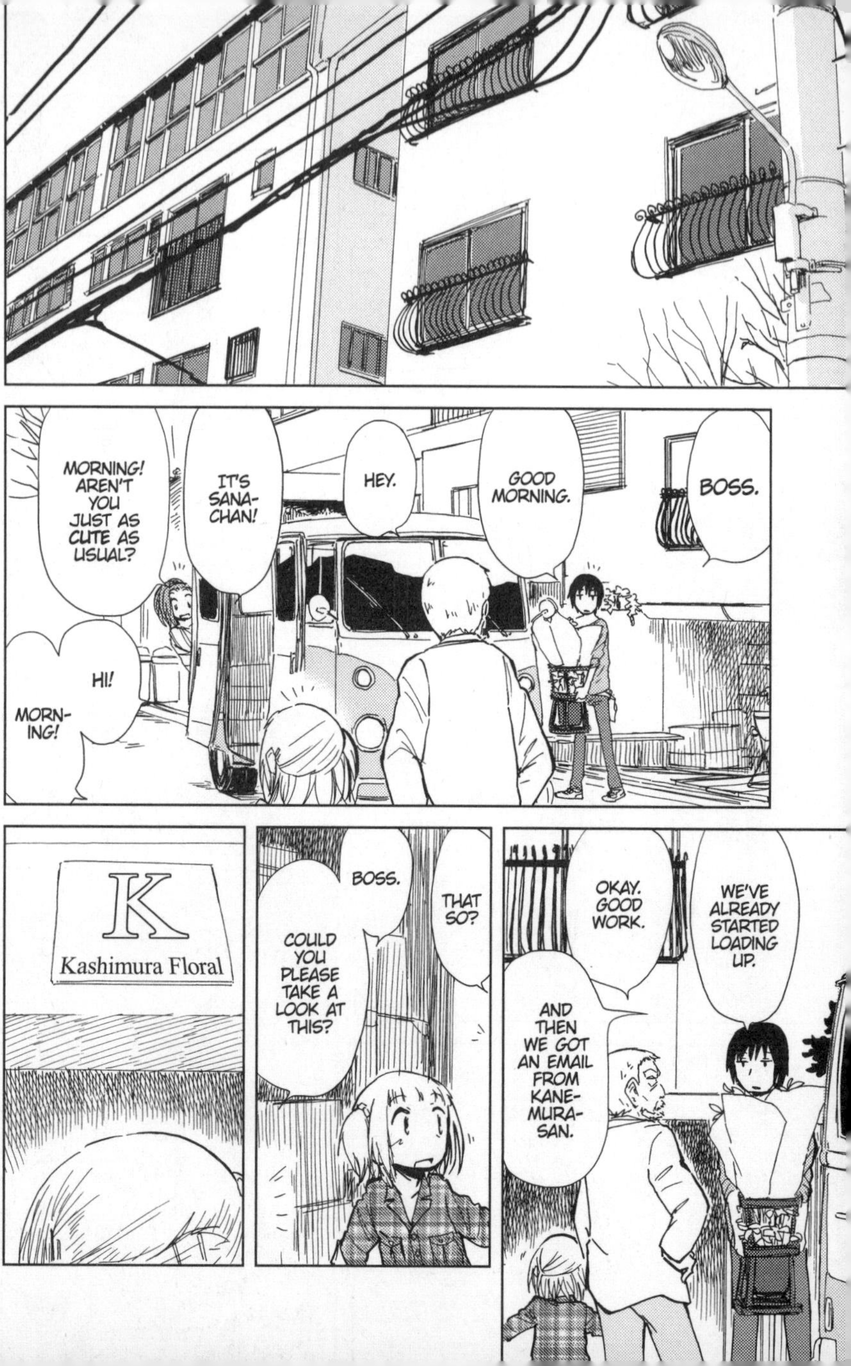
BOSS.
GOOD MORNING.
HEY.
IT'S SANA-CHAN!
MORNING! AREN'T YOU JUST AS CUTE AS USUAL?
HI!
MORN-ING!
WE'VE ALREADY STARTED LOADING UP.
OKAY. GOOD WORK.
AND THEN WE GOT AN EMAIL FROM KANE-MURA-SAN.
THAT SO?
BOSS.
COULD YOU PLEASE TAKE A LOOK AT THIS?
K
Kashimura Floral

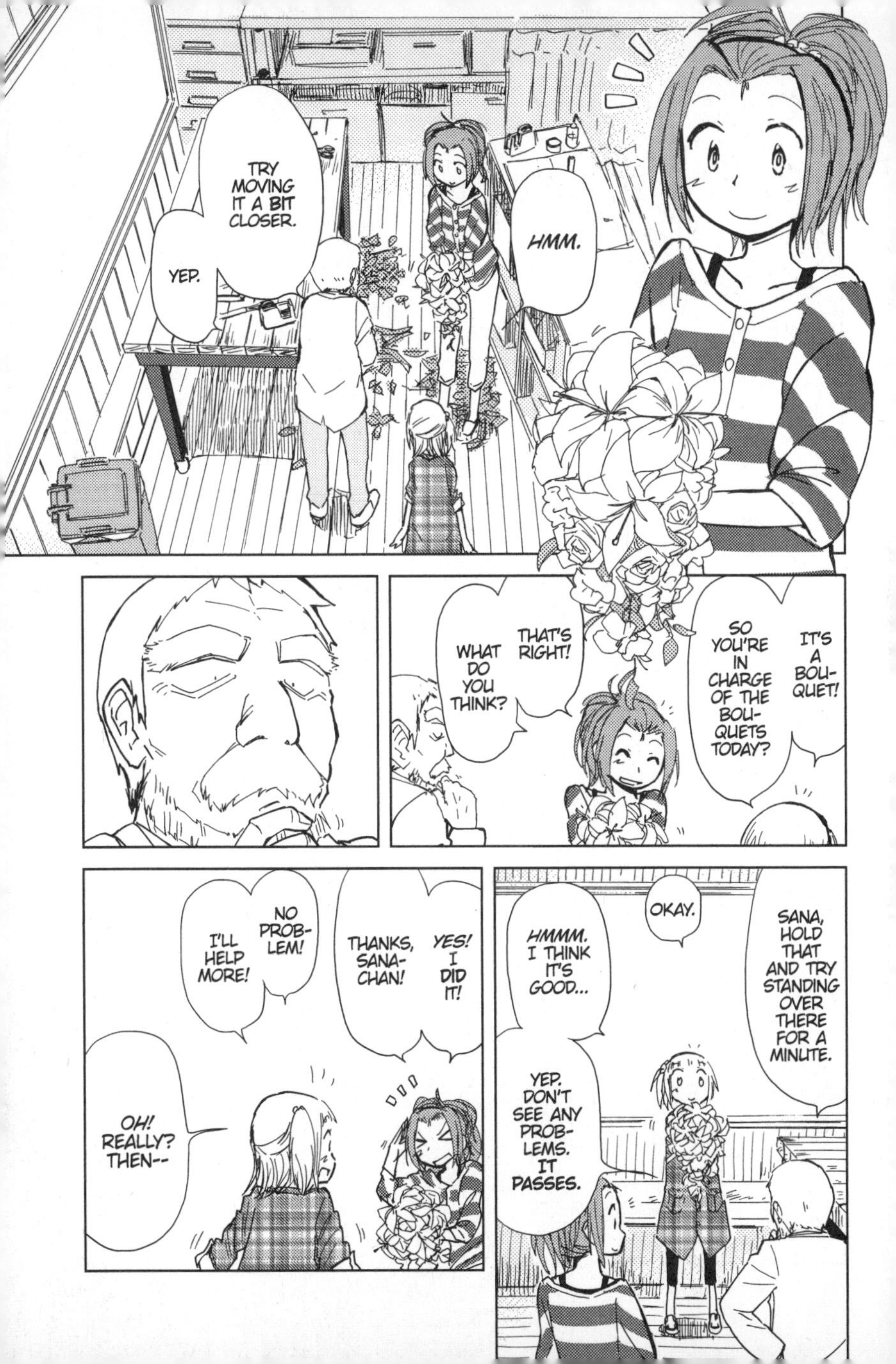
HMM.
TRY MOVING IT A BIT CLOSER.
YEP.
IT'S A BOU-QUET!
SO YOU'RE IN CHARGE OF THE BOU-QUETS TODAY?
THAT'S RIGHT!
WHAT DO YOU THINK?
SANA, HOLD THAT AND TRY STANDING OVER THERE FOR A MINUTE.
OKAY.
HMMM. I THINK IT'S GOOD...
YEP. DON'T SEE ANY PROB-LEMS. IT PASSES.
YES! I DID IT!
THANKS, SANA-CHAN!
NO PROB-LEM!
I'LL HELP MORE!
OH! REALLY? THEN--

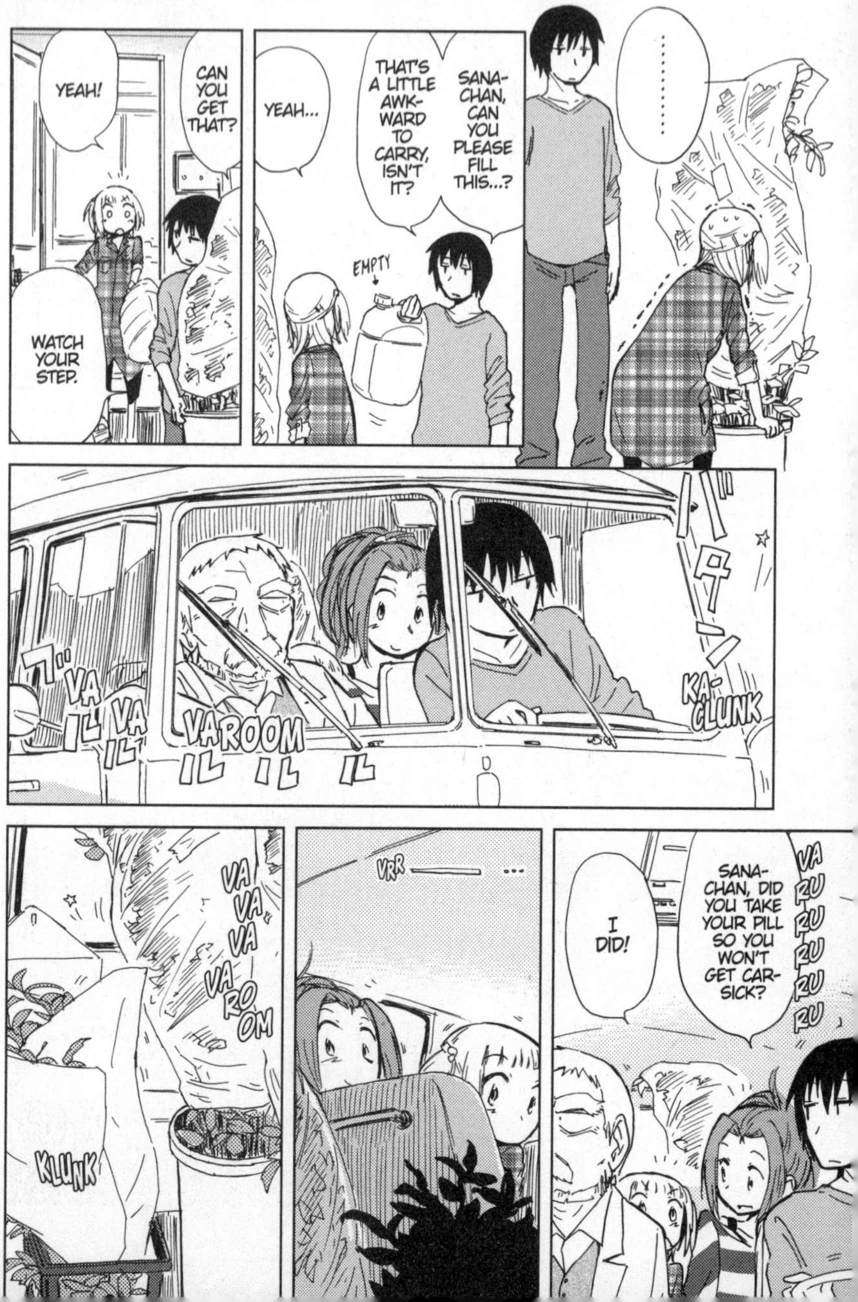
......
SANA-CHAN, CAN YOU PLEASE FILL THIS...?
THAT'S A LITTLE AWKWARD TO CARRY, ISN'T IT?
YEAH...
EMPTY
CAN YOU GET THAT?
YEAH!
WATCH YOUR STEP.
KA-CLUNK
VAROOM
VA VA
VARURURURURU
SANA-CHAN, DID YOU TAKE YOUR PILL SO YOU WON'T GET CAR-SICK?
I DID!
VRR ——— ...
VA VA VA VAROOM
KLUNK

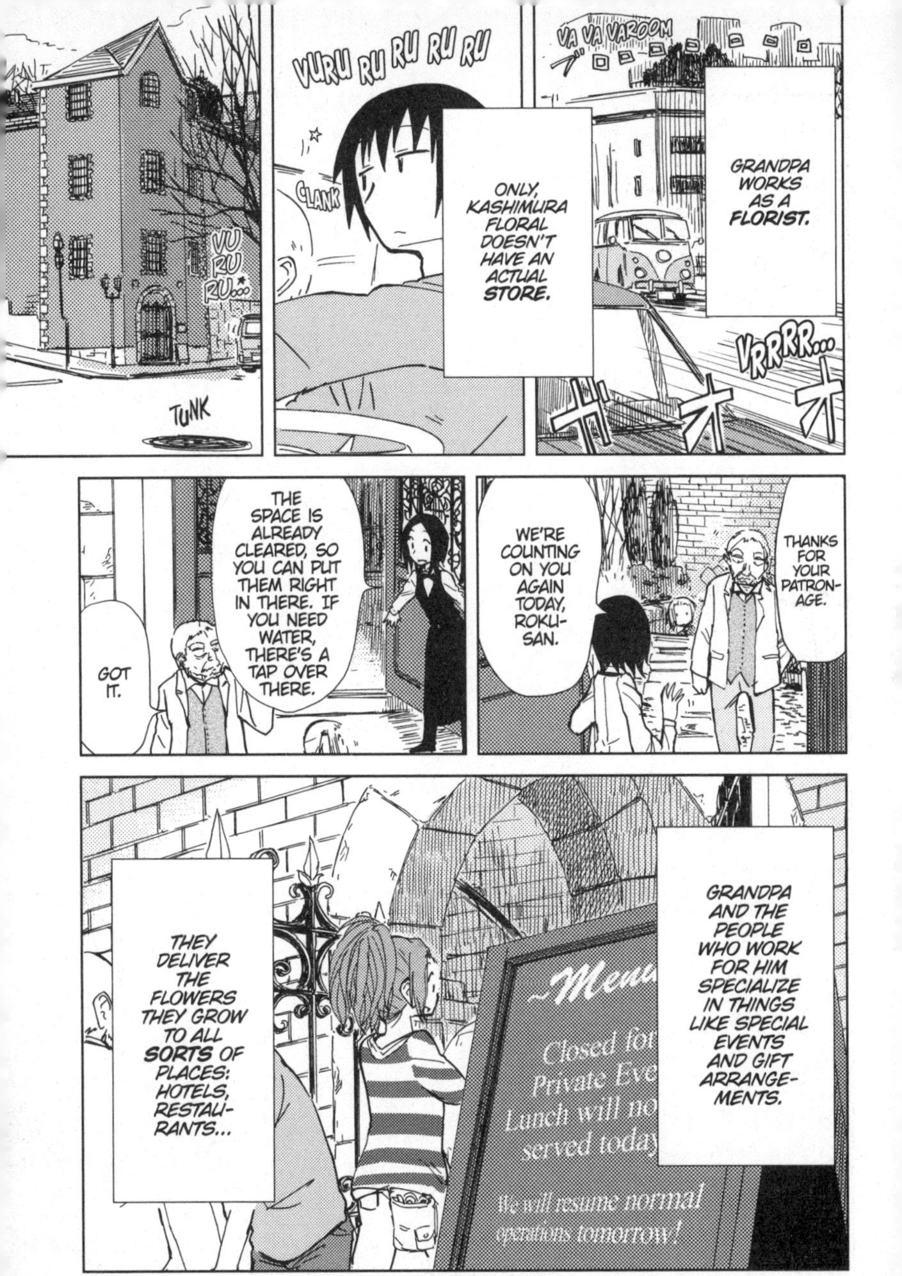
VA VA VAROOM
GRANDPA WORKS AS A **FLORIST.**
VRRRR...
VURU RU RU RU RU
CLANK
ONLY, KASHIMURA FLORAL DOESN'T HAVE AN ACTUAL **STORE.**
VU RU RU...
TUNK
THANKS FOR YOUR PATRON-AGE.
WE'RE COUNTING ON YOU AGAIN TODAY, ROKU-SAN.
THE SPACE IS ALREADY CLEARED, SO YOU CAN PUT THEM RIGHT IN THERE. IF YOU NEED WATER, THERE'S A TAP OVER THERE.
GOT IT.
GRANDPA AND THE PEOPLE WHO WORK FOR HIM SPECIALIZE IN THINGS LIKE SPECIAL EVENTS AND GIFT ARRANGE-MENTS.
THEY DELIVER THE FLOWERS THEY GROW TO ALL **SORTS** OF PLACES: HOTELS, RESTAU-RANTS...
We will resume normal operations tomorrow!

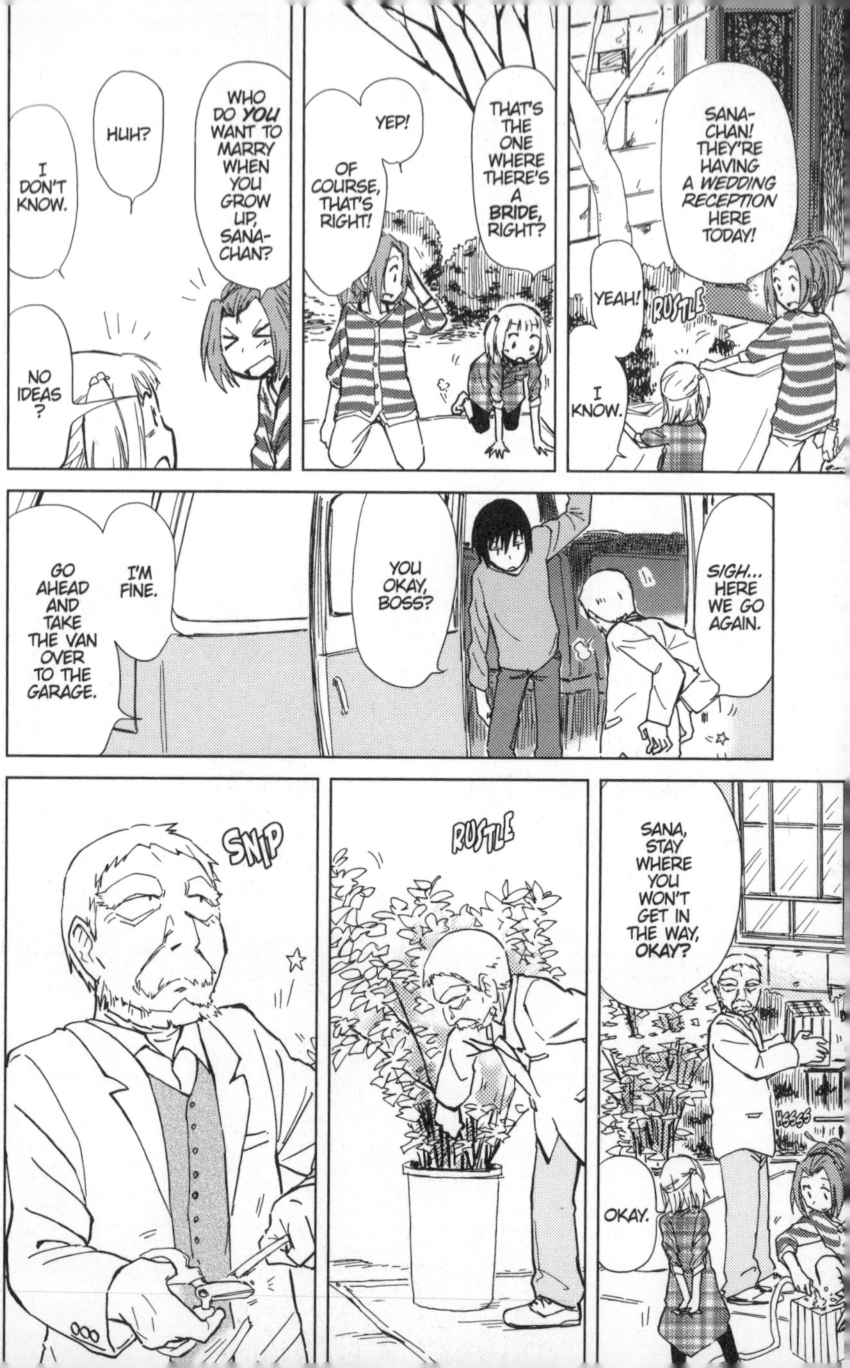
SANA-CHAN! THEY'RE HAVING A *WEDDING RECEPTION* HERE TODAY!
YEAH!
RUSTLE
I KNOW.
THAT'S THE ONE WHERE THERE'S A **BRIDE**, RIGHT?
YEP!
OF COURSE, THAT'S RIGHT!
WHO DO ***YOU*** WANT TO MARRY WHEN YOU GROW UP, SANA-CHAN?
HUH?
I DON'T KNOW.
NO IDEAS?
SIGH... HERE WE GO AGAIN.
YOU OKAY, BOSS?
I'M FINE.
GO AHEAD AND TAKE THE VAN OVER TO THE GARAGE.
SANA, STAY WHERE YOU WON'T GET IN THE WAY, **OKAY?**
HSSSS
OKAY.
RUSTLE
SNIP

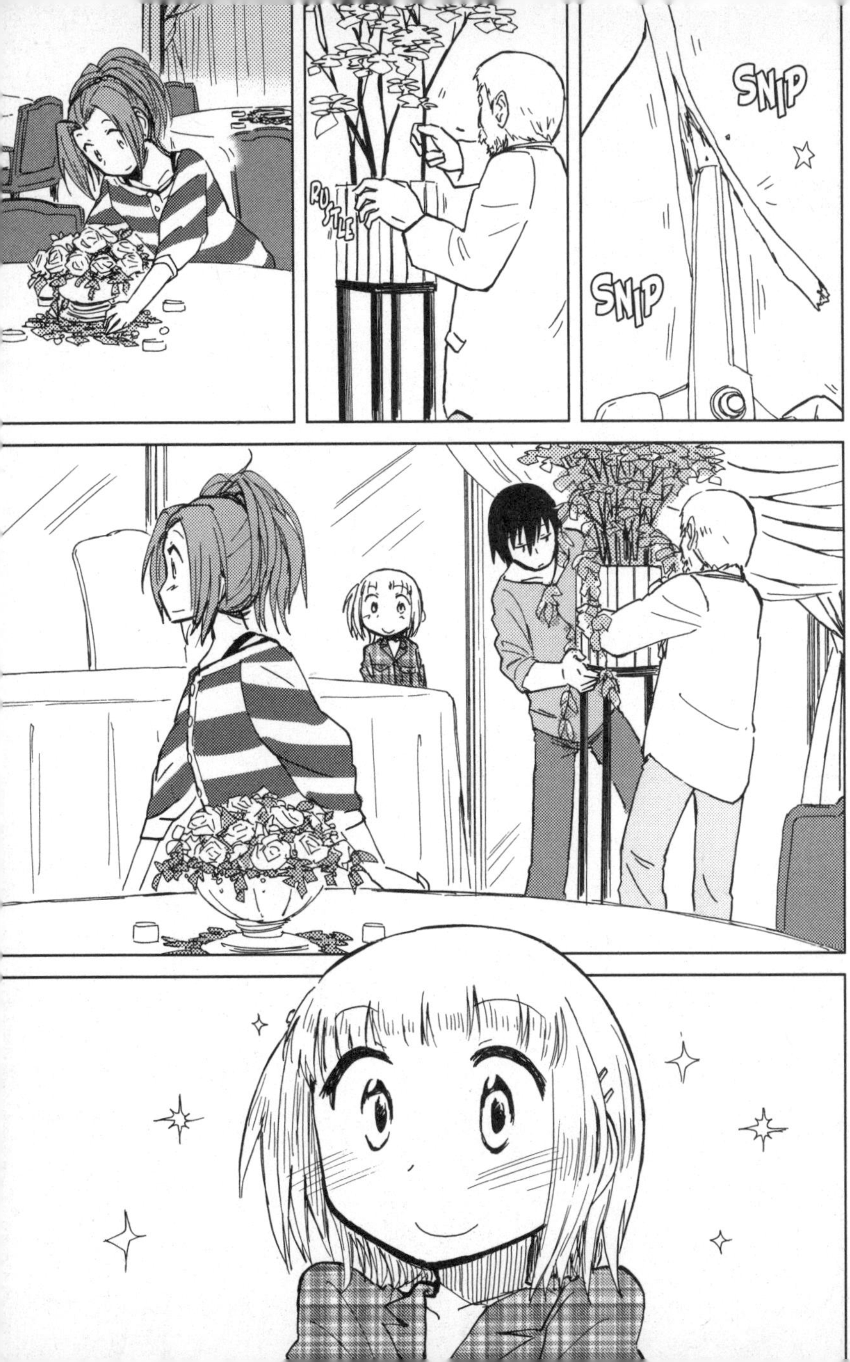
SNIP
SNIP
RUSTLE

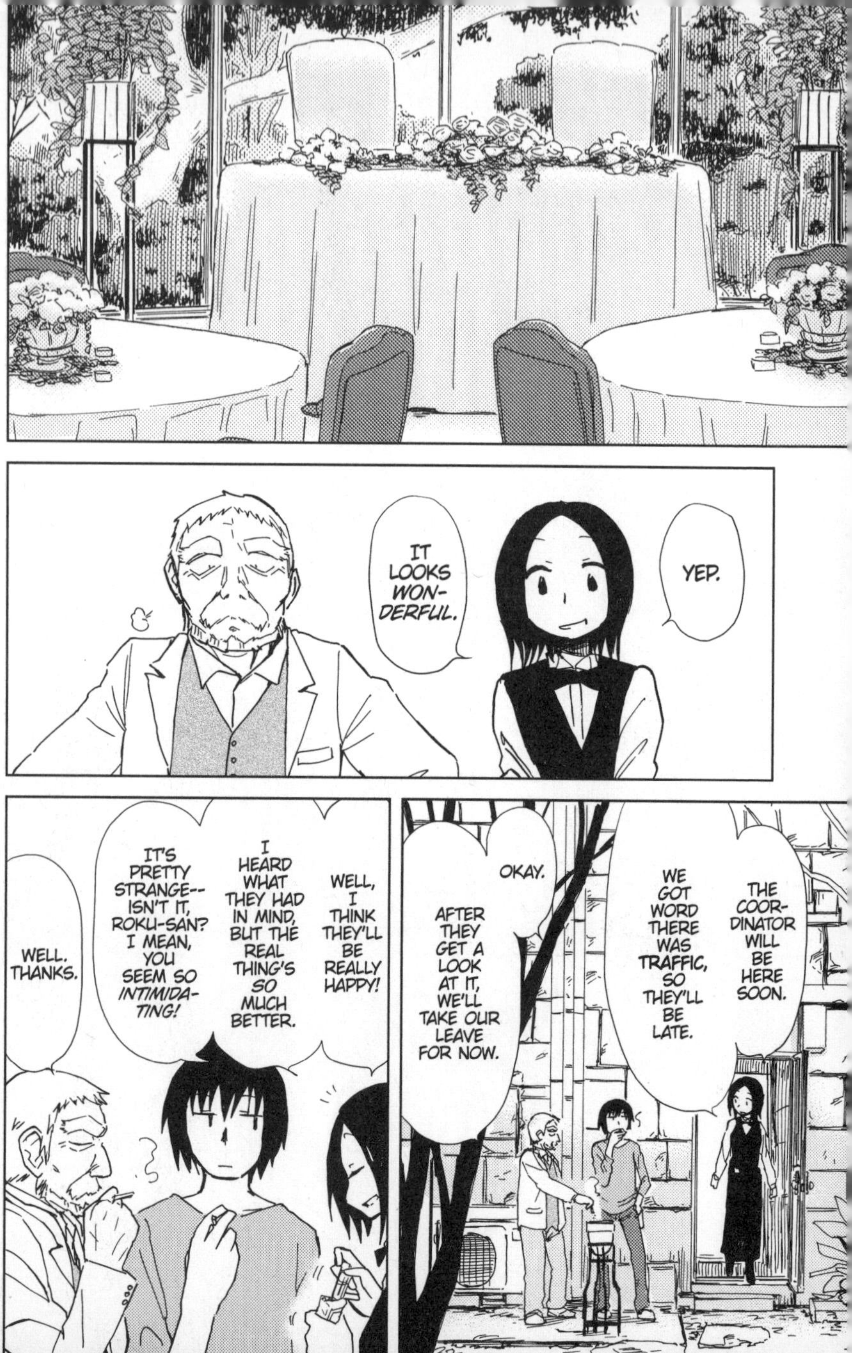
YEP.
IT LOOKS *WONDERFUL.*
THE COORDINATOR WILL BE HERE SOON.
WE GOT WORD THERE WAS TRAFFIC, SO THEY'LL BE LATE.
OKAY.
AFTER THEY GET A LOOK AT IT, WE'LL TAKE OUR LEAVE FOR NOW.
WELL, I THINK THEY'LL BE REALLY HAPPY!
I HEARD WHAT THEY HAD IN MIND, BUT THE REAL THING'S *SO* MUCH BETTER.
IT'S PRETTY STRANGE--ISN'T IT, ROKU-SAN? I MEAN, YOU SEEM SO *INTIMIDATING!*
WELL. THANKS.

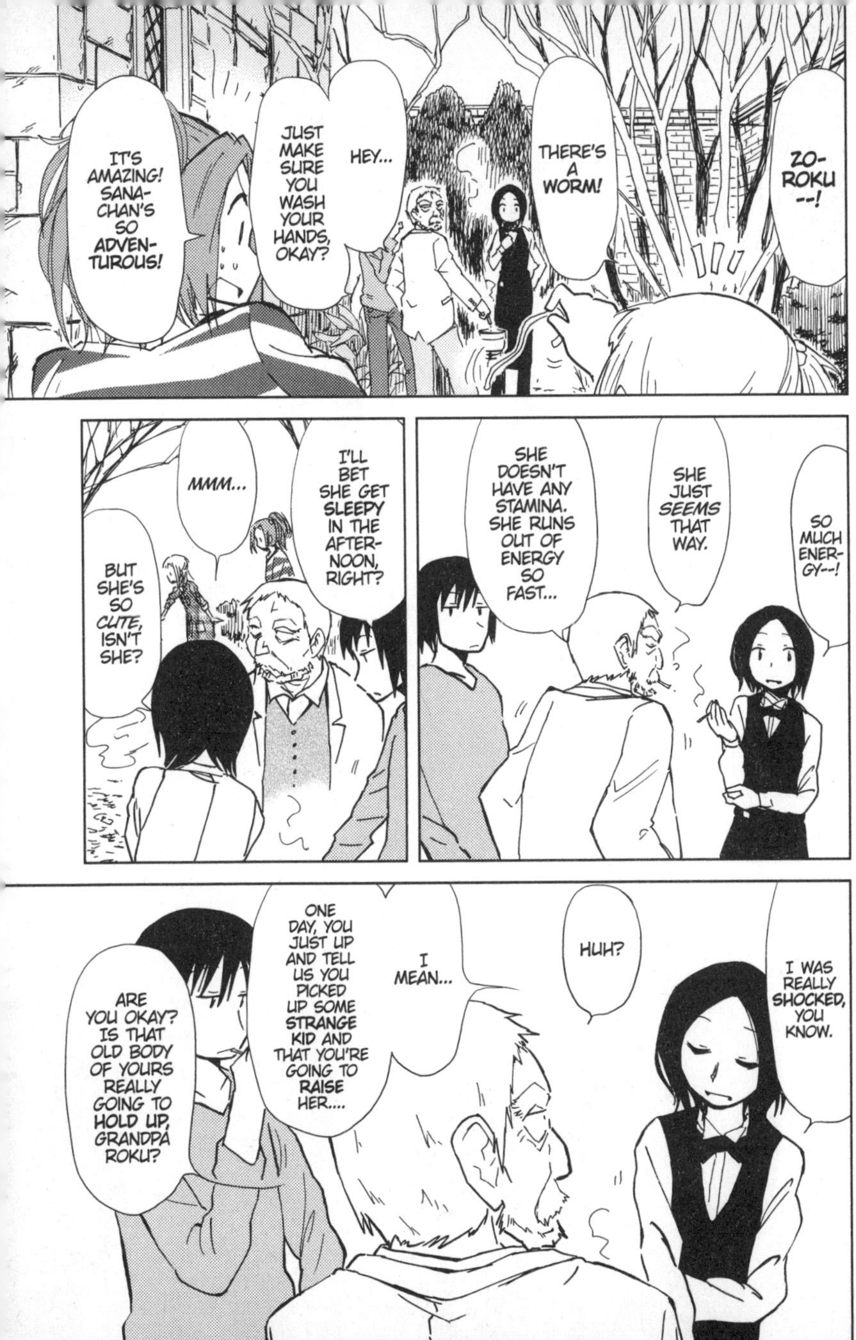
ZO-ROKU--!
THERE'S A WORM!
HEY...
JUST MAKE SURE YOU WASH YOUR HANDS, OKAY?
IT'S AMAZING! SANA-CHAN'S SO ADVENTUROUS!
SO MUCH ENERGY--!
SHE JUST SEEMS THAT WAY.
SHE DOESN'T HAVE ANY STAMINA. SHE RUNS OUT OF ENERGY SO FAST...
I'LL BET SHE GET SLEEPY IN THE AFTERNOON, RIGHT?
MMM...
BUT SHE'S SO CUTE, ISN'T SHE?
I WAS REALLY SHOCKED, YOU KNOW.
HUH?
I MEAN...
ONE DAY, YOU JUST UP AND TELL US YOU PICKED UP SOME STRANGE KID AND THAT YOU'RE GOING TO RAISE HER....
ARE YOU OKAY? IS THAT OLD BODY OF YOURS REALLY GOING TO HOLD UP, GRANDPA ROKU?

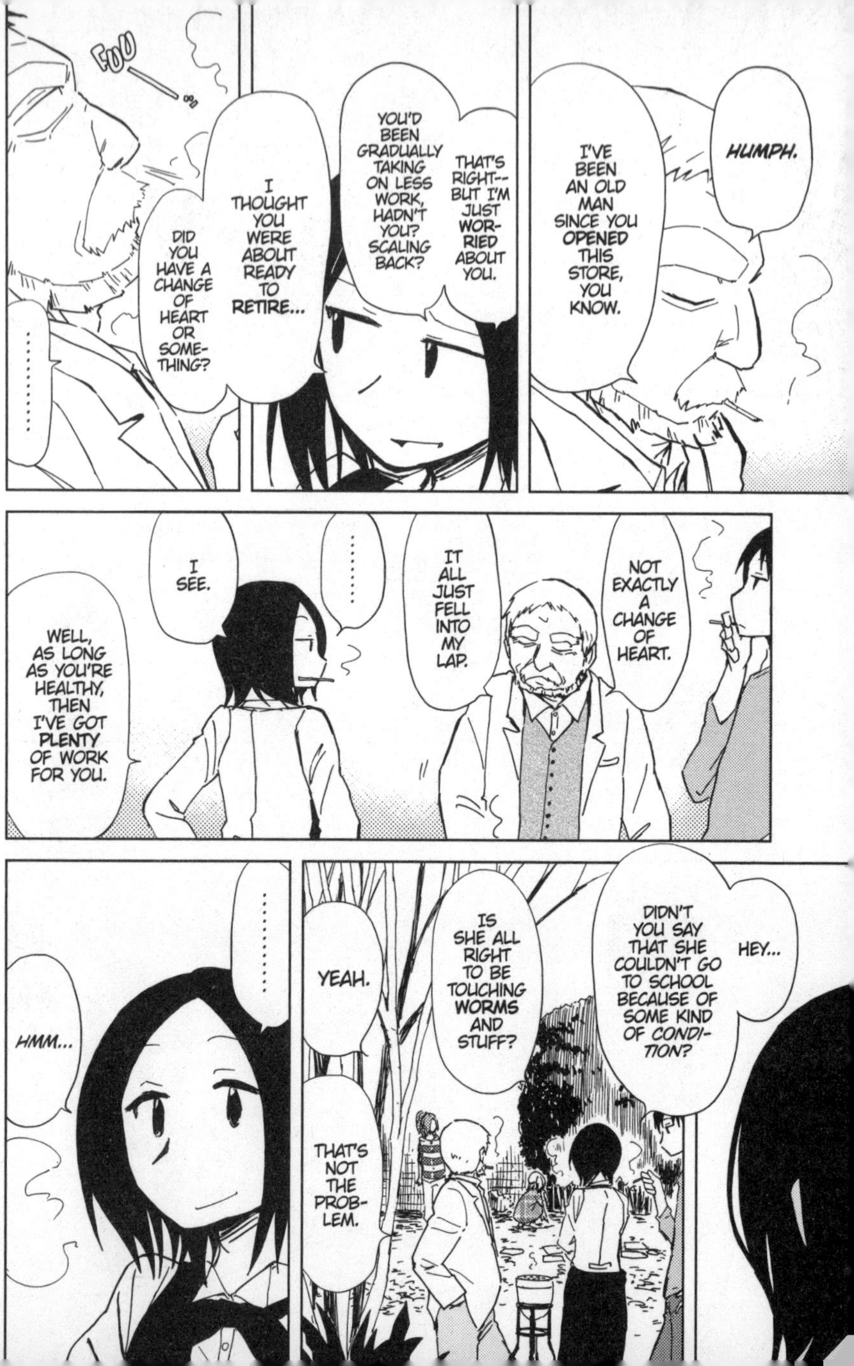
HUMPH.
I'VE BEEN AN OLD MAN SINCE YOU OPENED THIS STORE, YOU KNOW.
THAT'S RIGHT-- BUT I'M JUST WOR-RIED ABOUT YOU.
YOU'D BEEN GRADUALLY TAKING ON LESS WORK, HADN'T YOU? SCALING BACK?
FOU
I THOUGHT YOU WERE ABOUT READY TO RETIRE...
DID YOU HAVE A CHANGE OF HEART OR SOME-THING?
......
NOT EXACTLY A CHANGE OF HEART.
IT ALL JUST FELL INTO MY LAP.
......
I SEE.
WELL, AS LONG AS YOU'RE HEALTHY, THEN I'VE GOT PLENTY OF WORK FOR YOU.
HEY...
DIDN'T YOU SAY THAT SHE COULDN'T GO TO SCHOOL BECAUSE OF SOME KIND OF CONDI-TION?
IS SHE ALL RIGHT TO BE TOUCHING WORMS AND STUFF?
YEAH.
THAT'S NOT THE PROB-LEM.
......
HMM...

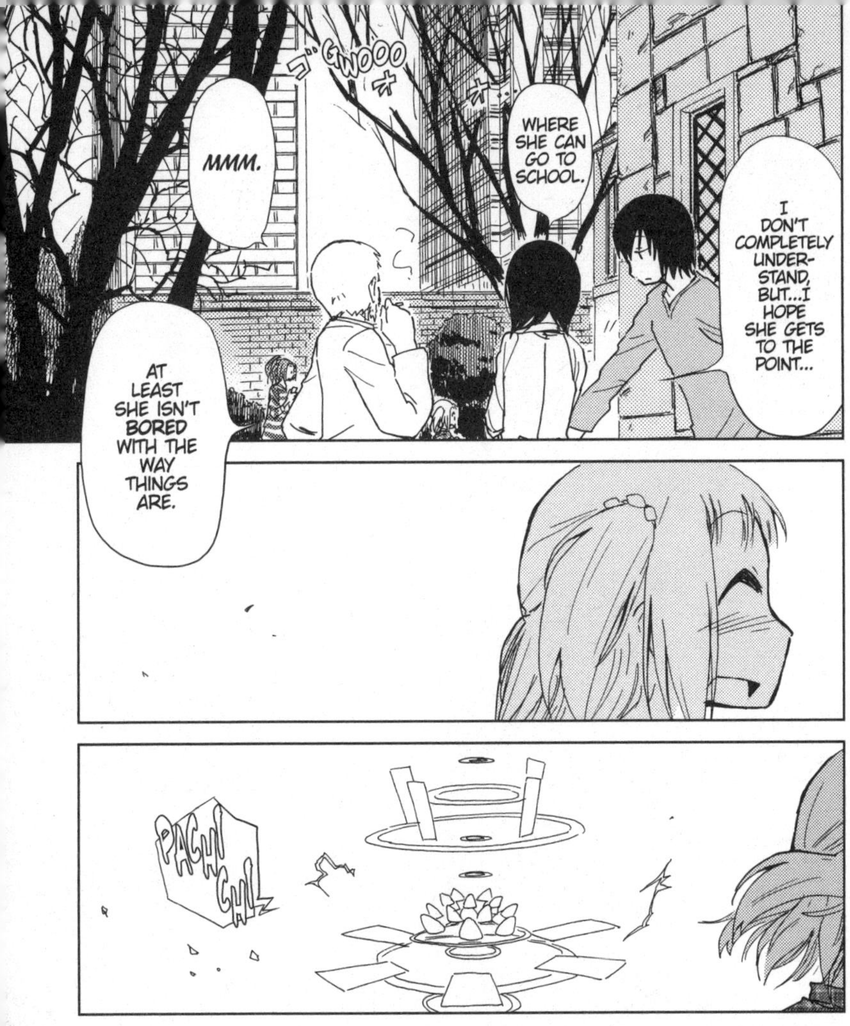
I DON'T COMPLETELY UNDER-STAND, BUT...I HOPE SHE GETS TO THE POINT...
WHERE SHE CAN GO TO SCHOOL.
GWOOO
MMM.
AT LEAST SHE ISN'T BORED WITH THE WAY THINGS ARE.
PACHI CHI

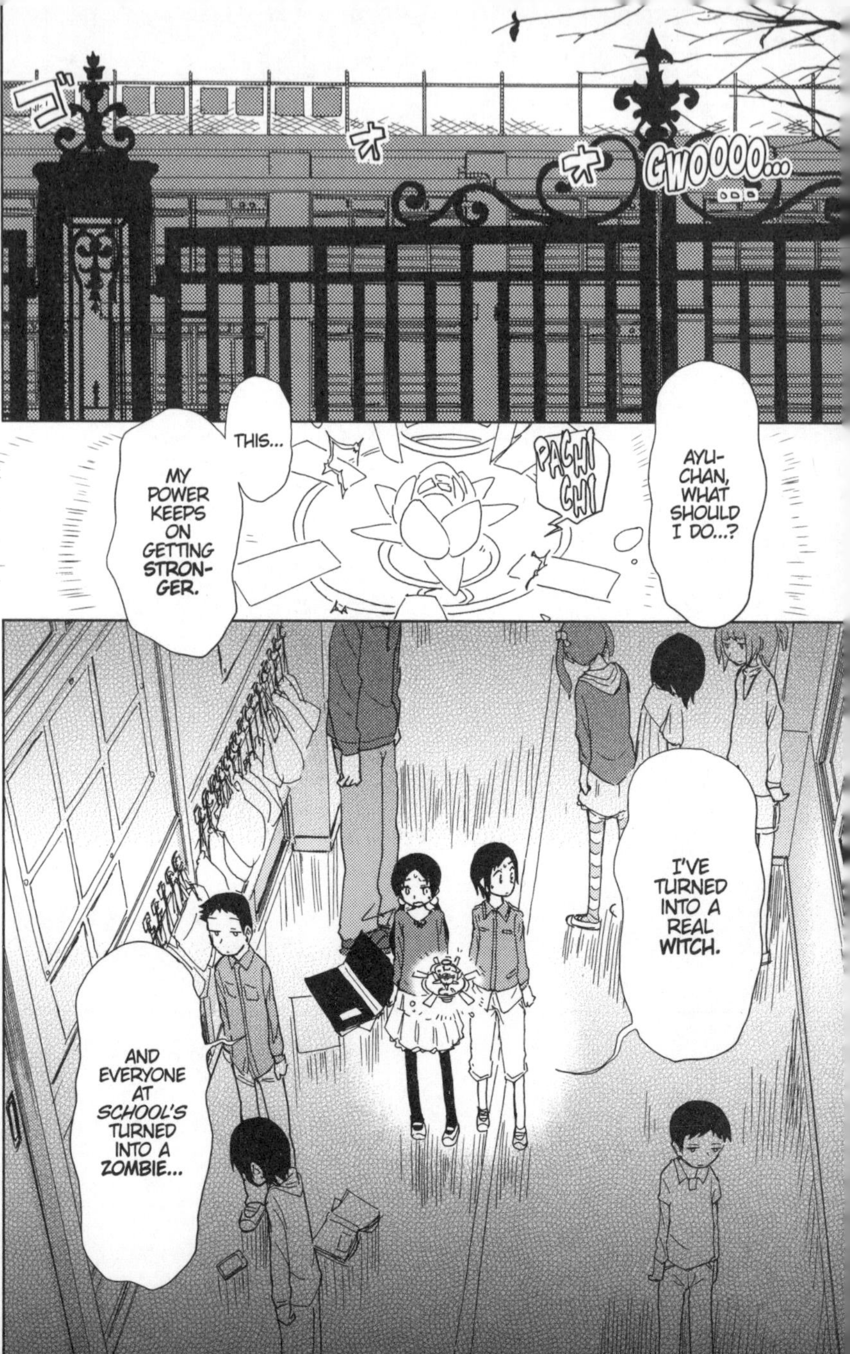
ゴ
オ
オ
GWOOOO...
AYU-CHAN, WHAT SHOULD I DO...?
PACHI CHI
THIS...
MY POWER KEEPS ON GETTING STRONGER.
I'VE TURNED INTO A REAL WITCH.
AND EVERYONE AT SCHOOL'S TURNED INTO A ZOMBIE...

Alice & Zoroku

INTERLUDE

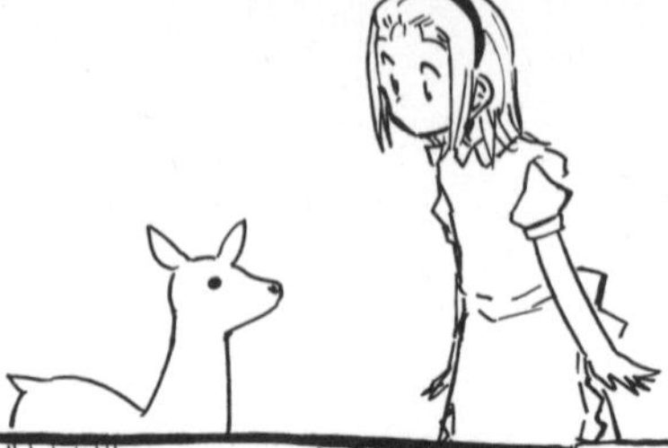

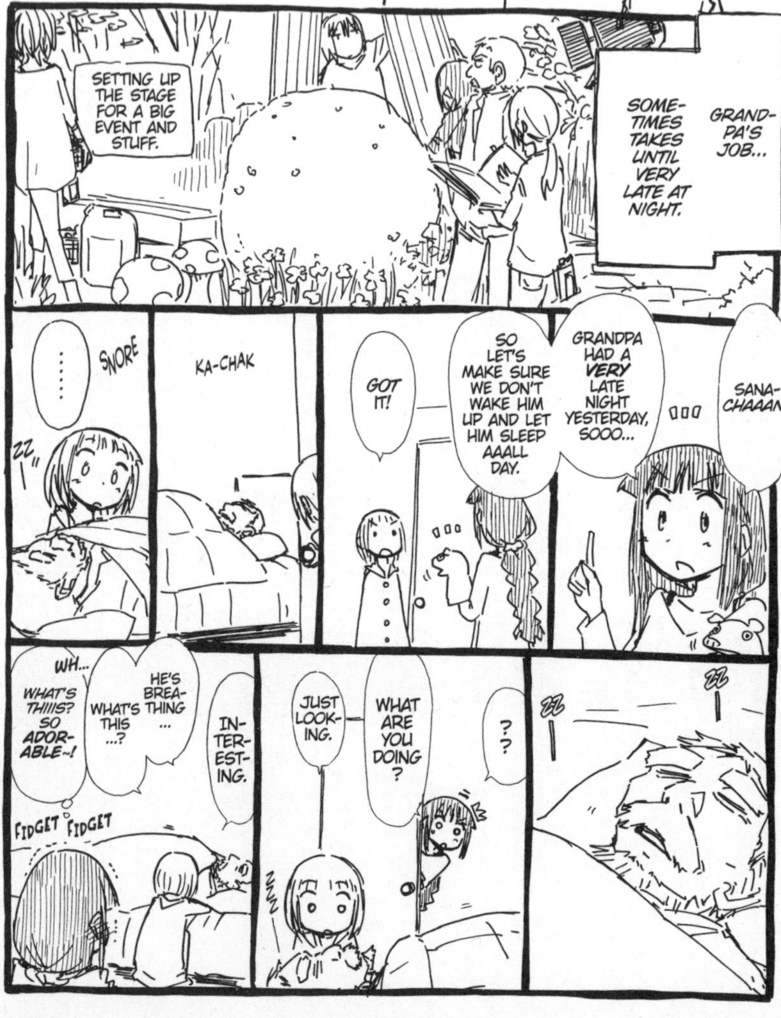

GRANDPA'S JOB...
SOMETIMES TAKES UNTIL VERY LATE AT NIGHT.
SETTING UP THE STAGE FOR A BIG EVENT AND STUFF.
SANA-CHAAAN!
GRANDPA HAD A VERY LATE NIGHT YESTERDAY, SOOO...
SO LET'S MAKE SURE WE DON'T WAKE HIM UP AND LET HIM SLEEP AAALL DAY.
GOT IT!
KA-CHAK
......
SNORE
?-?
WHAT ARE YOU DOING?
JUST LOOKING.
INTERESTING.
HE'S BREATHING...
WHAT'S THIS...?
WH... WHAT'S THIIIS? SO ADORABLE~!
FIDGET FIDGET

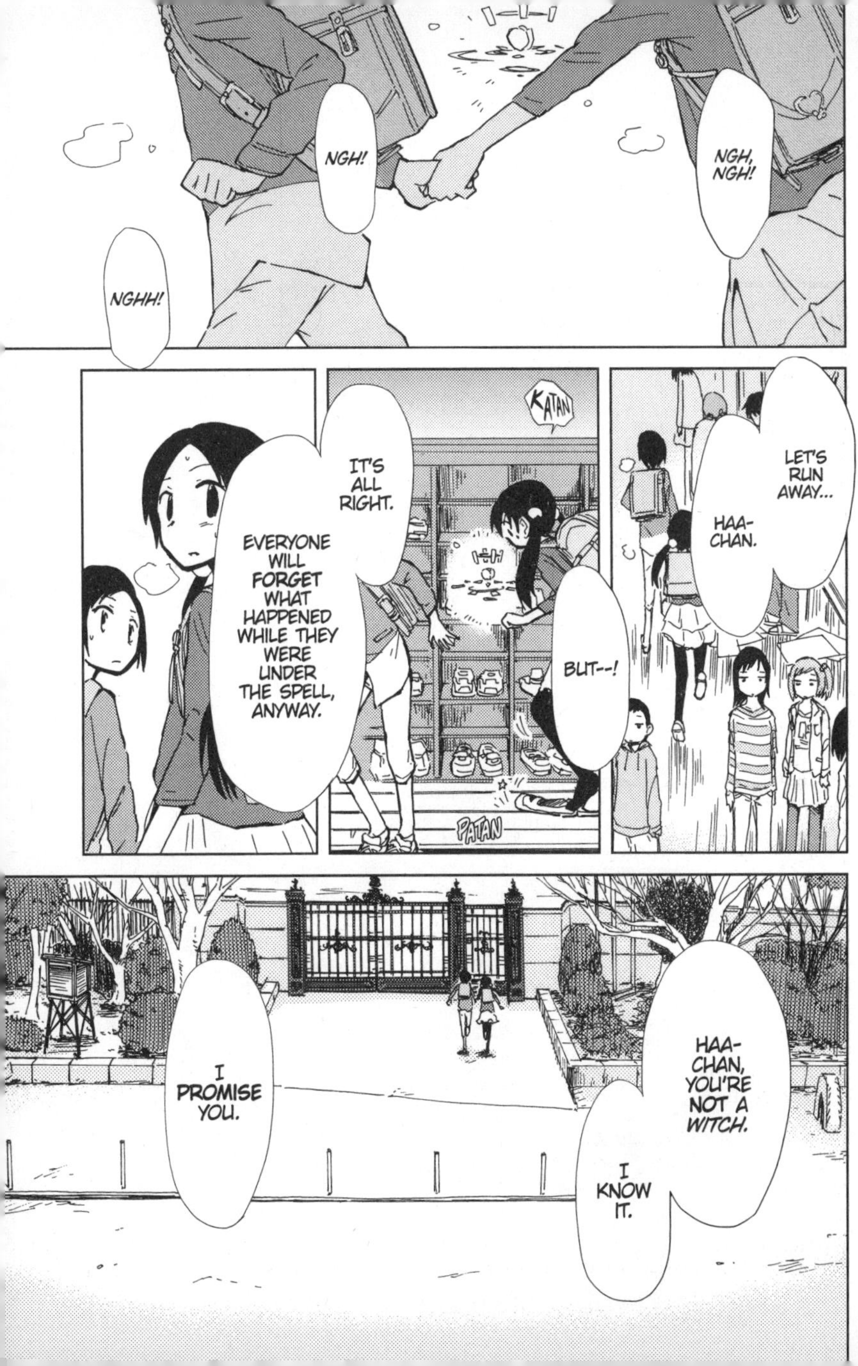
NGH, NGH!
NGH!
NGHH!
LET'S RUN AWAY...
HAA-CHAN.
BUT--!
KATAN
IT'S ALL RIGHT.
EVERYONE WILL FORGET WHAT HAPPENED WHILE THEY WERE UNDER THE SPELL, ANYWAY.
PATAN
HAA-CHAN, YOU'RE NOT A WITCH.
I KNOW IT.
I PROMISE YOU.

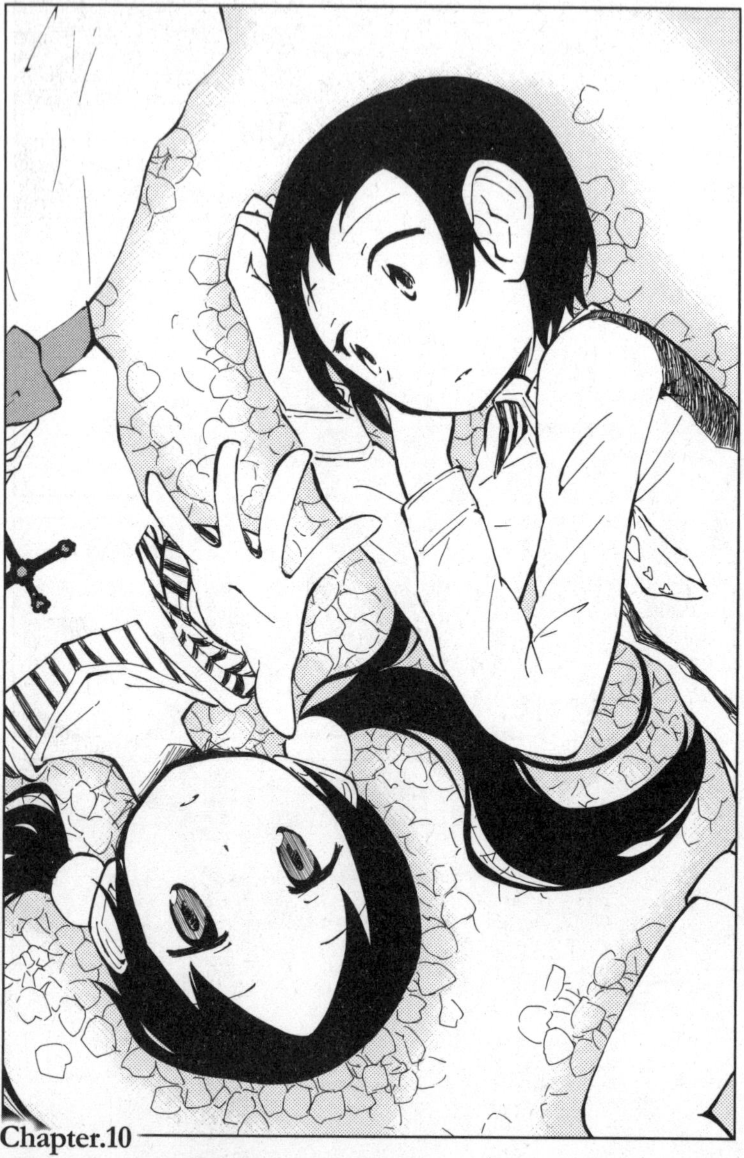

Chapter.10

A Tangled Rabbit Warren

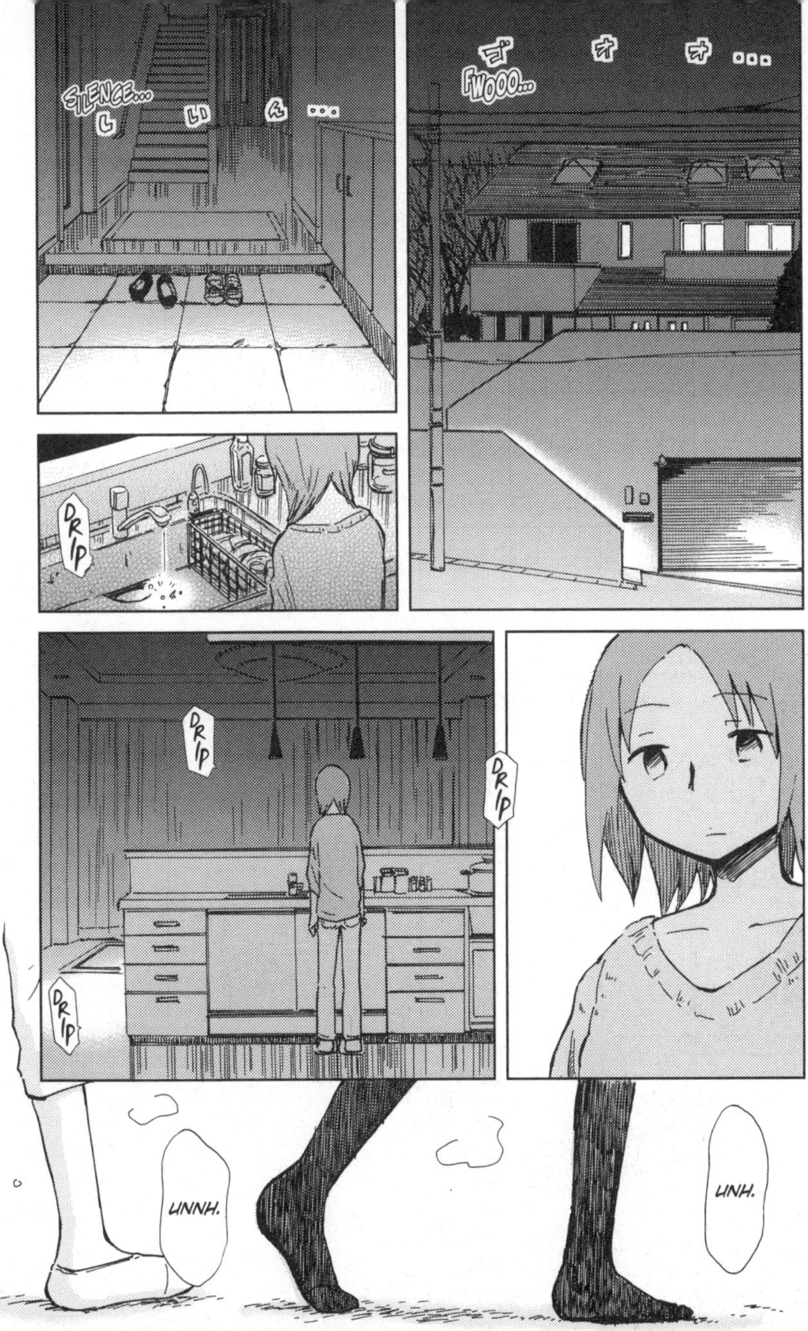
ゴオオ…
FWOOO…
SILENCE…
しいん…
DRIP
DRIP
DRIP
DRIP
UNH.
UNNH.

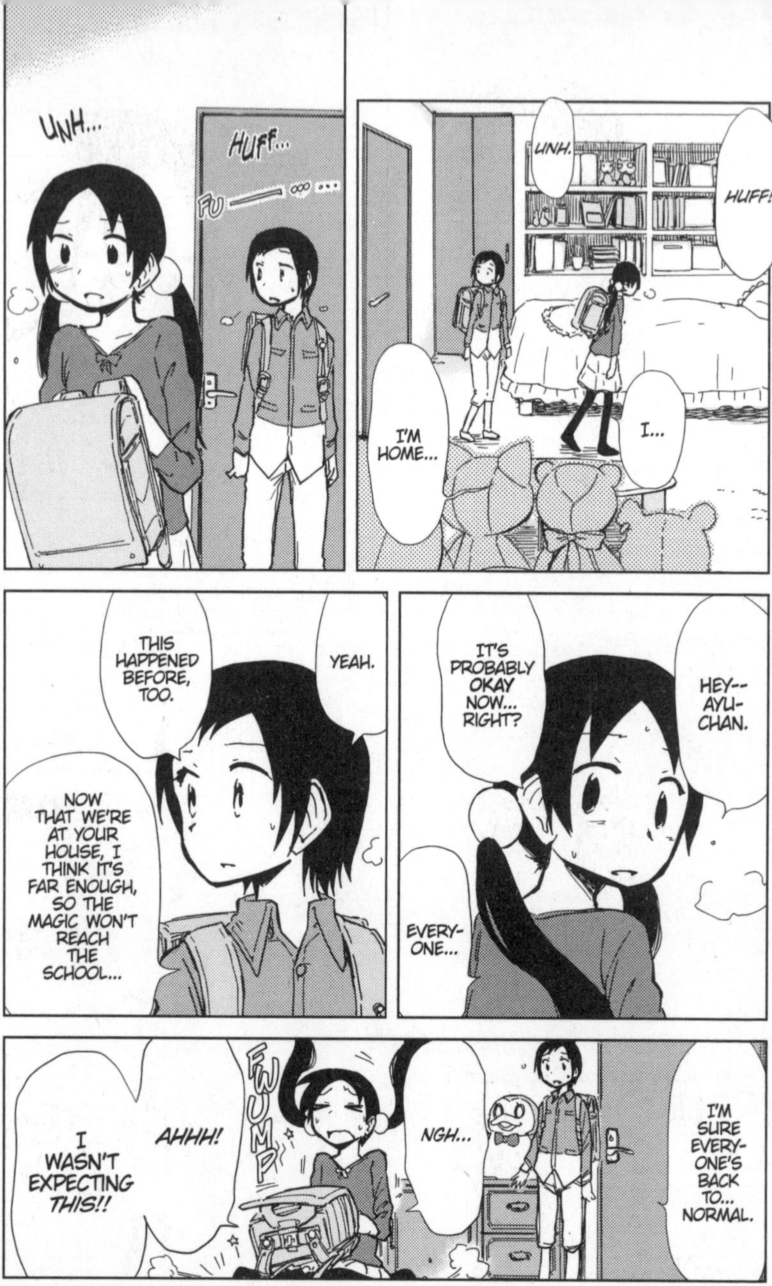
HUFF!
UNH.
I...
I'M HOME...
HUFF...
FU——ooo...
UNH...
HEY-- AYU-CHAN.
IT'S PROBABLY OKAY NOW... RIGHT?
EVERY-ONE...
YEAH.
THIS HAPPENED BEFORE, TOO.
NOW THAT WE'RE AT YOUR HOUSE, I THINK IT'S FAR ENOUGH, SO THE MAGIC WON'T REACH THE SCHOOL...
I'M SURE EVERY-ONE'S BACK TO... NORMAL.
NGH...
FWUMP
AHHH!
I WASN'T EXPECTING *THIS!!*

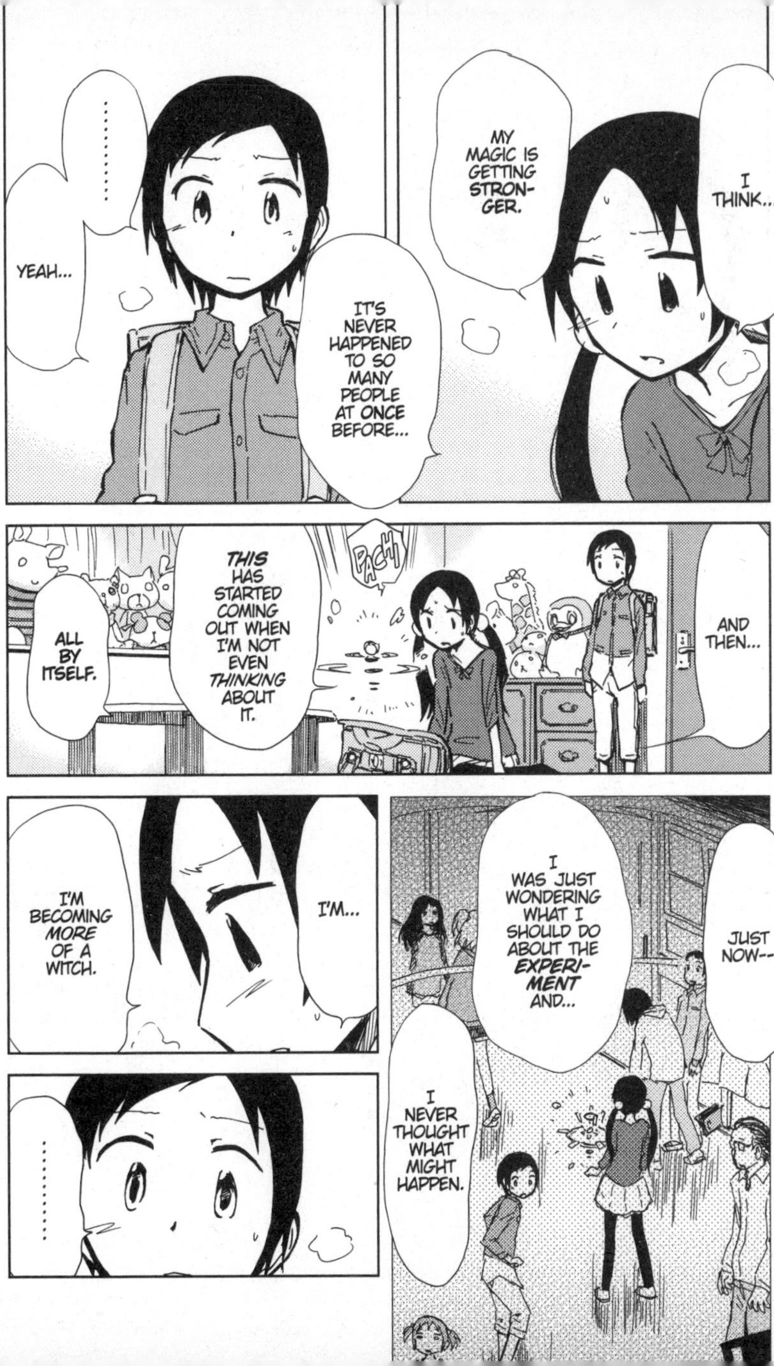
I THINK...
MY MAGIC IS GETTING STRONGER.
......
YEAH...
IT'S NEVER HAPPENED TO SO MANY PEOPLE AT ONCE BEFORE...
AND THEN...
PACH
THIS HAS STARTED COMING OUT WHEN I'M NOT EVEN *THINKING* ABOUT IT.
ALL BY ITSELF.
JUST NOW--
I WAS JUST WONDERING WHAT I SHOULD DO ABOUT THE *EXPERIMENT* AND...
I NEVER THOUGHT WHAT MIGHT HAPPEN.
I'M...
I'M BECOMING *MORE* OF A WITCH.
......

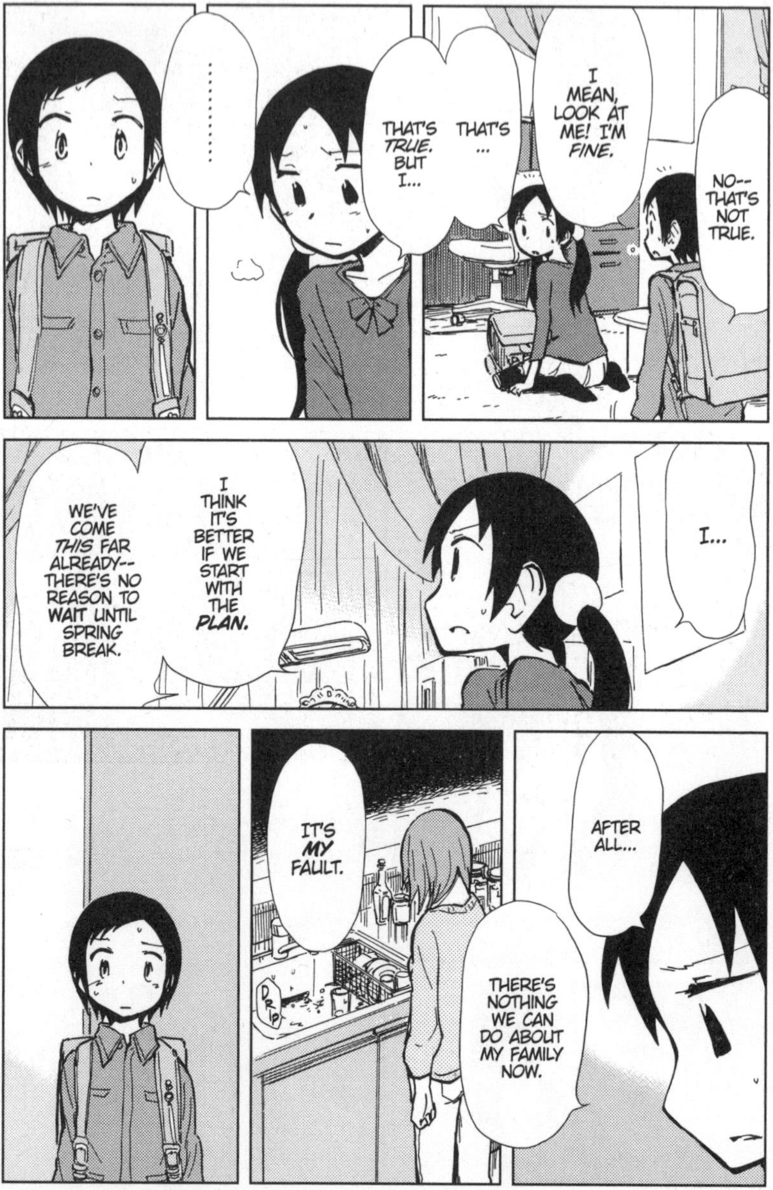
I MEAN, LOOK AT ME! I'M *FINE.*
NO-- THAT'S NOT TRUE.
THAT'S ...
THAT'S *TRUE.* BUT I...
......
I...
I THINK IT'S BETTER IF WE START WITH THE **PLAN.**
WE'VE COME *THIS* FAR ALREADY-- THERE'S NO REASON TO WAIT UNTIL SPRING BREAK.
AFTER ALL...
THERE'S NOTHING WE CAN DO ABOUT MY FAMILY NOW.
IT'S ***MY*** FAULT.
DRIP

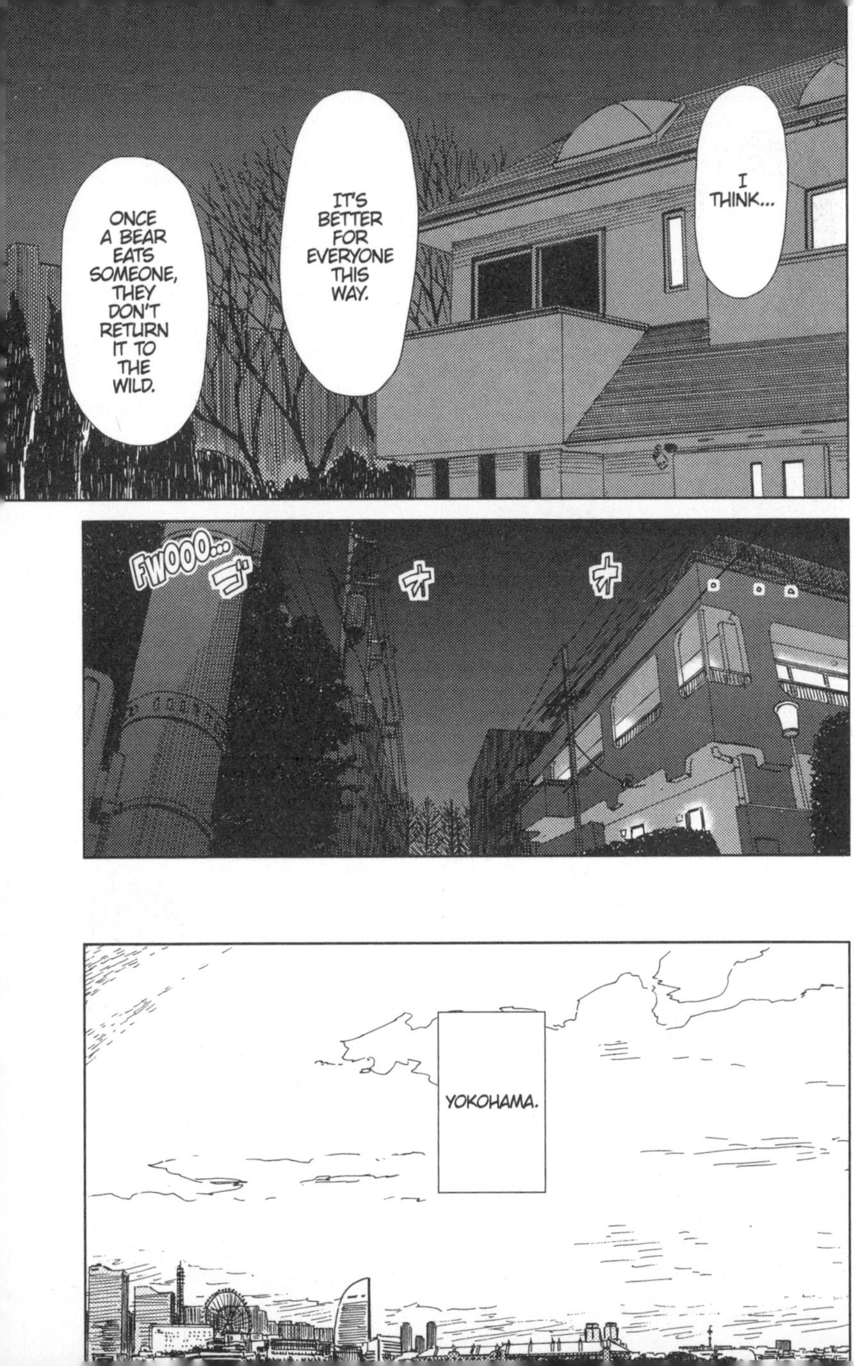
I THINK...
IT'S BETTER FOR EVERYONE THIS WAY.
ONCE A BEAR EATS SOMEONE, THEY DON'T RETURN IT TO THE WILD.
FWOOO...
ゴ
オ
オ
YOKOHAMA.

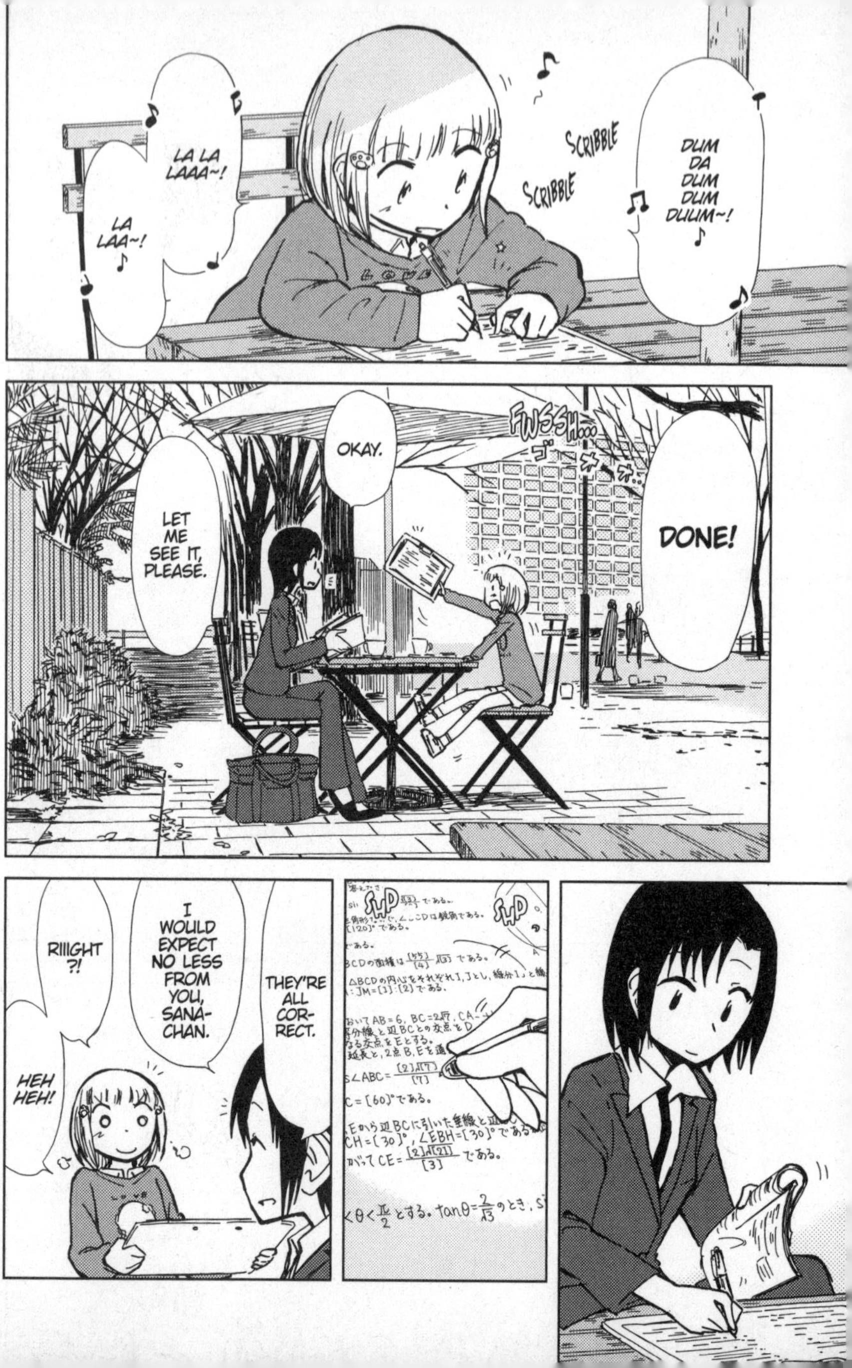
DUM DA DUM DUM DUUM~!
SCRIBBLE
SCRIBBLE
LA LA LAAA~!
LA LAA~!
DONE!
FWSSH...
OKAY.
LET ME SEE IT, PLEASE.
SHP
SHP
THEY'RE ALL CORRECT.
I WOULD EXPECT NO LESS FROM YOU, SANA-CHAN.
RIIIGHT?!
HEH HEH!

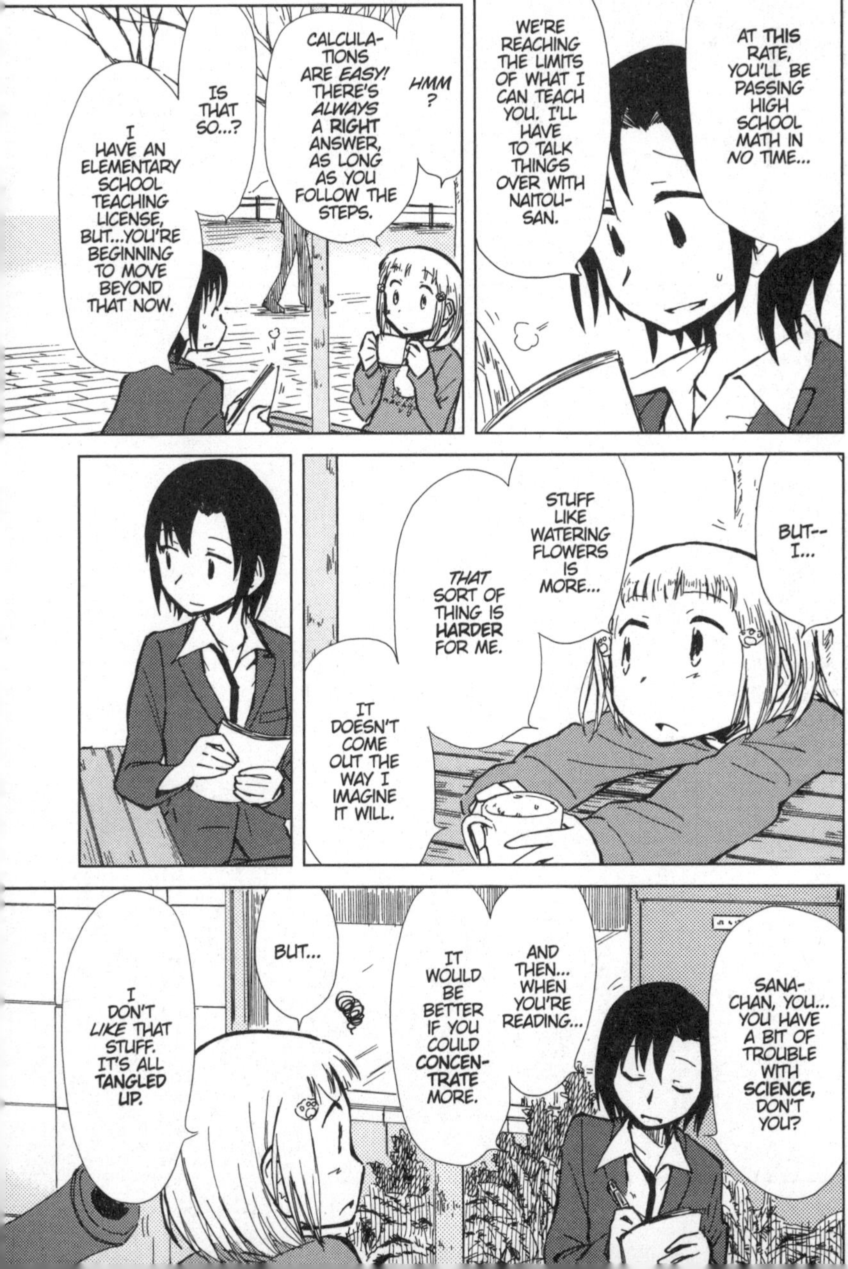
AT THIS RATE, YOU'LL BE PASSING HIGH SCHOOL MATH IN *NO TIME*...
WE'RE REACHING THE LIMITS OF WHAT I CAN TEACH YOU. I'LL HAVE TO TALK THINGS OVER WITH NAITOU-SAN.
HMM ?
CALCULATIONS ARE *EASY!* THERE'S *ALWAYS* A RIGHT ANSWER, AS LONG AS YOU FOLLOW THE STEPS.
IS THAT SO...?
I HAVE AN ELEMENTARY SCHOOL TEACHING LICENSE, BUT...YOU'RE BEGINNING TO MOVE BEYOND THAT NOW.
BUT-- I...
STUFF LIKE WATERING FLOWERS IS MORE...
THAT SORT OF THING IS **HARDER** FOR ME.
IT DOESN'T COME OUT THE WAY I IMAGINE IT WILL.
SANA-CHAN, YOU... YOU HAVE A BIT OF TROUBLE WITH **SCIENCE**, DON'T YOU?
AND THEN... WHEN YOU'RE READING...
IT WOULD BE BETTER IF YOU COULD **CONCENTRATE** MORE.
BUT...
I DON'T *LIKE* THAT STUFF. IT'S ALL **TANGLED UP**.

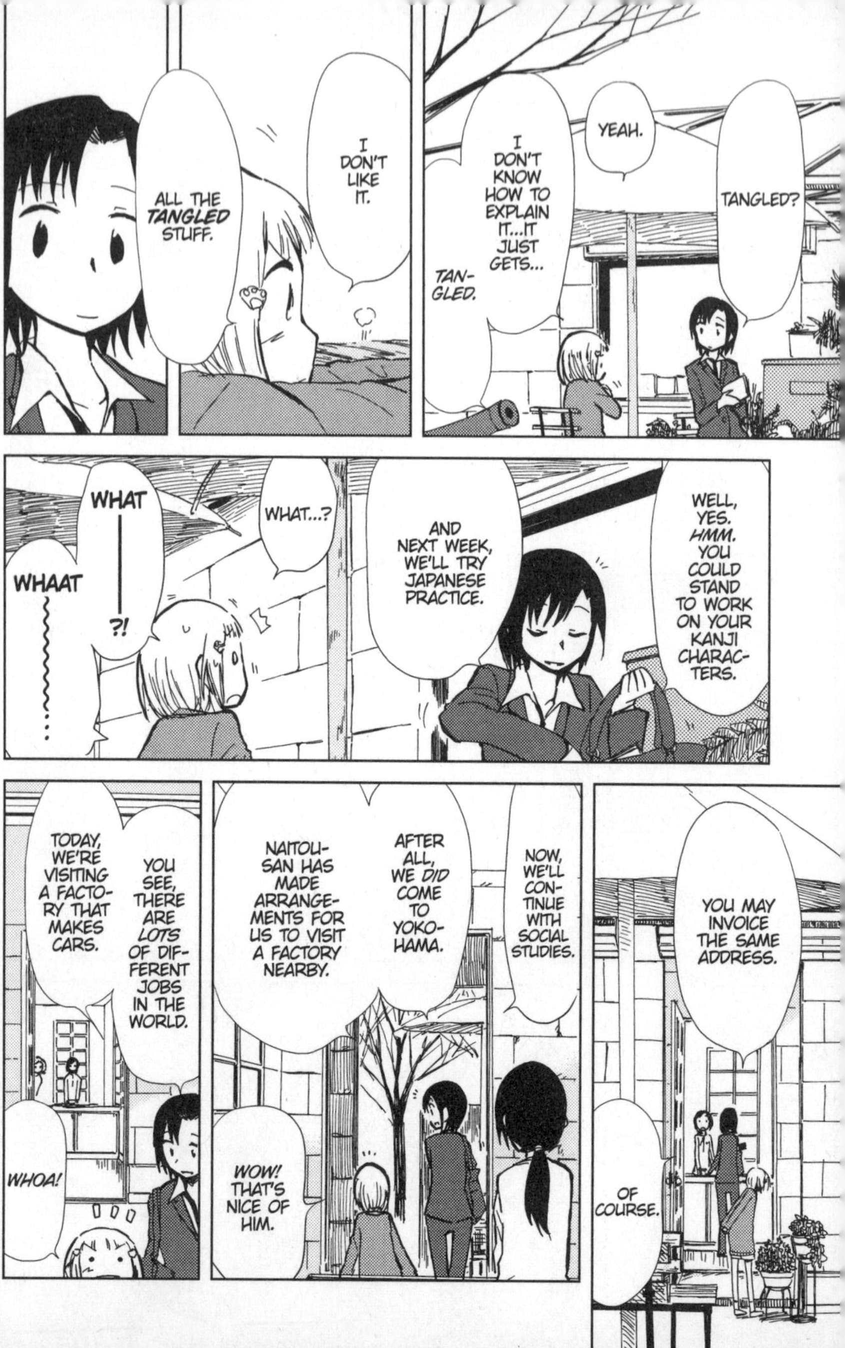
TANGLED?
YEAH.
I DON'T KNOW HOW TO EXPLAIN IT...IT JUST GETS... TANGLED.
I DON'T LIKE IT.
ALL THE TANGLED STUFF.
WELL, YES. HMM. YOU COULD STAND TO WORK ON YOUR KANJI CHARACTERS.
AND NEXT WEEK, WE'LL TRY JAPANESE PRACTICE.
WHAT...?
WHAT—?!
WHAAT......
YOU MAY INVOICE THE SAME ADDRESS.
OF COURSE.
NOW, WE'LL CONTINUE WITH SOCIAL STUDIES.
AFTER ALL, WE DID COME TO YOKOHAMA.
NAITOU-SAN HAS MADE ARRANGEMENTS FOR US TO VISIT A FACTORY NEARBY.
WOW! THAT'S NICE OF HIM.
YOU SEE, THERE ARE LOTS OF DIFFERENT JOBS IN THE WORLD.
TODAY, WE'RE VISITING A FACTORY THAT MAKES CARS.
WHOA!

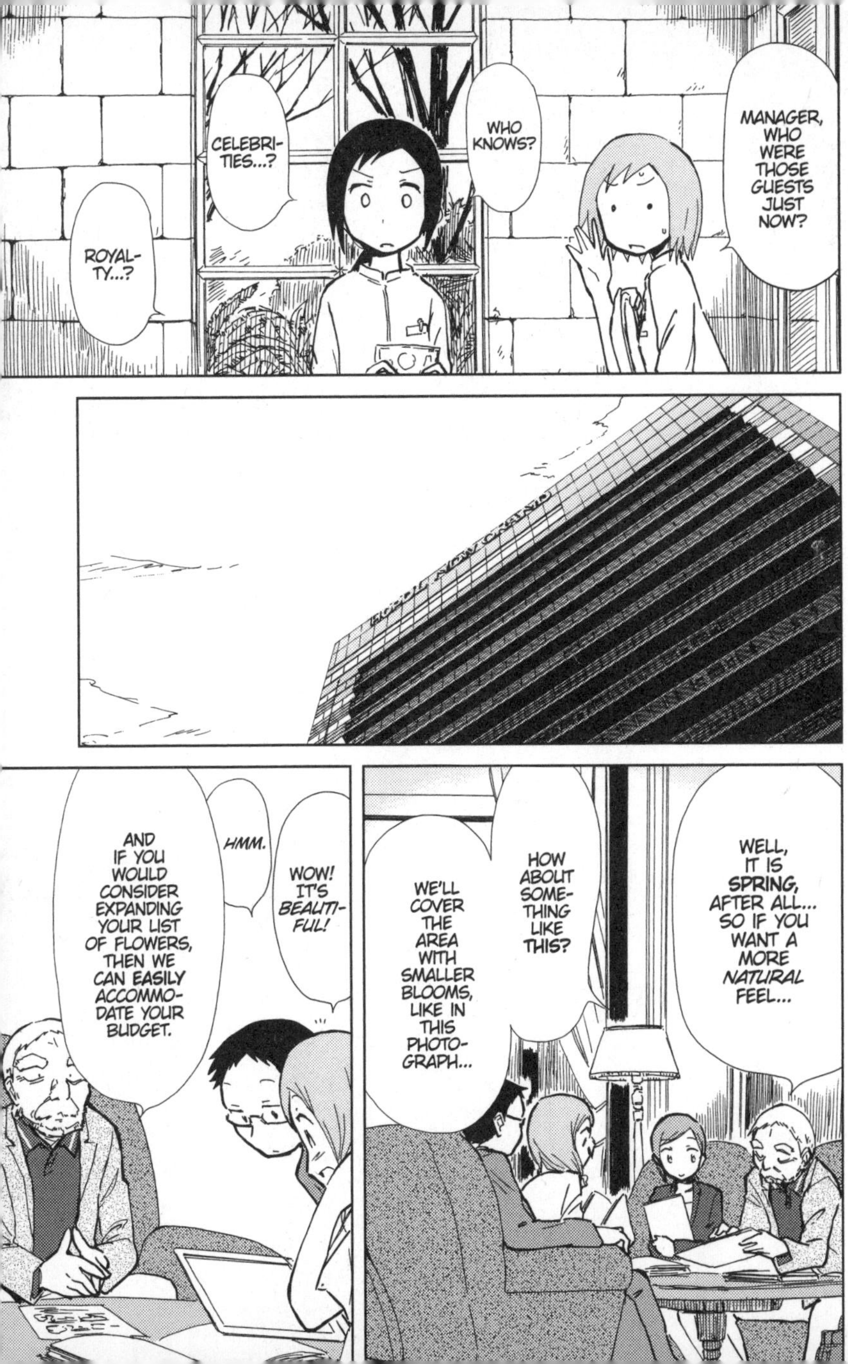
MANAGER, WHO WERE THOSE GUESTS JUST NOW?
WHO KNOWS?
CELEBRITIES...?
ROYALTY...?
WELL, IT IS SPRING, AFTER ALL... SO IF YOU WANT A MORE NATURAL FEEL...
HOW ABOUT SOMETHING LIKE THIS?
WE'LL COVER THE AREA WITH SMALLER BLOOMS, LIKE IN THIS PHOTOGRAPH...
WOW! IT'S BEAUTIFUL!
HMM.
AND IF YOU WOULD CONSIDER EXPANDING YOUR LIST OF FLOWERS, THEN WE CAN EASILY ACCOMMODATE YOUR BUDGET.

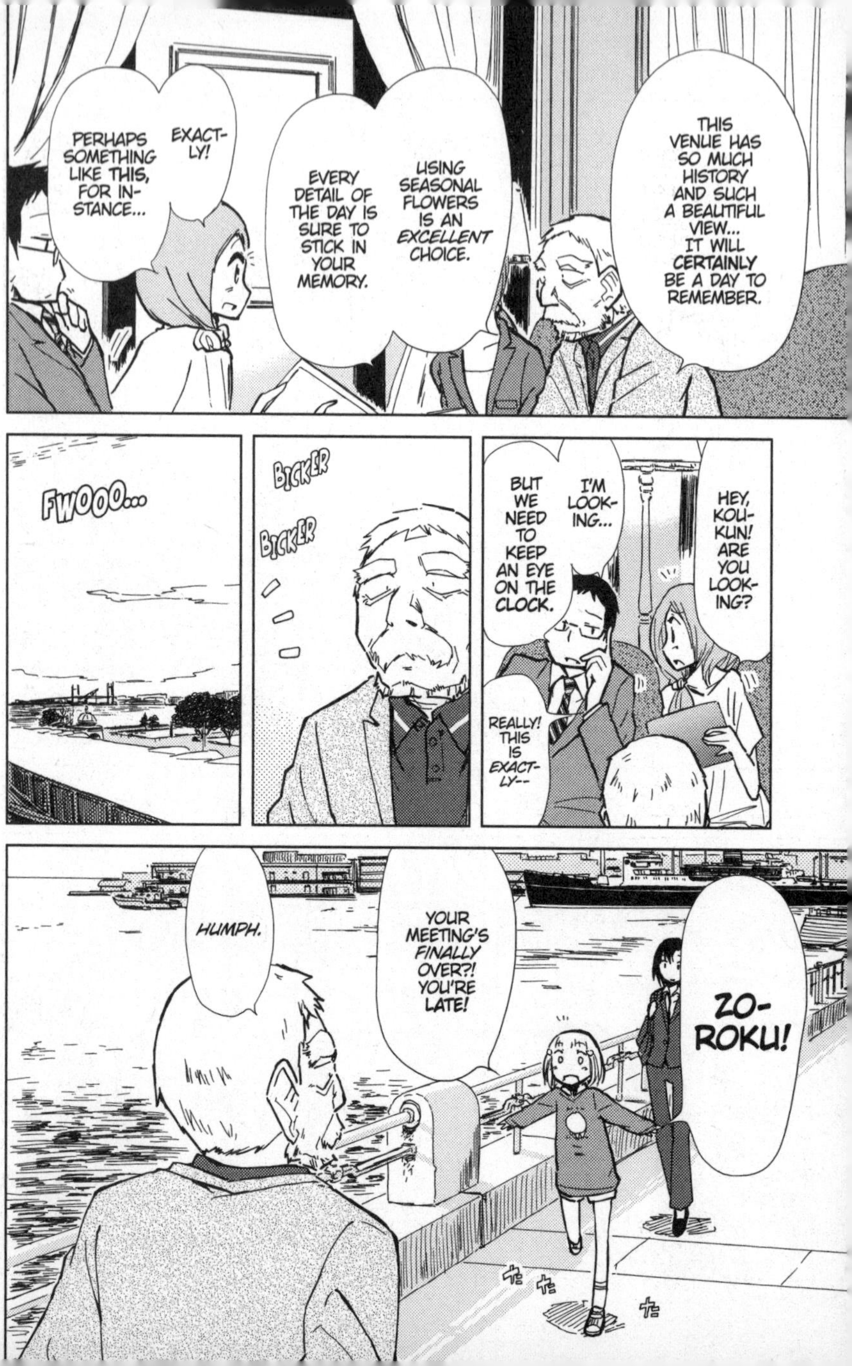
THIS VENUE HAS SO MUCH HISTORY AND SUCH A BEAUTIFUL VIEW... IT WILL CERTAINLY BE A DAY TO REMEMBER.
USING SEASONAL FLOWERS IS AN EXCELLENT CHOICE.
EVERY DETAIL OF THE DAY IS SURE TO STICK IN YOUR MEMORY.
EXACT-LY!
PERHAPS SOMETHING LIKE THIS, FOR IN-STANCE...
HEY, KOU-KUN! ARE YOU LOOK-ING?
I'M LOOK-ING...
BUT WE NEED TO KEEP AN EYE ON THE CLOCK.
REALLY! THIS IS EXACT-LY--
BICKER
BICKER
FWOOO...
ZO-ROKU!
YOUR MEETING'S FINALLY OVER?! YOU'RE LATE!
HUMPH.

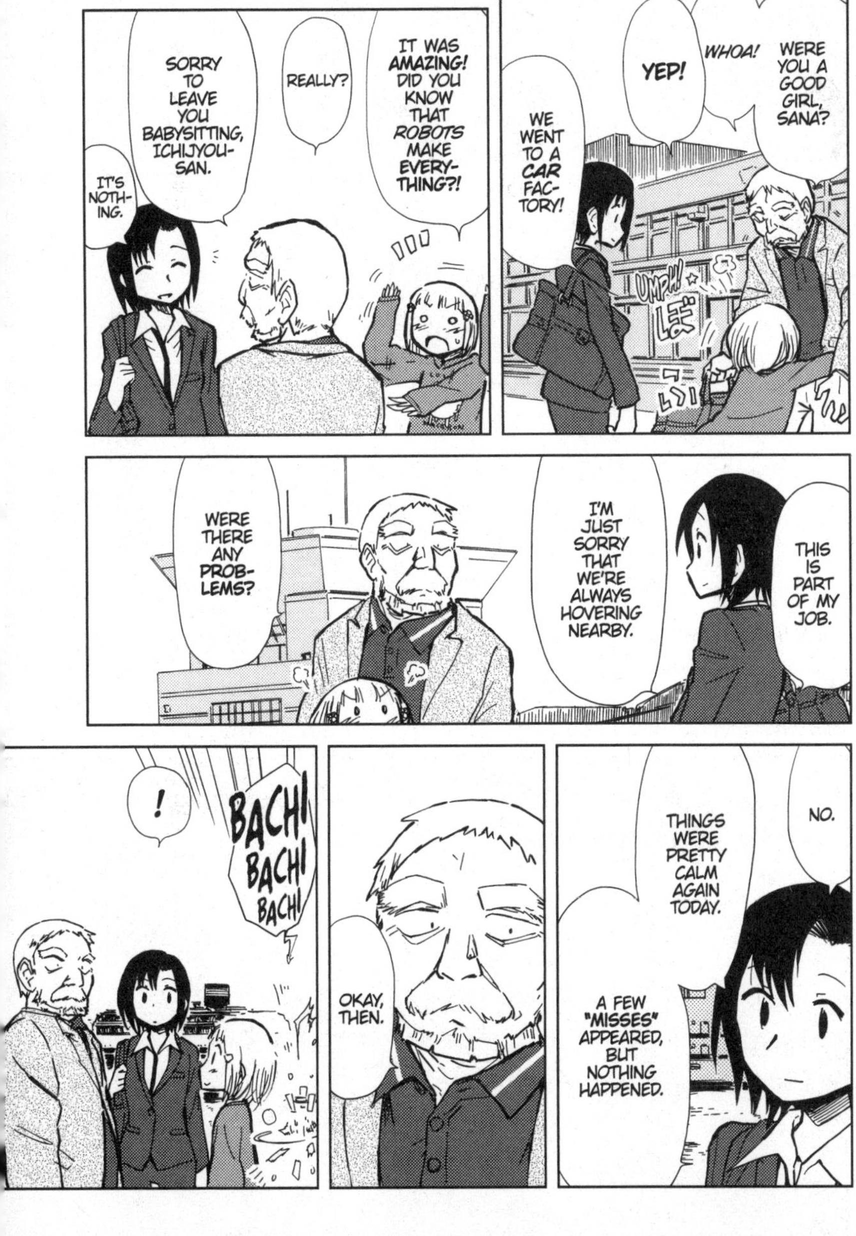
WERE YOU A GOOD GIRL, SANA?
WHOA!
YEP!
WE WENT TO A CAR FACTORY!
UMPH!
IT WAS AMAZING! DID YOU KNOW THAT ROBOTS MAKE EVERYTHING?!
REALLY?
SORRY TO LEAVE YOU BABYSITTING, ICHIJYOU-SAN.
IT'S NOTHING.
THIS IS PART OF MY JOB.
I'M JUST SORRY THAT WE'RE ALWAYS HOVERING NEARBY.
WERE THERE ANY PROBLEMS?
NO.
THINGS WERE PRETTY CALM AGAIN TODAY.
A FEW "MISSES" APPEARED, BUT NOTHING HAPPENED.
OKAY, THEN.
!
BACHI BACHI BACHI

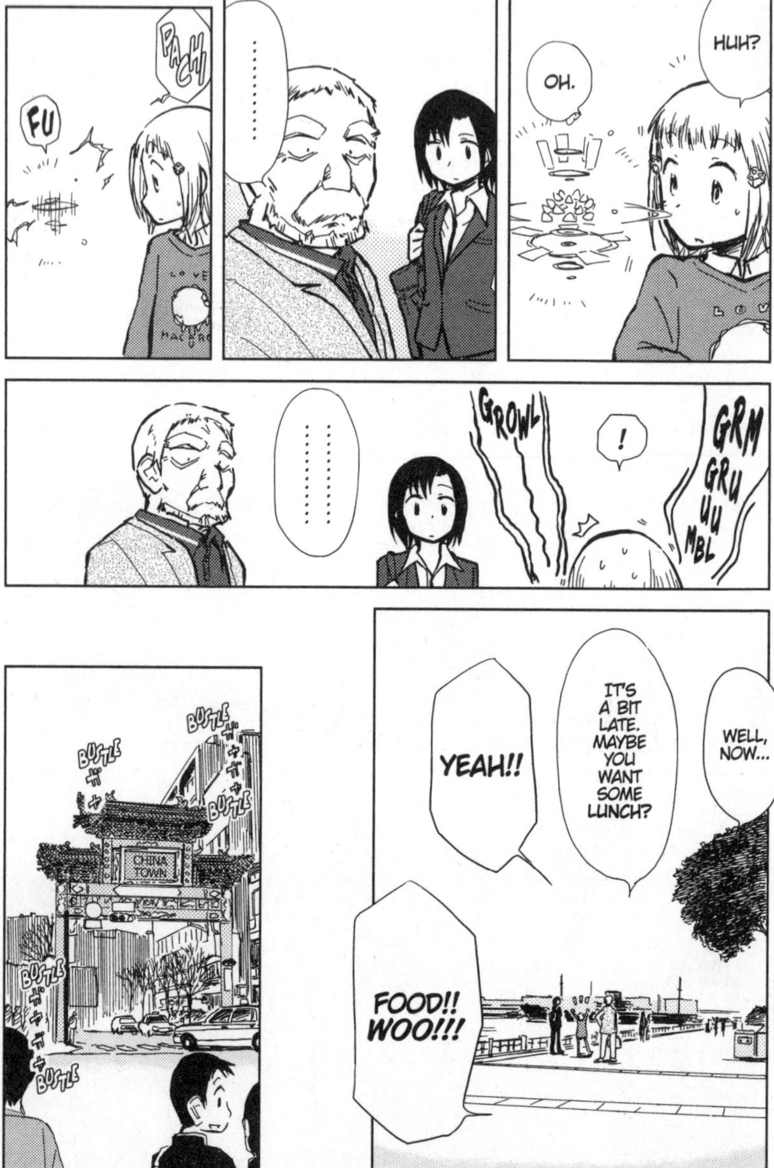
HUH?
OH.
......
PACHI
FU
GRM GRU UU MBL
!
GROWL
......
WELL, NOW...
IT'S A BIT LATE. MAYBE YOU WANT SOME LUNCH?
YEAH!!
FOOD!! WOO!!!
BUSTLE
BUSTLE
CHINA TOWN
BUSTLE
BUSTLE
BUSTLE

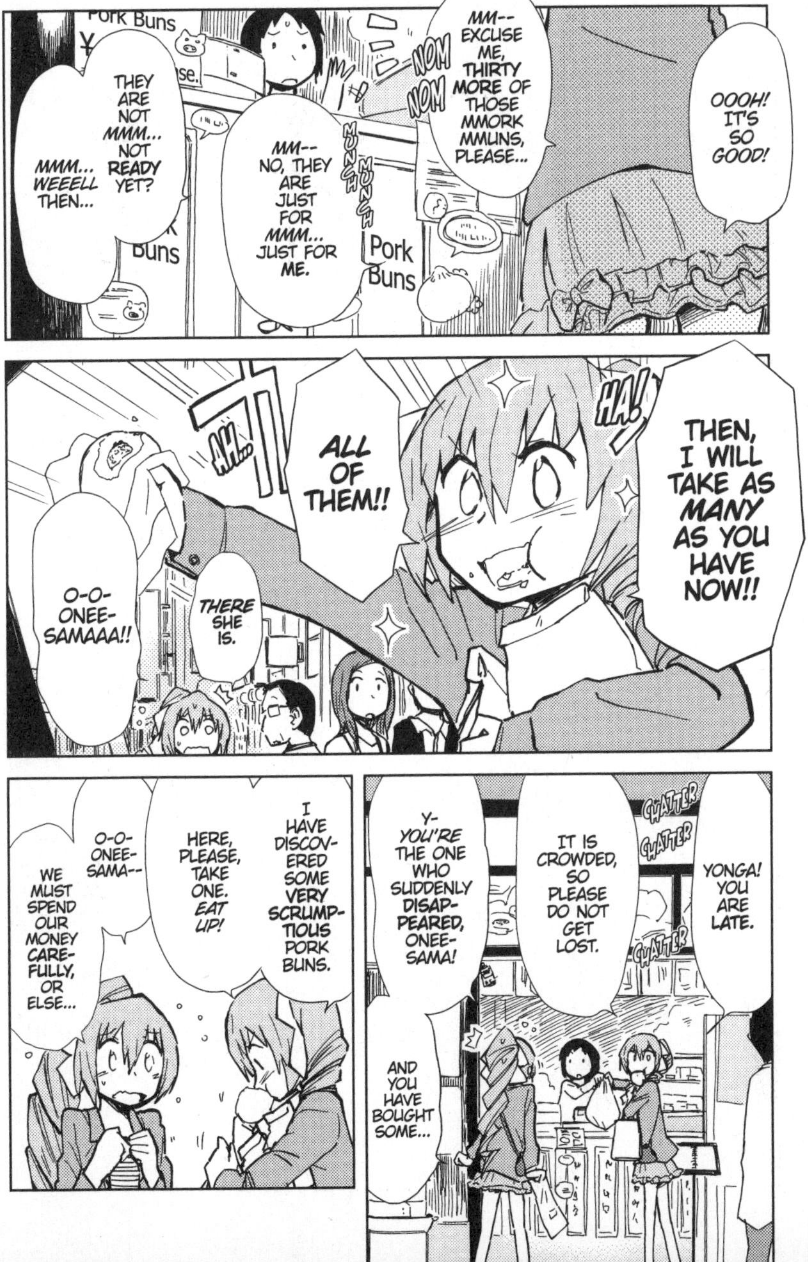
OOOH! IT'S SO GOOD!
MM-- EXCUSE ME, THIRTY MORE OF THOSE MMORK MMUNS, PLEASE...
NOM NOM
Pork Buns
MUNCH MUNCH
MM-- NO, THEY ARE JUST FOR MMM... JUST FOR ME.
Pork Buns
THEY ARE NOT MMM... NOT READY YET?
MMM... WEEELL THEN...
Pork Buns
HA!
THEN, I WILL TAKE AS MANY AS YOU HAVE NOW!!
ALL OF THEM!!
AH...
THERE SHE IS.
O-O-ONEE-SAMAAA!!
YONGA! YOU ARE LATE.
CHATTER
CHATTER
CHATTER
IT IS CROWDED, SO PLEASE DO NOT GET LOST.
Y-YOU'RE THE ONE WHO SUDDENLY DISAPPEARED, ONEE-SAMA!
AND YOU HAVE BOUGHT SOME...
I HAVE DISCOVERED SOME VERY SCRUMPTIOUS PORK BUNS.
HERE, PLEASE, TAKE ONE. EAT UP!
O-O-ONEE-SAMA--
WE MUST SPEND OUR MONEY CAREFULLY, OR ELSE...

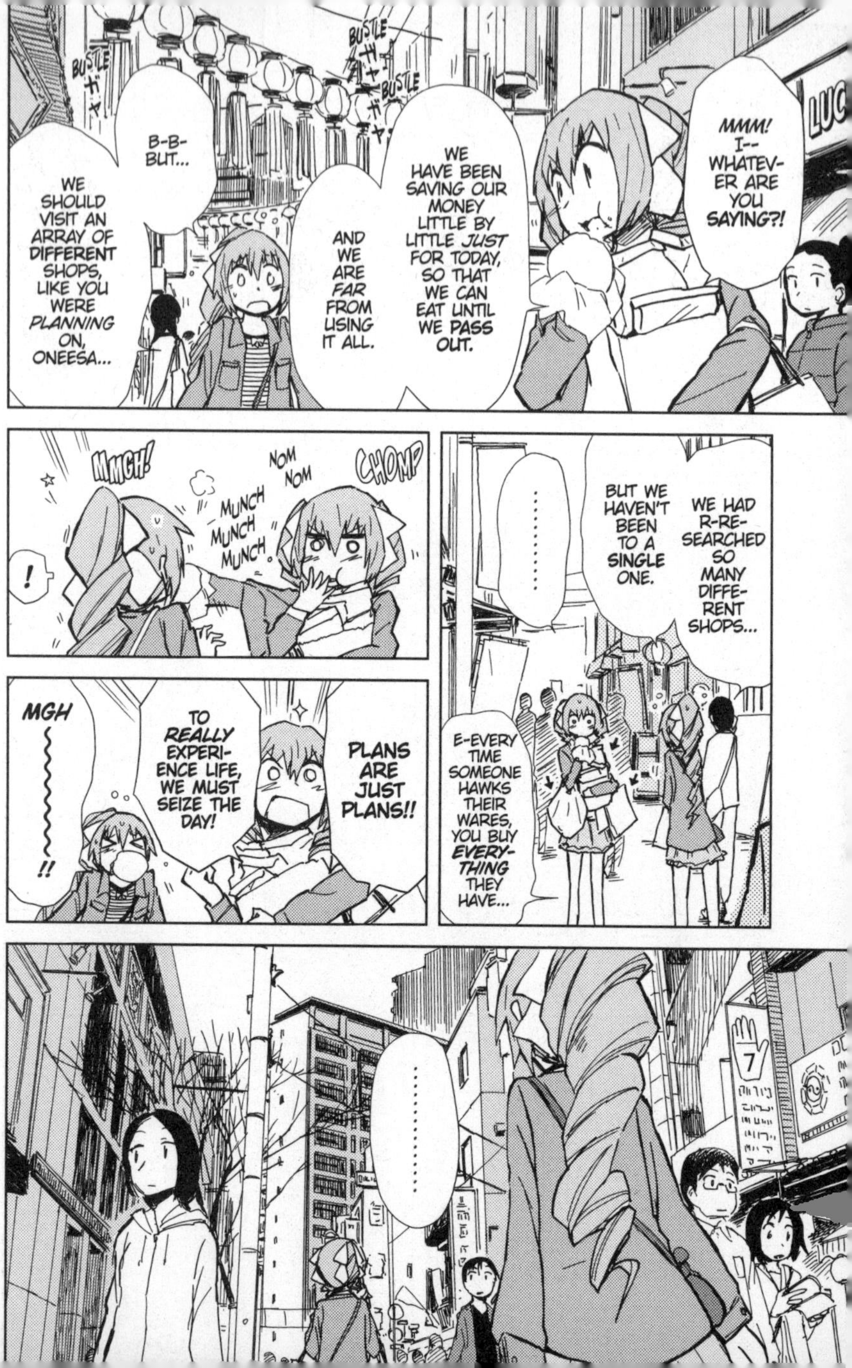
BUSTLE
BUSTLE
BUSTLE
MMM! I-- WHATEVER ARE YOU SAYING?!
WE HAVE BEEN SAVING OUR MONEY LITTLE BY LITTLE *JUST* FOR TODAY, SO THAT WE CAN EAT UNTIL WE PASS OUT.
AND WE ARE *FAR* FROM USING IT ALL.
B-B-BUT...
WE SHOULD VISIT AN ARRAY OF DIFFERENT SHOPS, LIKE YOU WERE *PLANNING* ON, ONEESA...
WE HAD R-RE-SEARCHED SO MANY DIFFE-RENT SHOPS...
BUT WE HAVEN'T BEEN TO A SINGLE ONE.
......
E-EVERY TIME SOMEONE HAWKS THEIR WARES, YOU BUY ***EVERY-THING*** THEY HAVE...
CHOMP
NOM NOM
MUNCH MUNCH MUNCH
MMGH!
!
PLANS ARE JUST PLANS!!
TO ***REALLY*** EXPERI-ENCE LIFE, WE MUST SEIZE THE DAY!
MGH ~~~ !!
......

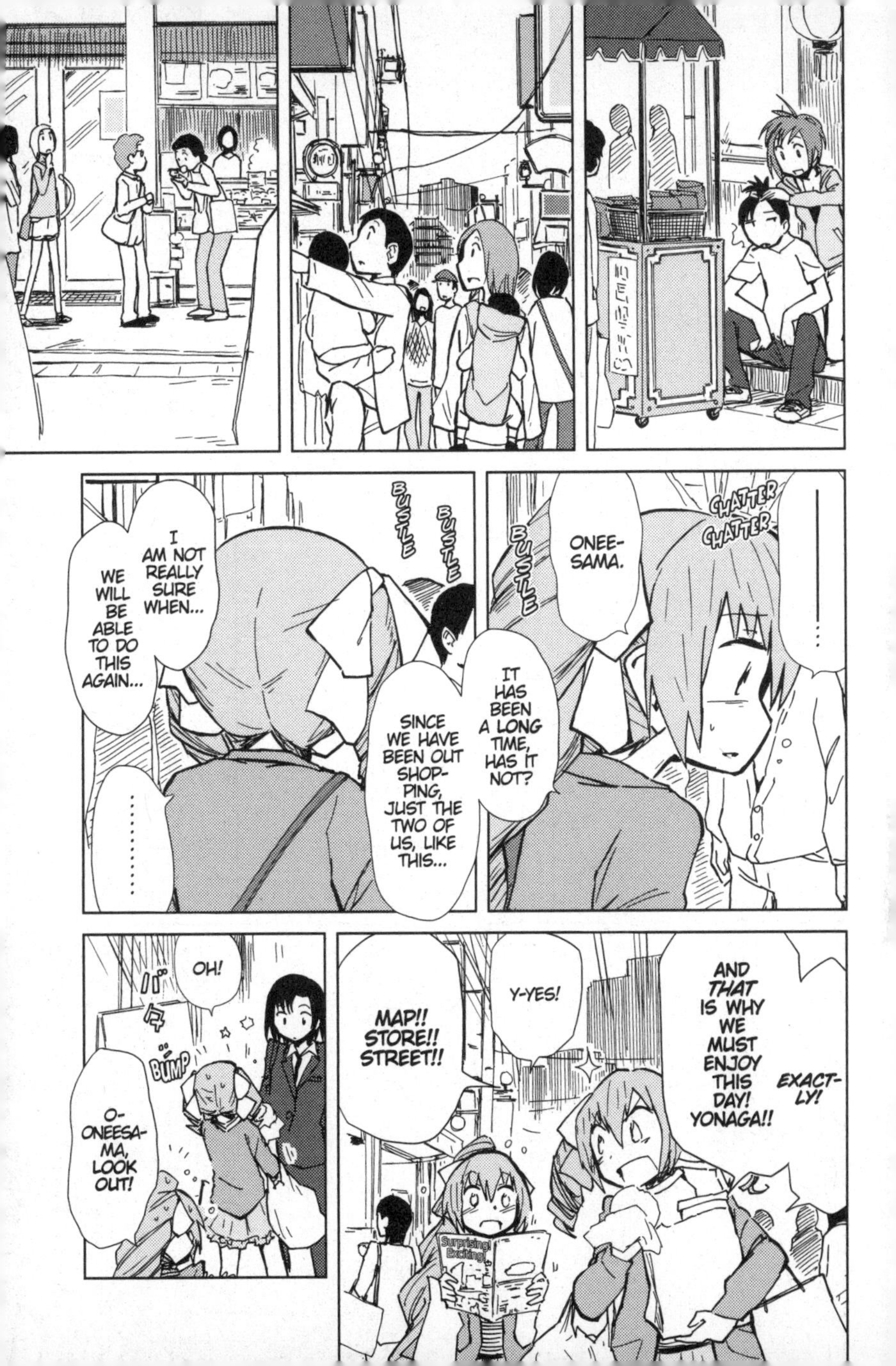

......
CHATTER CHATTER
ONEE-SAMA.
BUSTLE
IT HAS BEEN A LONG TIME, HAS IT NOT?
SINCE WE HAVE BEEN OUT SHOPPING, JUST THE TWO OF US, LIKE THIS...
BUSTLE
BUSTLE
I AM NOT REALLY SURE WHEN...
WE WILL BE ABLE TO DO THIS AGAIN...
......
EXACTLY!
AND *THAT* IS WHY WE MUST ENJOY THIS DAY! YONAGA!!
Y-YES!
MAP!! STORE!! STREET!!
Surprising! Exciting!
OH!
BUMP
O-ONEESAMA, LOOK OUT!

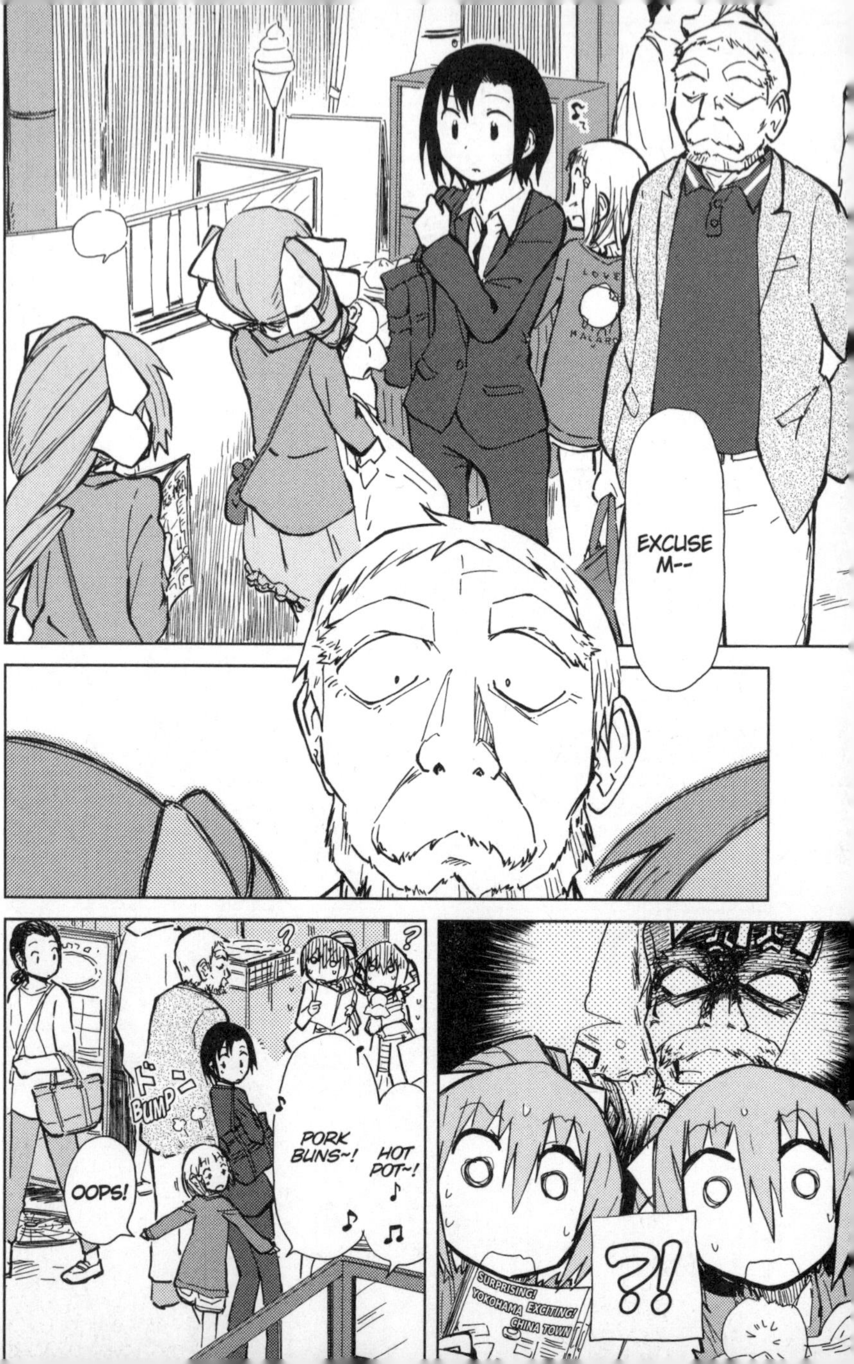
EXCUSE M--
?!
SURPRISING!
YOKOHAMA EXCITING!
CHINA TOWN
HOT POT~!
PORK BUNS~!
BUMP
OOPS!

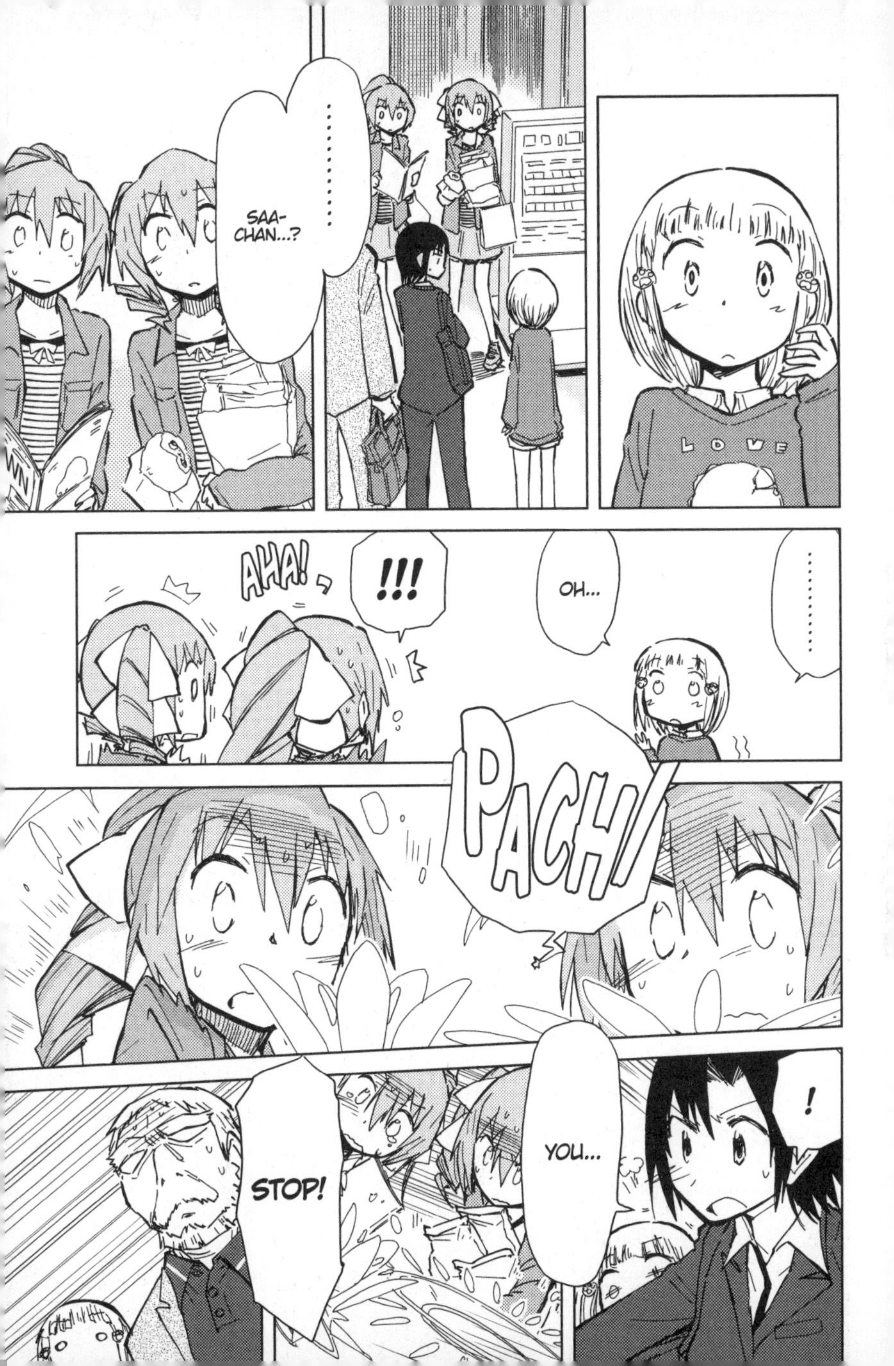

......
SAA-CHAN...?
......
OH...
!!!
AHA!
PACH!
!
YOU...
STOP!

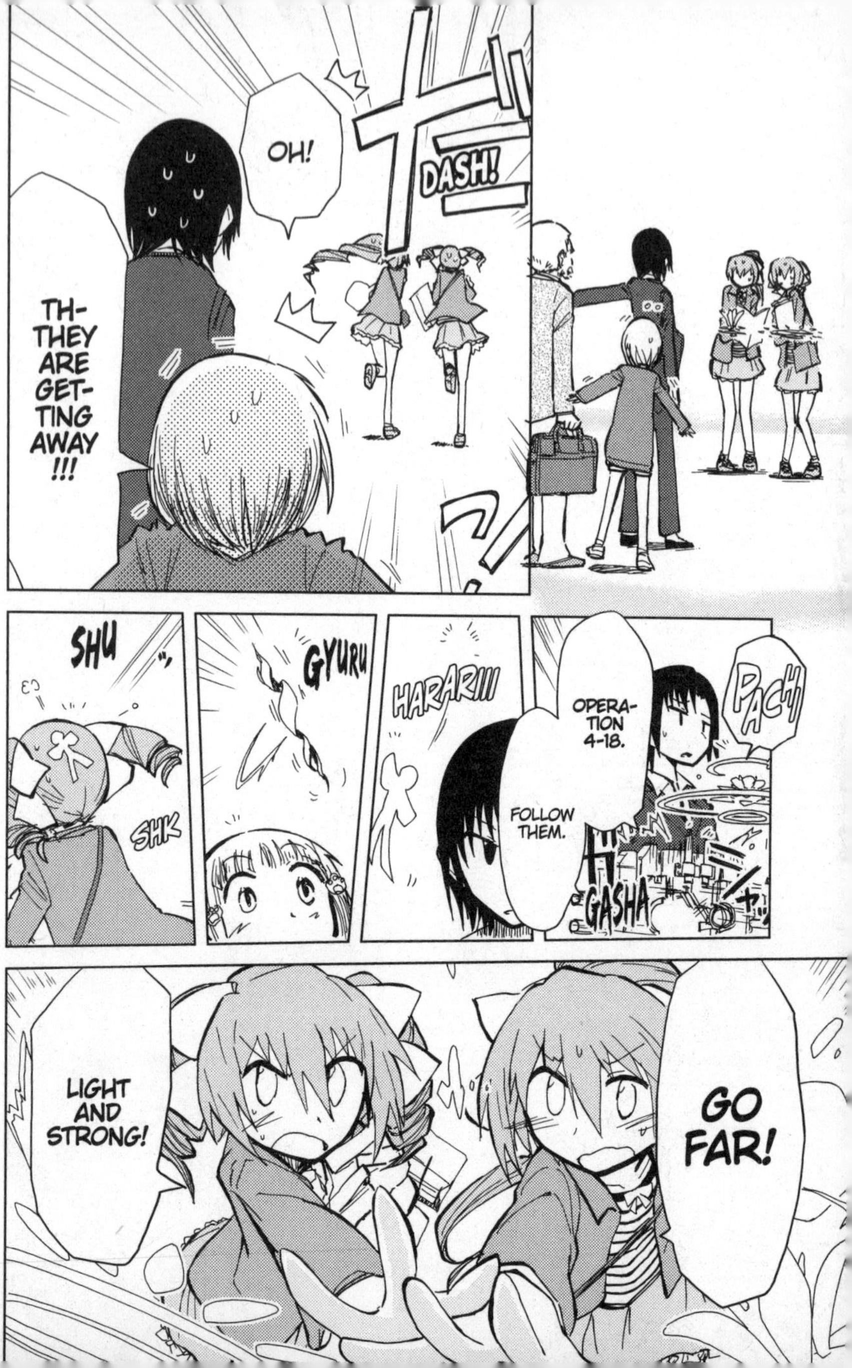
DASH!
OH!
TH-THEY ARE GETTING AWAY!!!
PACH
OPERATION 4-18.
FOLLOW THEM.
GASHA
HARARI!!!
GYURU
SHU
SHK
GO FAR!
LIGHT AND STRONG!

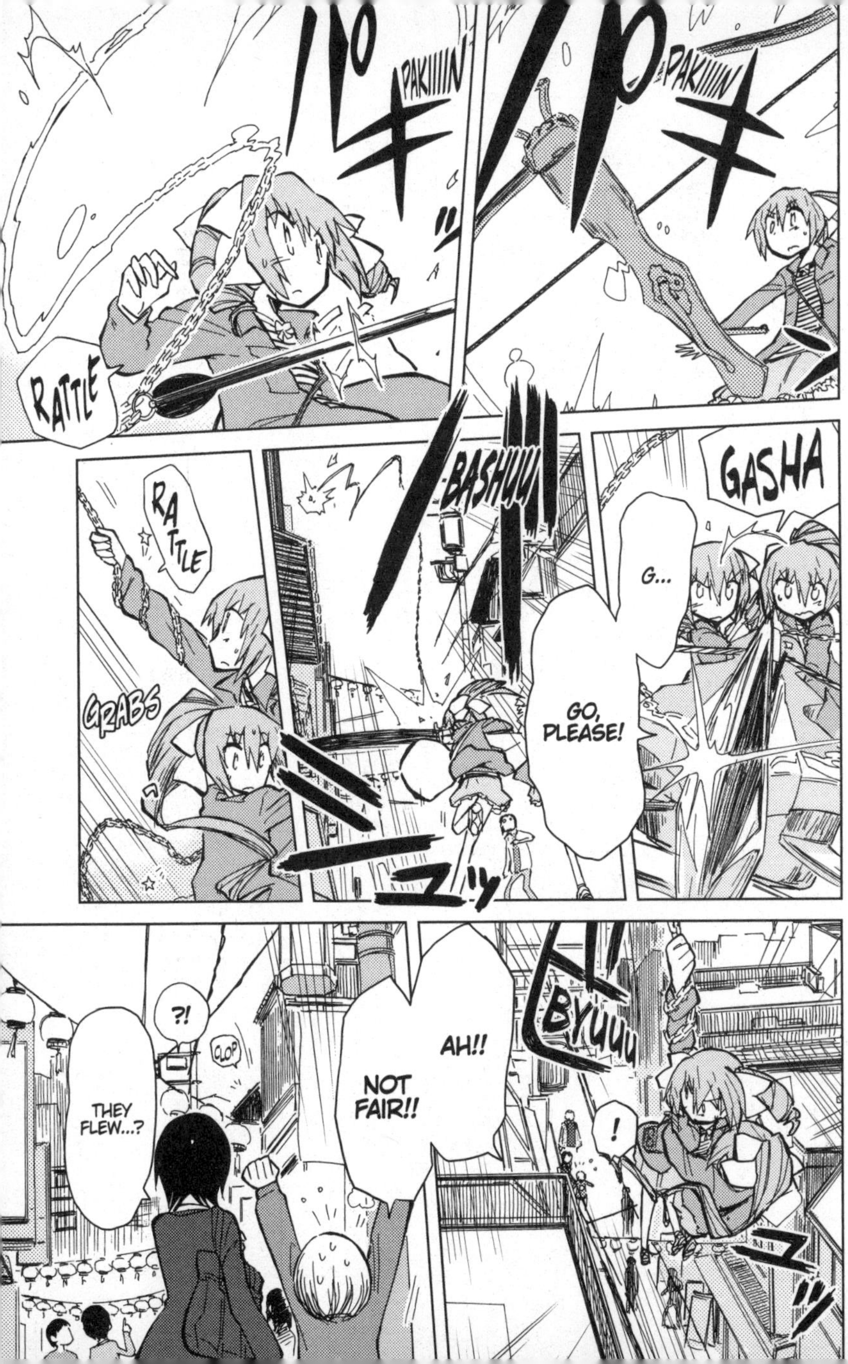

PAKIIIN
PAKIIIN
RATTLE
GASHA
G...
GO, PLEASE!
BASHUUU
RATTLE RATTLE
GRABS
BYUUU
!
AH!!
NOT FAIR!!
?!
CLOP
THEY FLEW...?

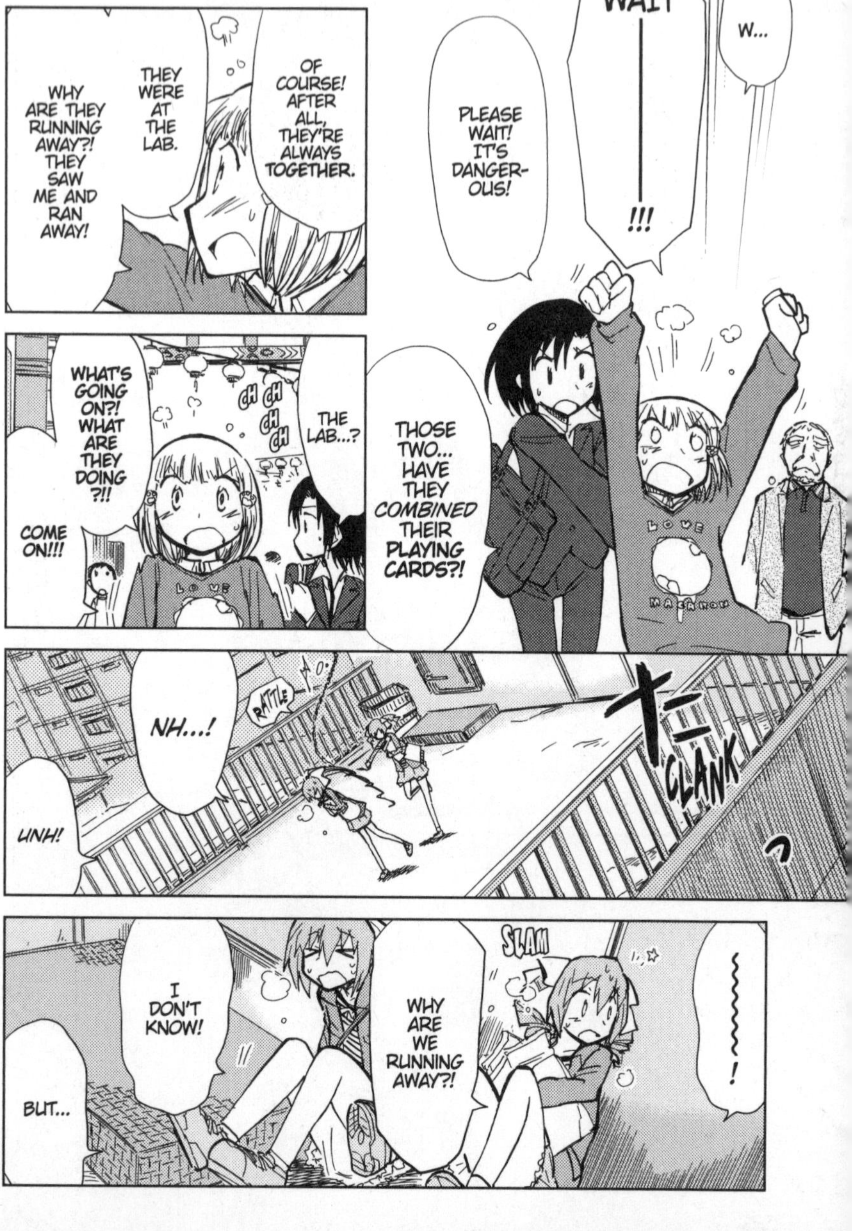
W...
WAIT—!!!
PLEASE WAIT! IT'S DANGEROUS!
THOSE TWO... HAVE THEY COMBINED THEIR PLAYING CARDS?!
OF COURSE! AFTER ALL, THEY'RE ALWAYS TOGETHER.
THEY WERE AT THE LAB.
WHY ARE THEY RUNNING AWAY?! THEY SAW ME AND RAN AWAY!
THE LAB...?
CH CH CH CH
WHAT'S GOING ON?! WHAT ARE THEY DOING?!!
COME ON!!!
CLANK
NH...!
RATTLE
UNH!
~~~~!
SLAM
WHY ARE WE RUNNING AWAY?!
I DON'T KNOW!
BUT...
~~~~

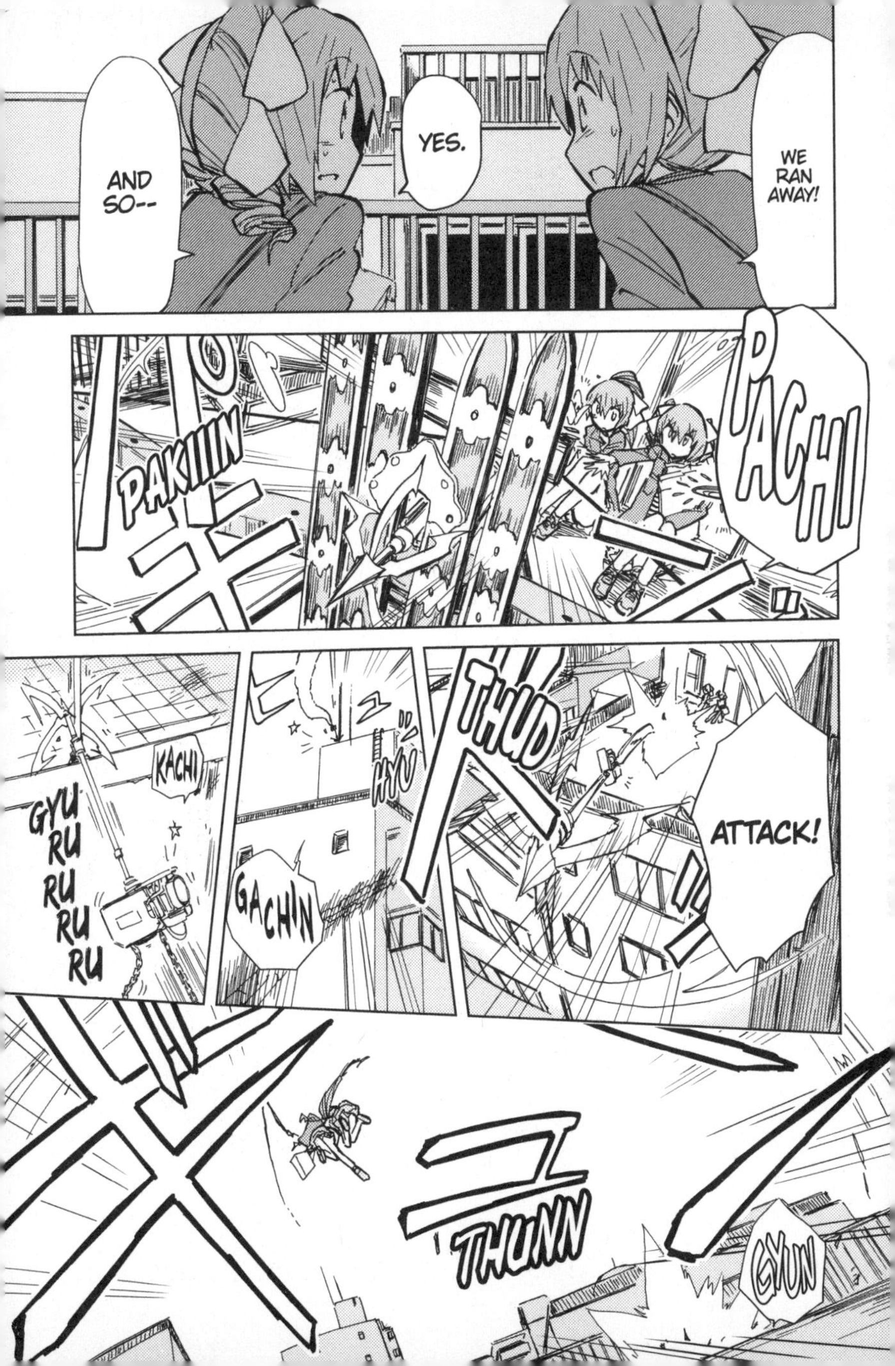

AND SO--
YES.
WE RAN AWAY!
PAKIIIN
PACHI
KACHI
GYU RU RU RU RU RU
HYU
GACHIN
THUD
ATTACK!
THUNN
GYUN

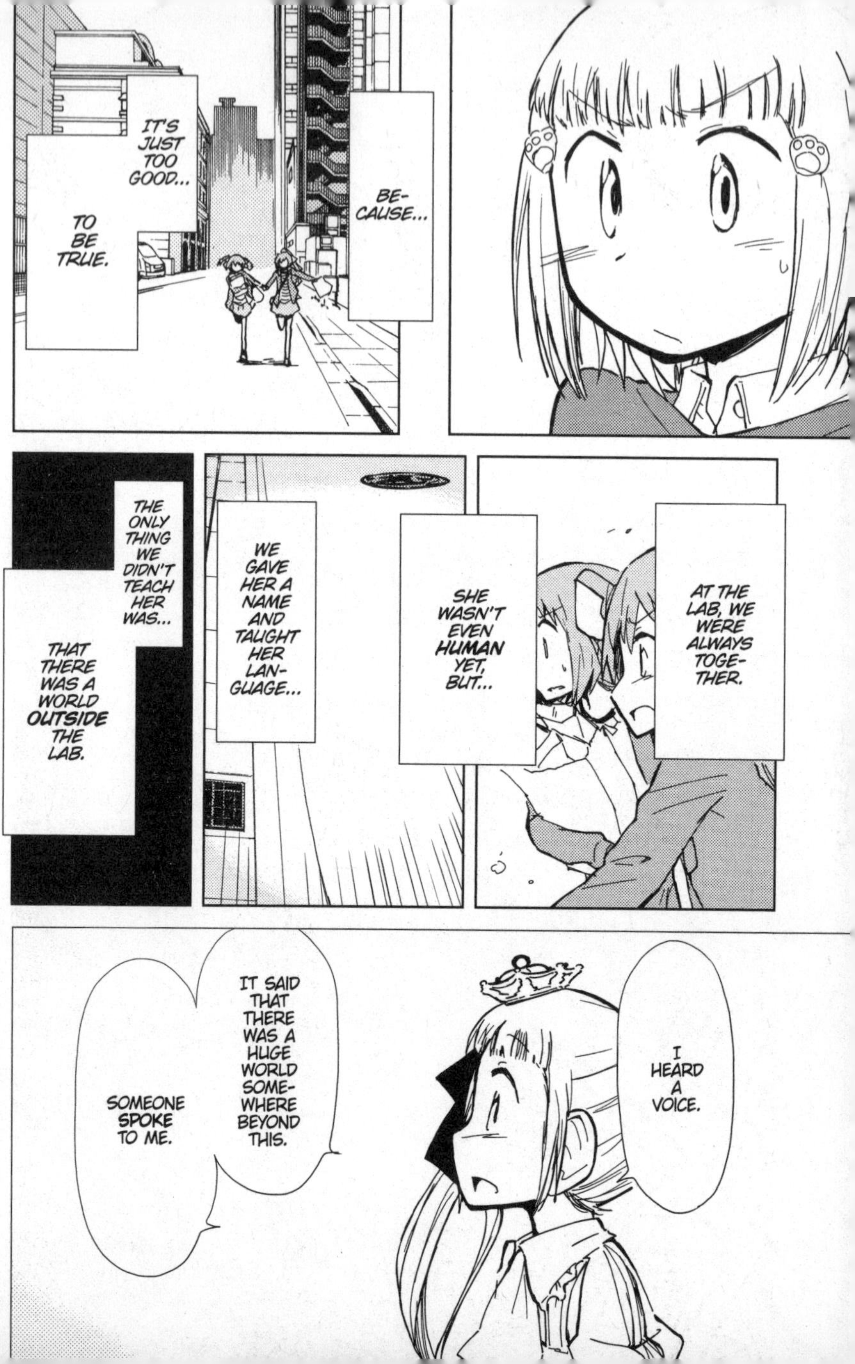

BE-CAUSE...
IT'S JUST TOO GOOD...
TO BE TRUE.
AT THE LAB, WE WERE ALWAYS TOGE-THER.
SHE WASN'T EVEN HUMAN YET, BUT...
WE GAVE HER A NAME AND TAUGHT HER LAN-GUAGE...
THE ONLY THING WE DIDN'T TEACH HER WAS...
THAT THERE WAS A WORLD OUTSIDE THE LAB.
I HEARD A VOICE.
IT SAID THAT THERE WAS A HUGE WORLD SOME-WHERE BEYOND THIS.
SOMEONE SPOKE TO ME.

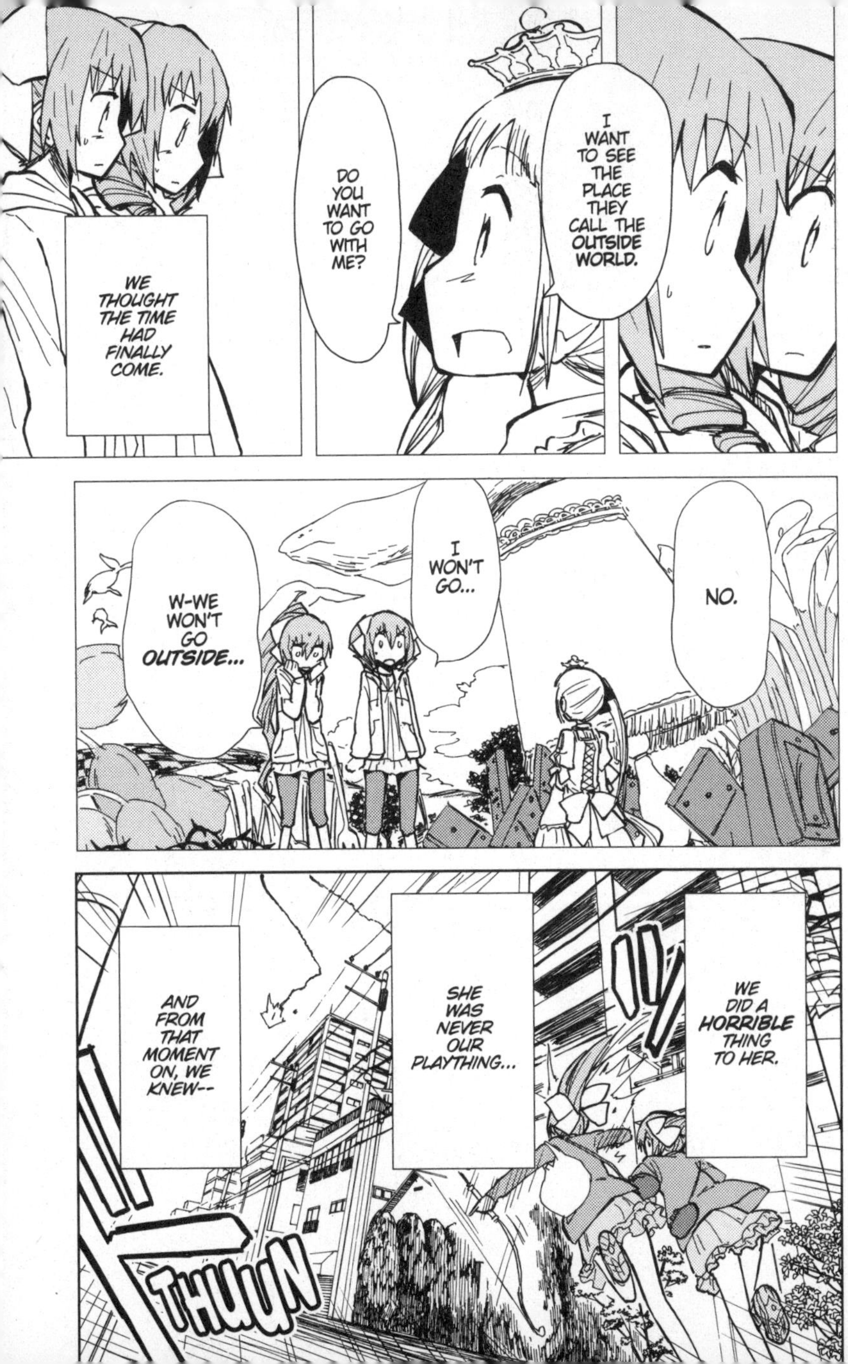
I WANT TO SEE THE PLACE THEY CALL THE OUTSIDE WORLD.
DO YOU WANT TO GO WITH ME?
WE THOUGHT THE TIME HAD FINALLY COME.
NO.
I WON'T GO...
W-WE WON'T GO OUTSIDE...
WE DID A HORRIBLE THING TO HER.
SHE WAS NEVER OUR PLAYTHING...
AND FROM THAT MOMENT ON, WE KNEW--
THUUN

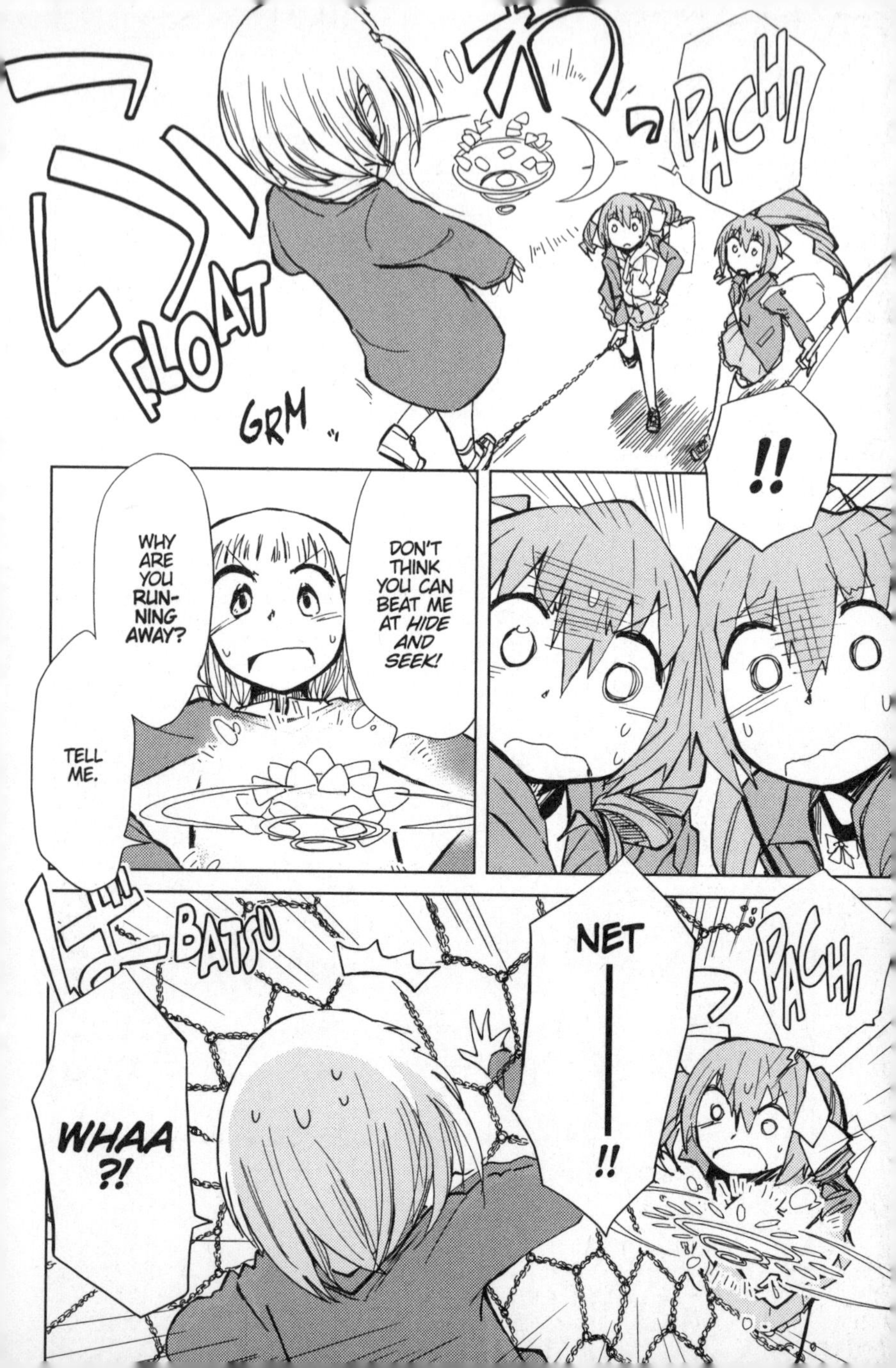
PACHI
FLOAT
GRM
!!
DON'T THINK YOU CAN BEAT ME AT HIDE AND SEEK!
WHY ARE YOU RUN-NING AWAY?
TELL ME.
PACHI
NET—!!
BATSU
WHAA?!

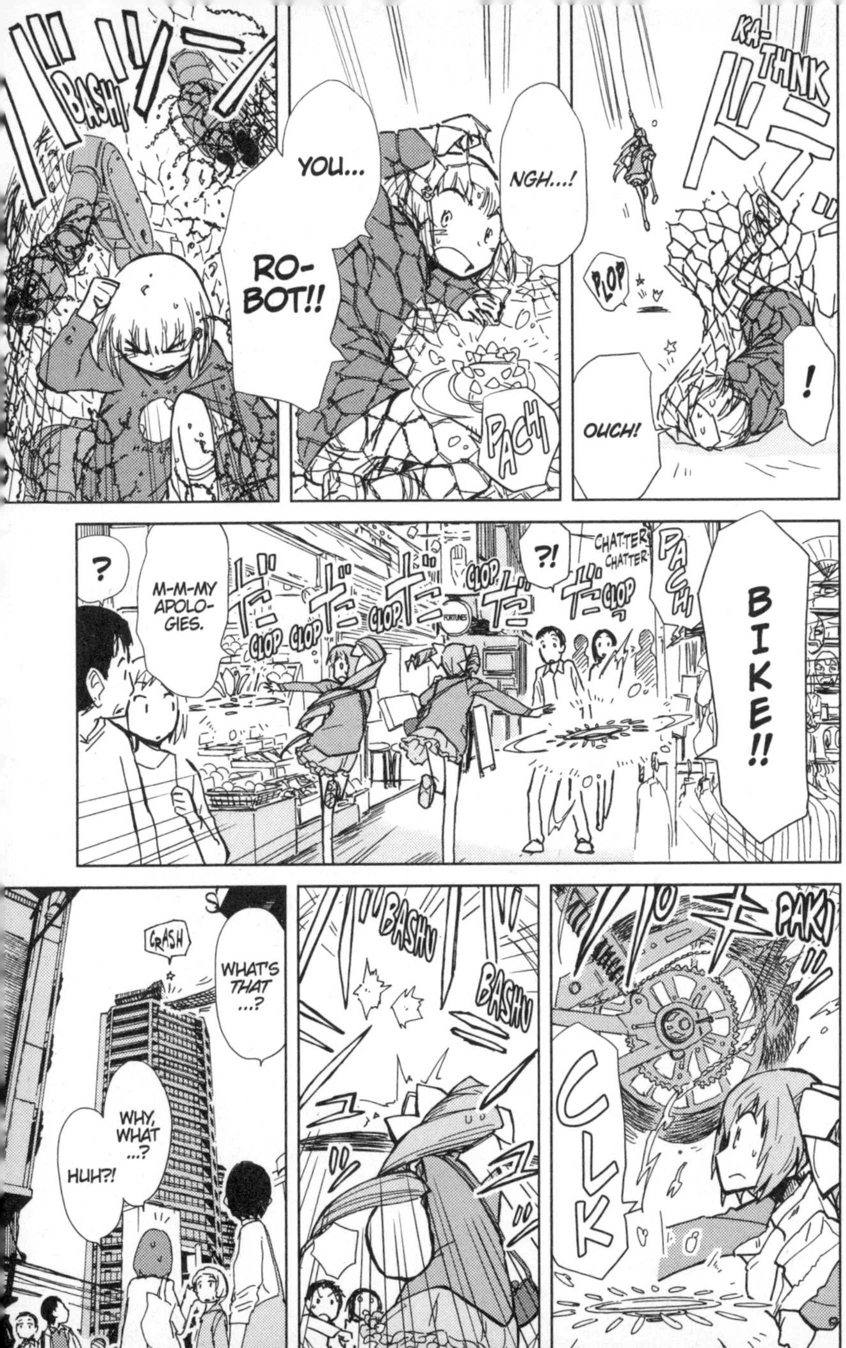

KA-THNK
PLOP
!
OUCH!
NGH...!
PACH
YOU...
RO-BOT!!
BASH
BIKE!!
PACHI
CHATTER CHATTER
?!
CLOP
CLOP
FORTUNES
CLOP
CLOP
CLOP
M-M-MY APOLOGIES.
?
PAKI
CLK
BASHU
BASHU
CRASH
WHAT'S THAT ...?
WHY, WHAT ...?
HUH?!

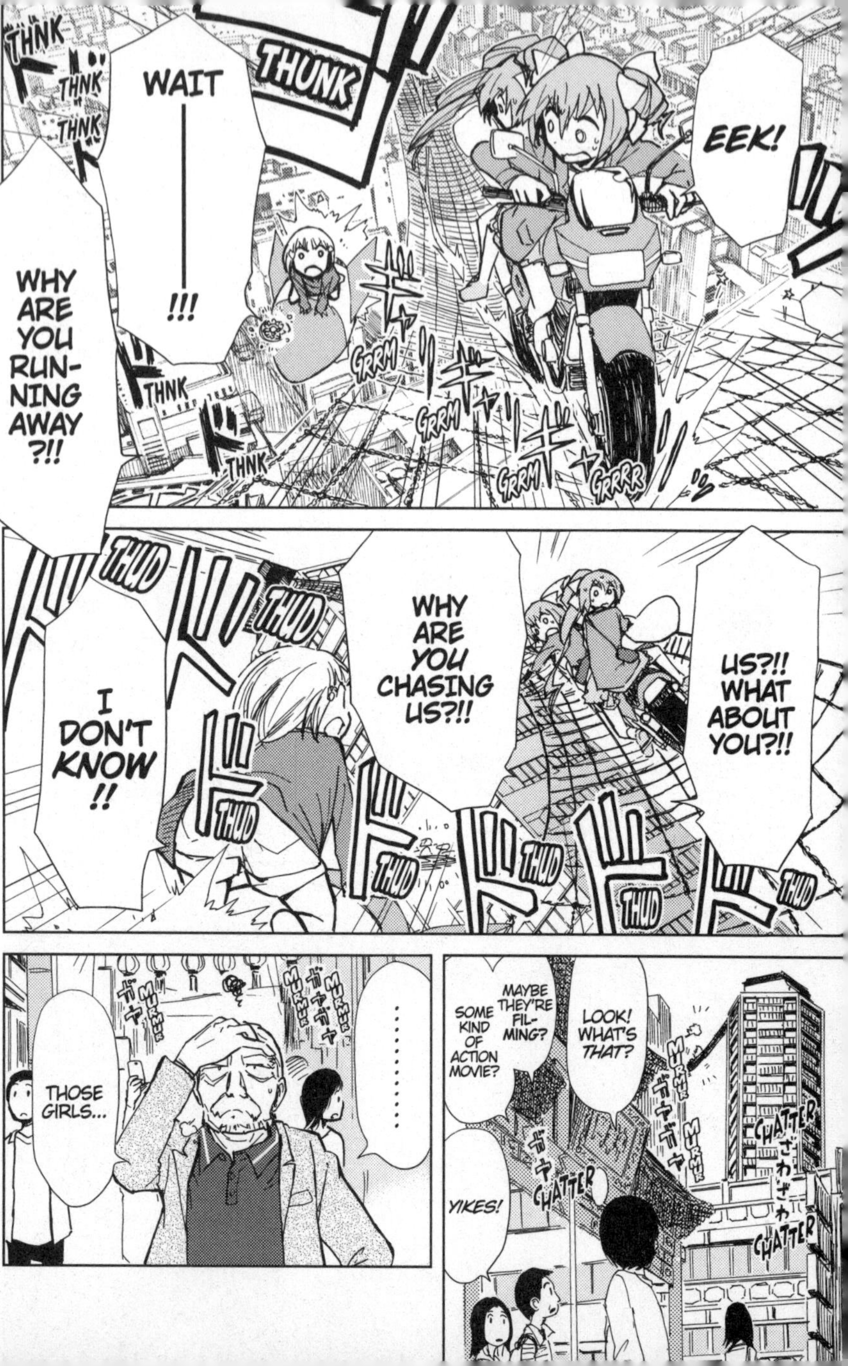
EEK!
THUNK
THNK
THNK
THNK
WAIT
!!!
WHY ARE YOU RUN-NING AWAY?!!
THNK
THNK
GRRM
GRRM
GRRM
GRRRR
US?!! WHAT ABOUT YOU?!!
WHY ARE YOU CHASING US?!!
THUD
THUD
I DON'T KNOW!!
THUD
THUD
THUD
THUD
THUD
LOOK! WHAT'S THAT?
MAYBE THEY'RE FIL-MING?
SOME KIND OF ACTION MOVIE?
MURMUR
MURMUR
CHATTER
CHATTER
CHATTER
YIKES!
MURMUR
MURMUR
MURMUR
......
THOSE GIRLS...

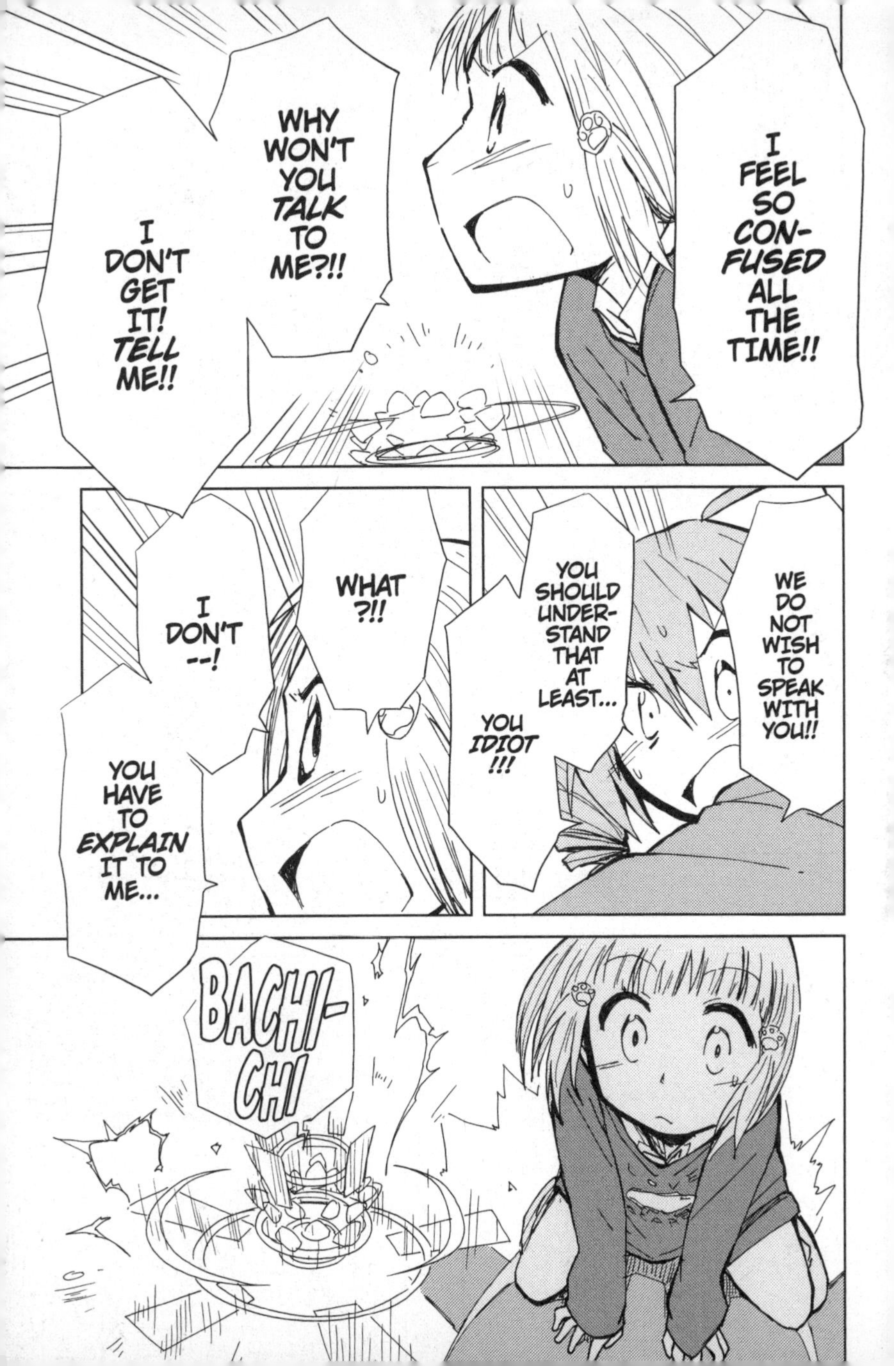
I FEEL SO CON-FUSED ALL THE TIME!!
WHY WON'T YOU TALK TO ME?!!
I DON'T GET IT! TELL ME!!
WE DO NOT WISH TO SPEAK WITH YOU!!
YOU SHOULD UNDER-STAND THAT AT LEAST...
YOU IDIOT!!!
WHAT?!!
I DON'T--!
YOU HAVE TO EXPLAIN IT TO ME...
BACHI-CHI

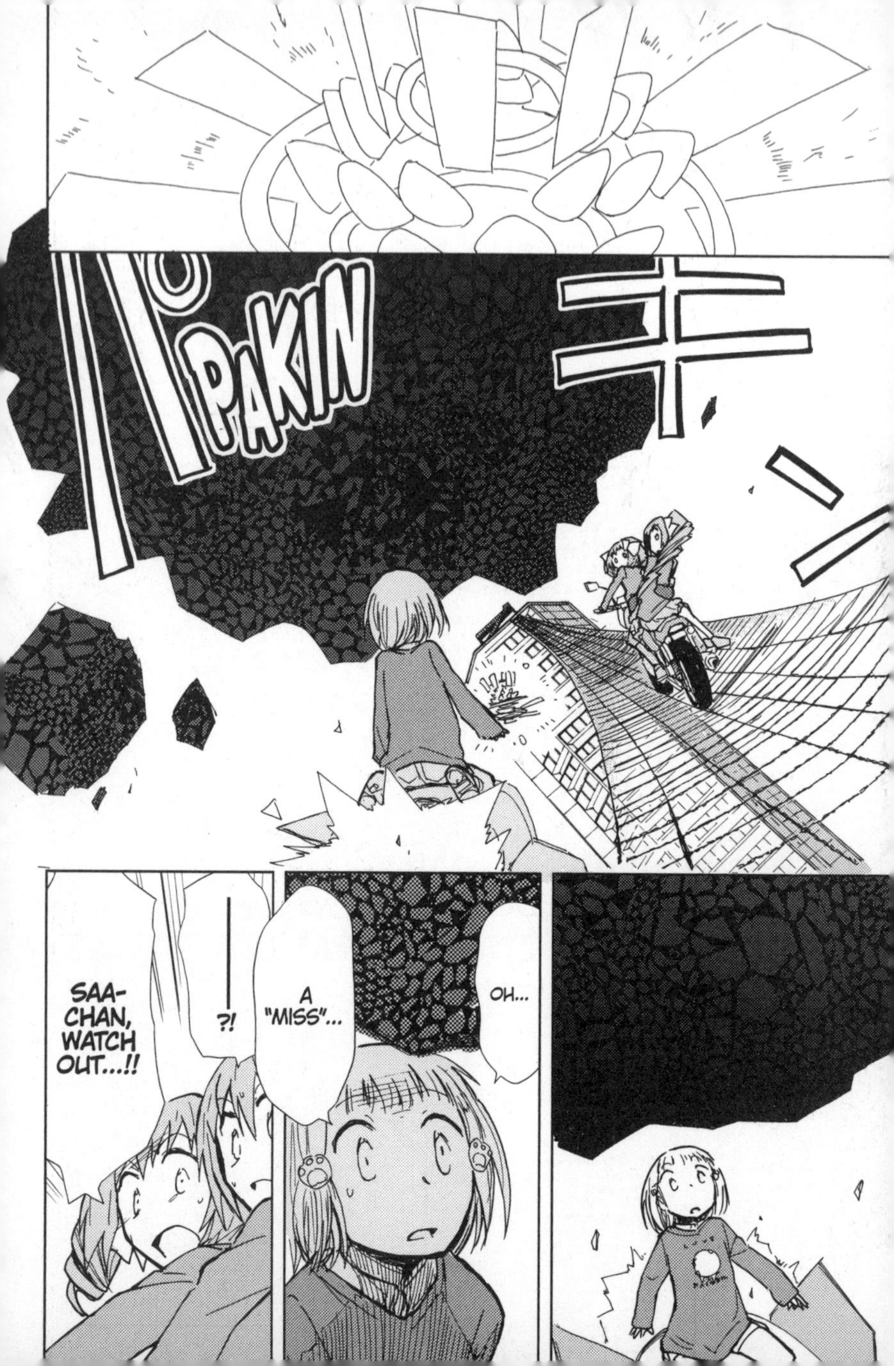
PAKIN
OH...
A "MISS"...
?!
SAA-CHAN, WATCH OUT...!!

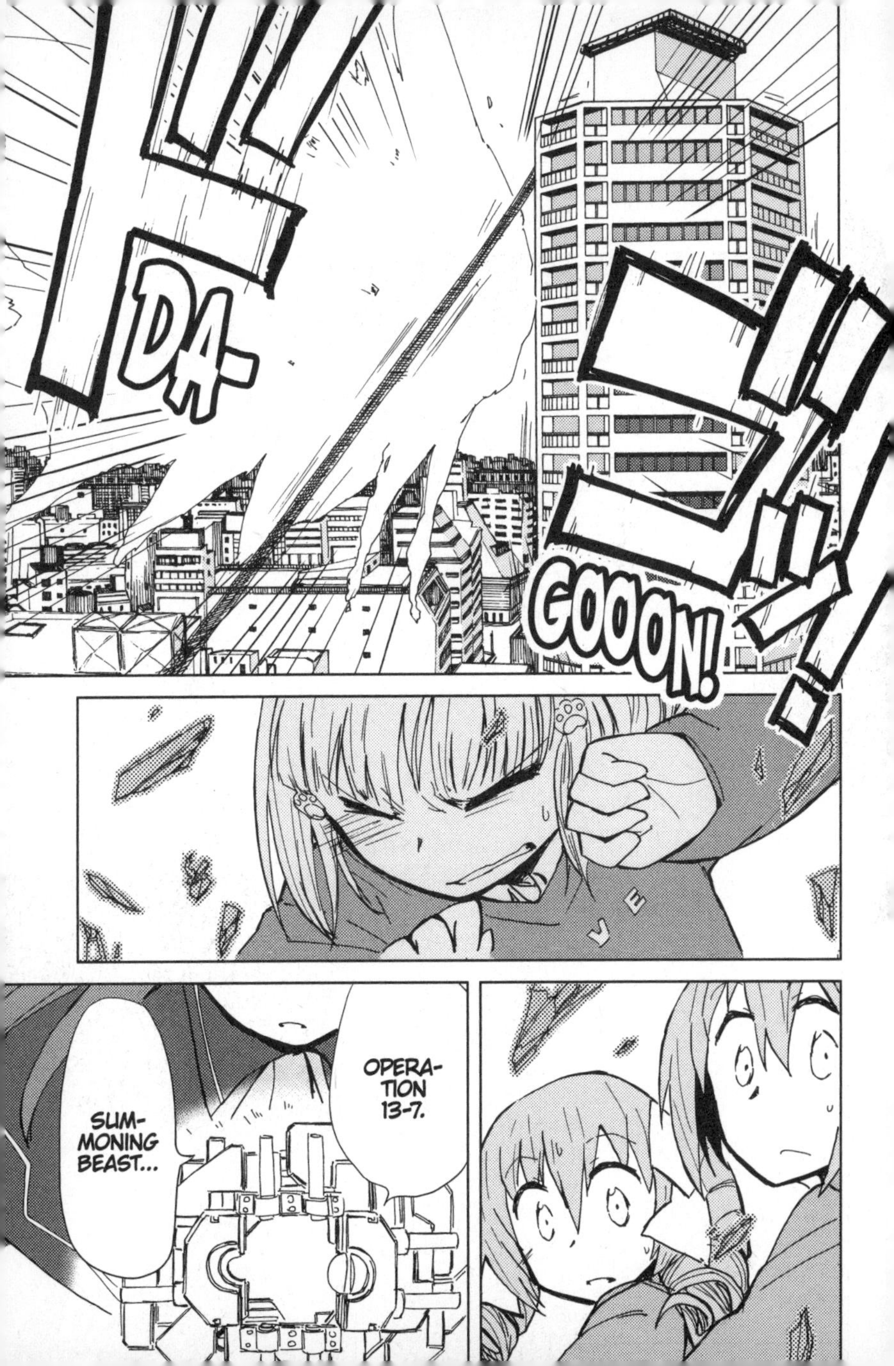
DA-
GOOON!
OPERA-TION 13-7.
SUM-MONING BEAST...

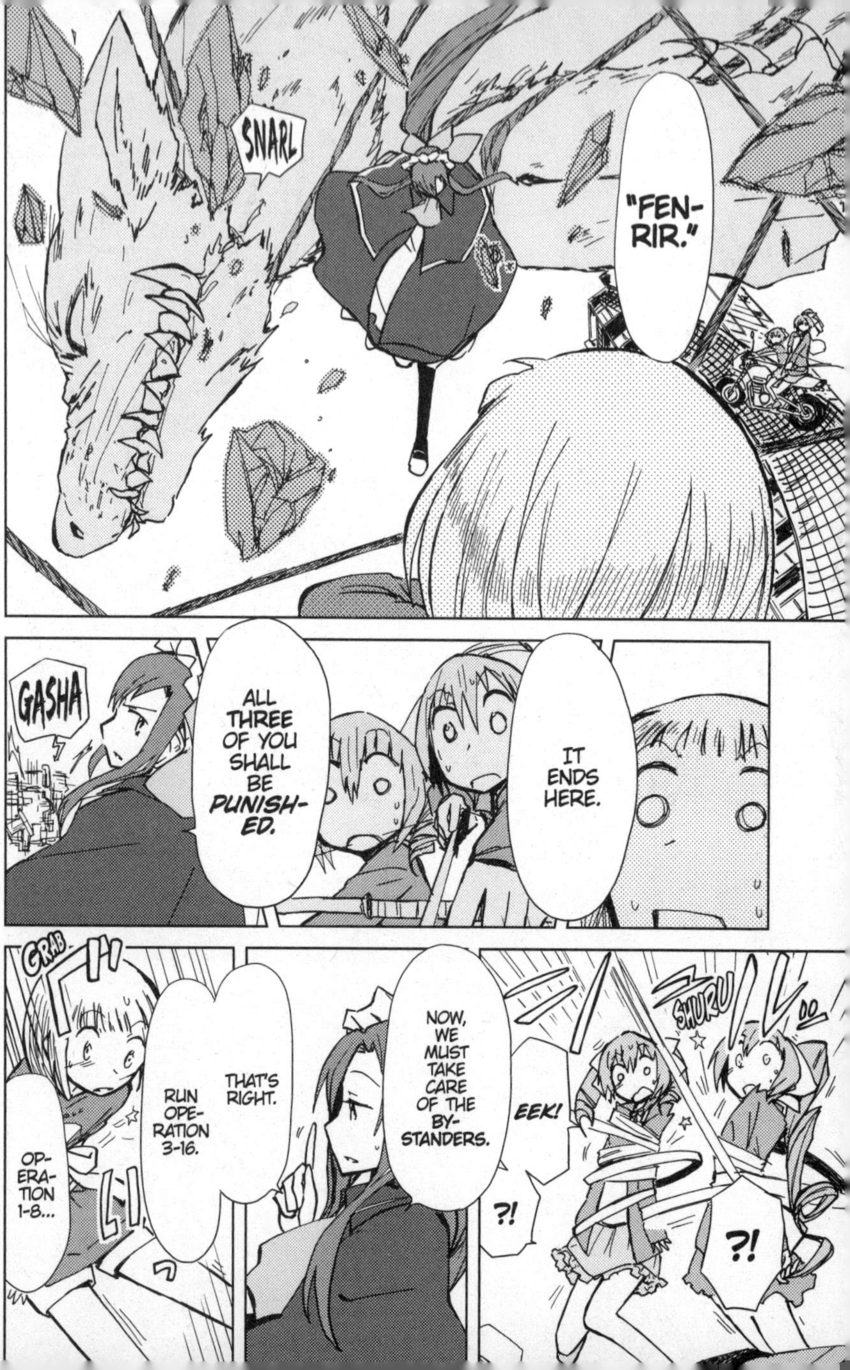
"FEN-
RIR."
SNARL
IT ENDS HERE.
ALL THREE OF YOU SHALL BE *PUNISHED.*
GASHA
SHURU
DO
EEK!
?!
?!
NOW, WE MUST TAKE CARE OF THE BYSTANDERS.
THAT'S RIGHT.
RUN OPERATION 3-16.
GRAB
OPERATION 1-8...

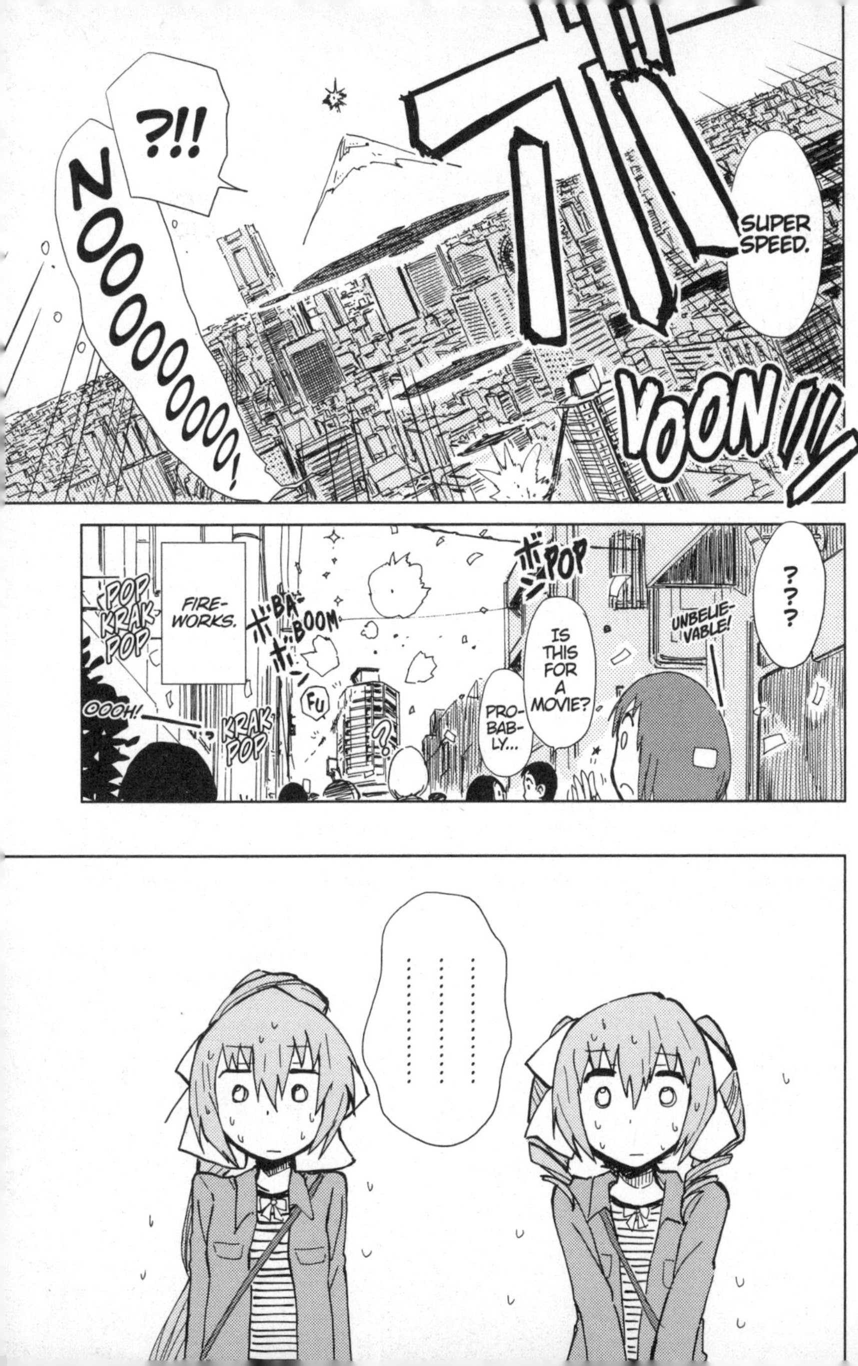
SUPER SPEED.
VOON!!
?!!
NOOOOOOOOOO!
???
UNBELIEVABLE!
IS THIS FOR A MOVIE?
PROBABLY...
POP
BA-BOOM
FIREWORKS.
POP KRAK POP
FU
OOOH!
KRAK POP
......

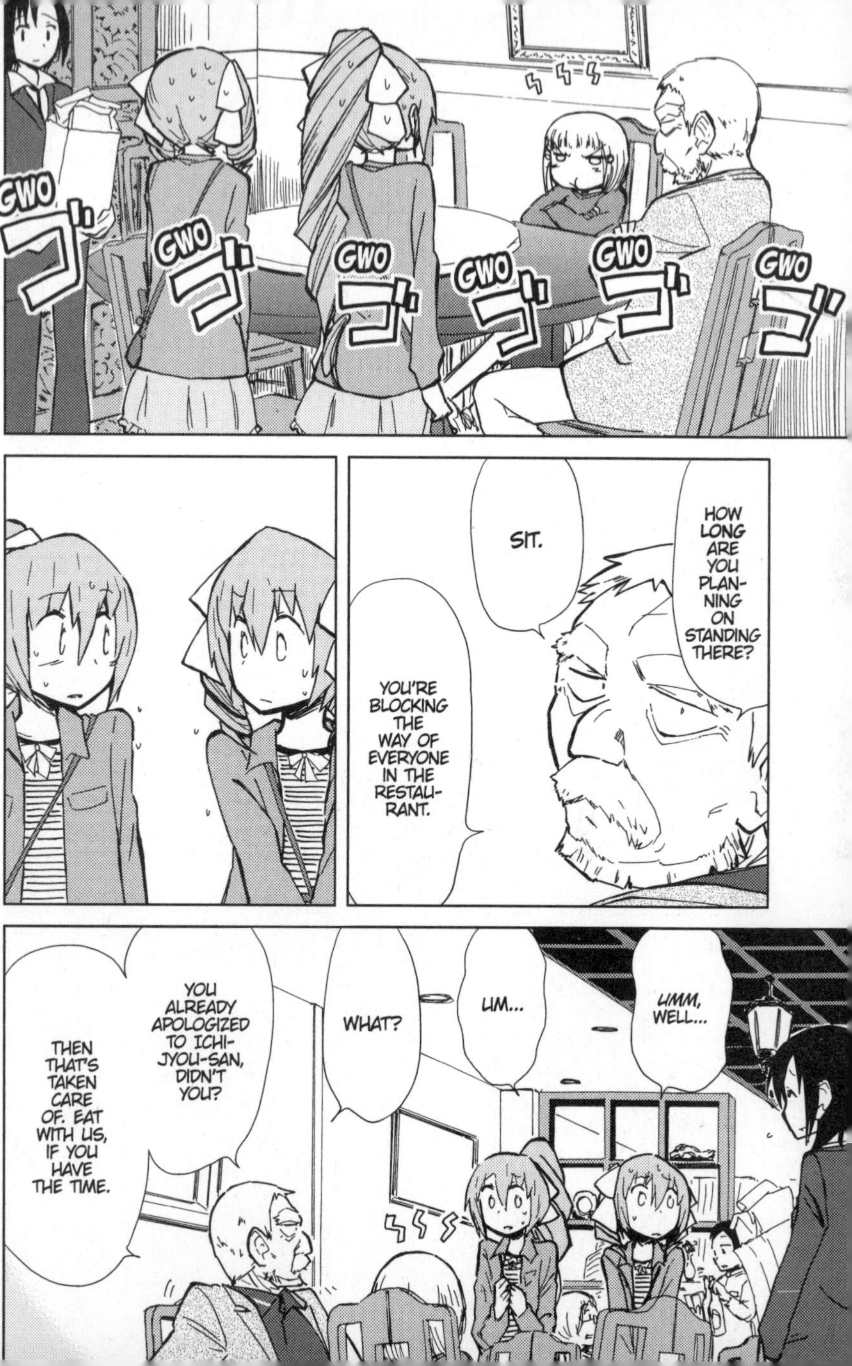
GWO ゴ
GWO ゴ
GWO ゴ
GWO ゴ
GWO ゴ
GWO ゴ
HOW LONG ARE YOU PLANNING ON STANDING THERE?
SIT.
YOU'RE BLOCKING THE WAY OF EVERYONE IN THE RESTAURANT.
UMM, WELL...
UM...
WHAT?
YOU ALREADY APOLOGIZED TO ICHIJYOU-SAN, DIDN'T YOU?
THEN THAT'S TAKEN CARE OF. EAT WITH US, IF YOU HAVE THE TIME.

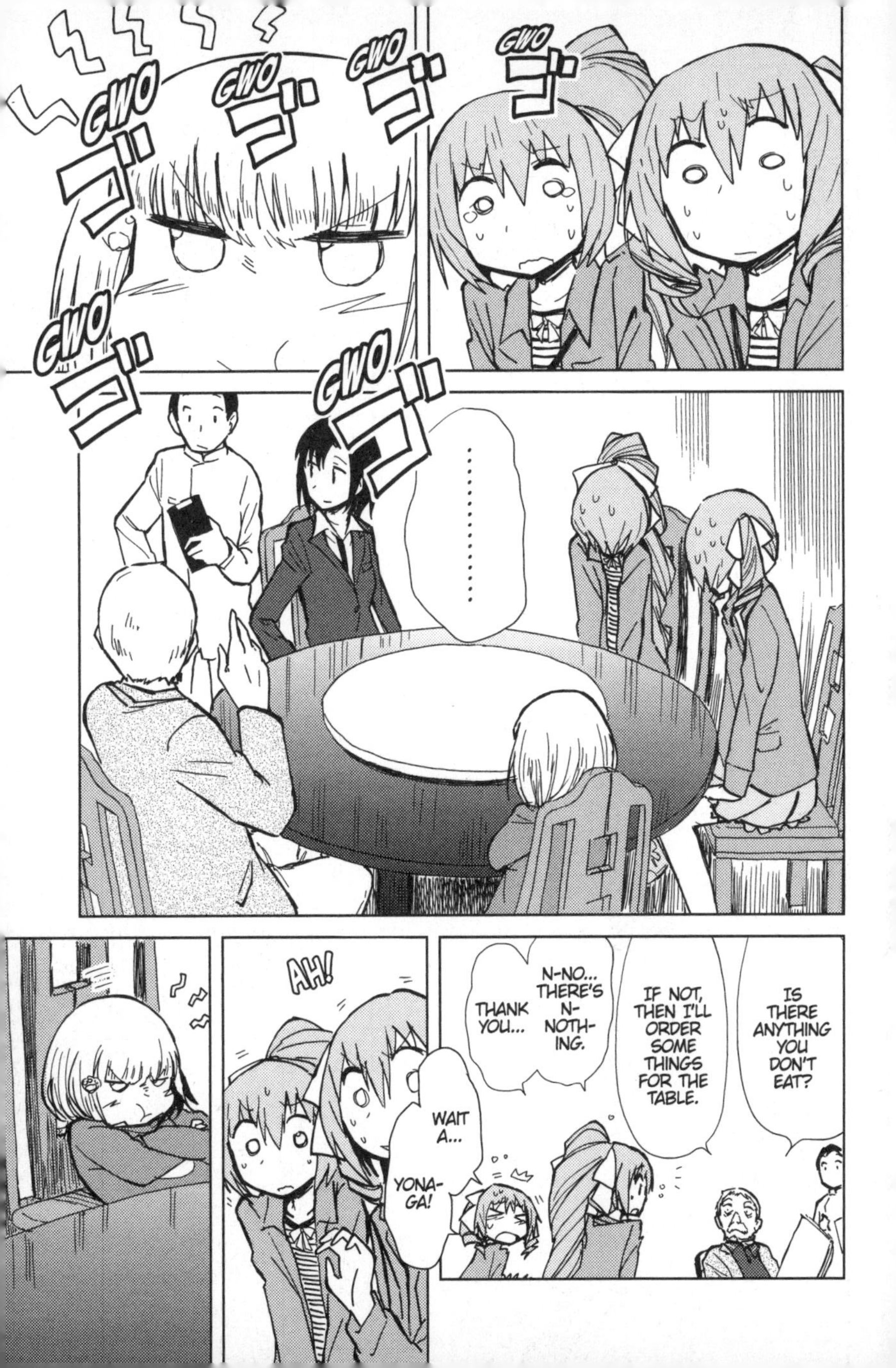

GWO
ゴ
GWO
ゴ
GWO
ゴ
GWO
ゴ
GWO
ゴ
GWO
ゴ
......
IS THERE ANYTHING YOU DON'T EAT?
IF NOT, THEN I'LL ORDER SOME THINGS FOR THE TABLE.
N-NO... THERE'S N-NOTH-ING.
THANK YOU...
AH!
WAIT A...
YONA-GA!

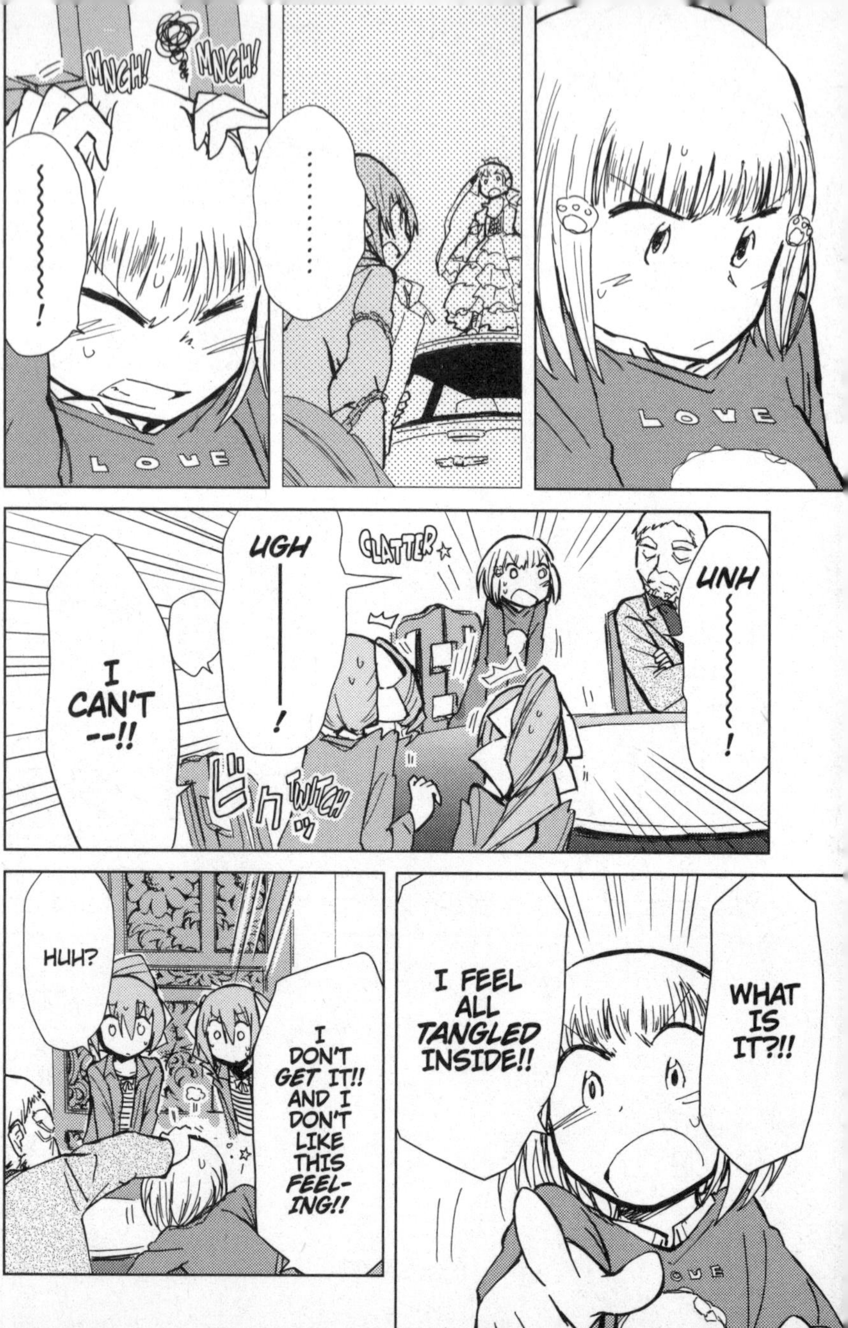
......
MNGH! MNGH!
~!
UNH~!
CLATTER
UGH—!
I CAN'T--!!
TWITCH
WHAT IS IT?!!
I FEEL ALL TANGLED INSIDE!!
I DON'T GET IT!! AND I DON'T LIKE THIS FEELING!!
HUH?

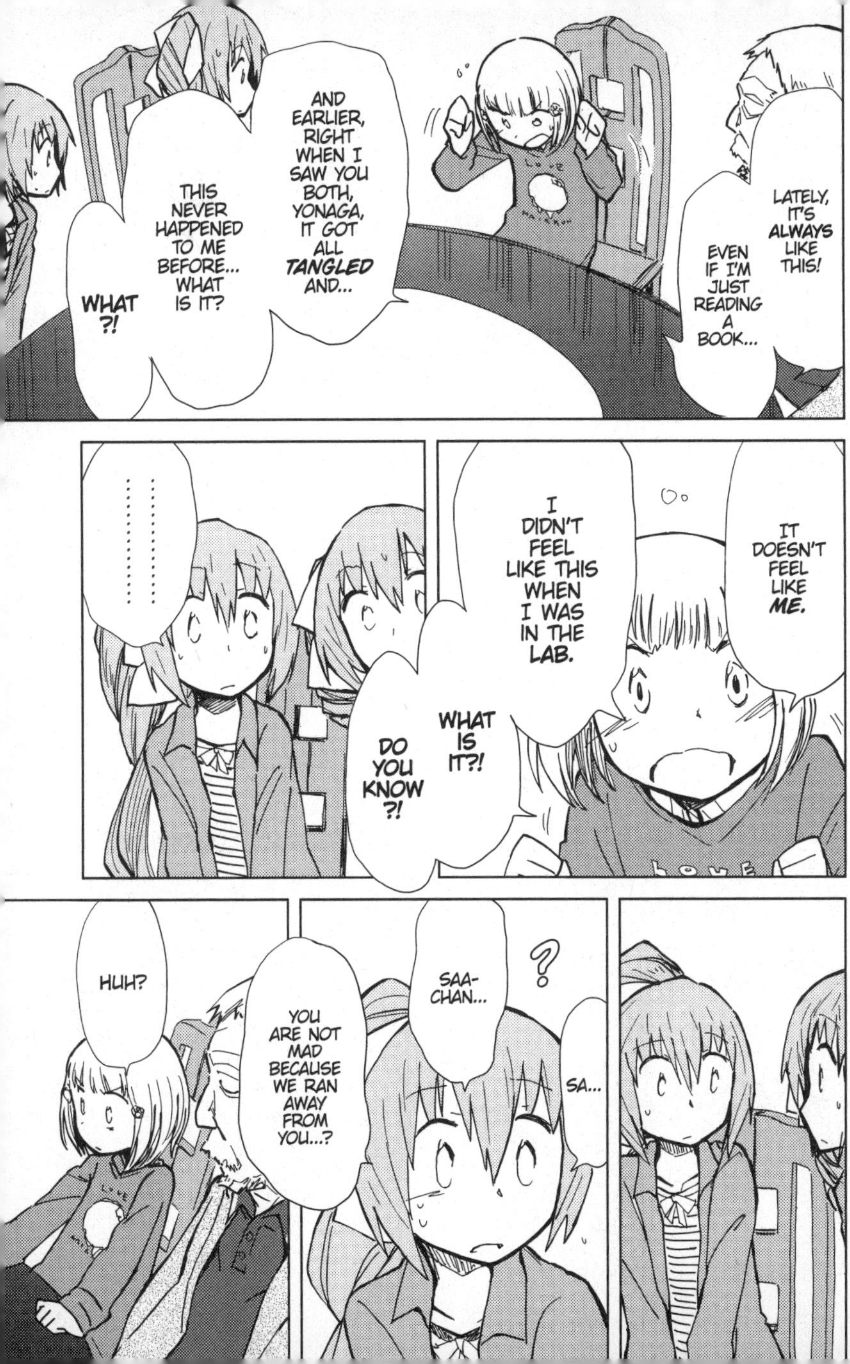
LATELY, IT'S **ALWAYS** LIKE THIS!
EVEN IF I'M JUST READING A BOOK...
AND EARLIER, RIGHT WHEN I SAW YOU BOTH, YONAGA, IT GOT ALL ***TANGLED*** AND...
THIS NEVER HAPPENED TO ME BEFORE... WHAT IS IT?
WHAT?!
IT DOESN'T FEEL LIKE ***ME.***
I DIDN'T FEEL LIKE THIS WHEN I WAS IN THE LAB.
WHAT IS IT?!
DO YOU KNOW?!
......
SA...
SAA-CHAN...
YOU ARE NOT MAD BECAUSE WE RAN AWAY FROM YOU...?
HUH?

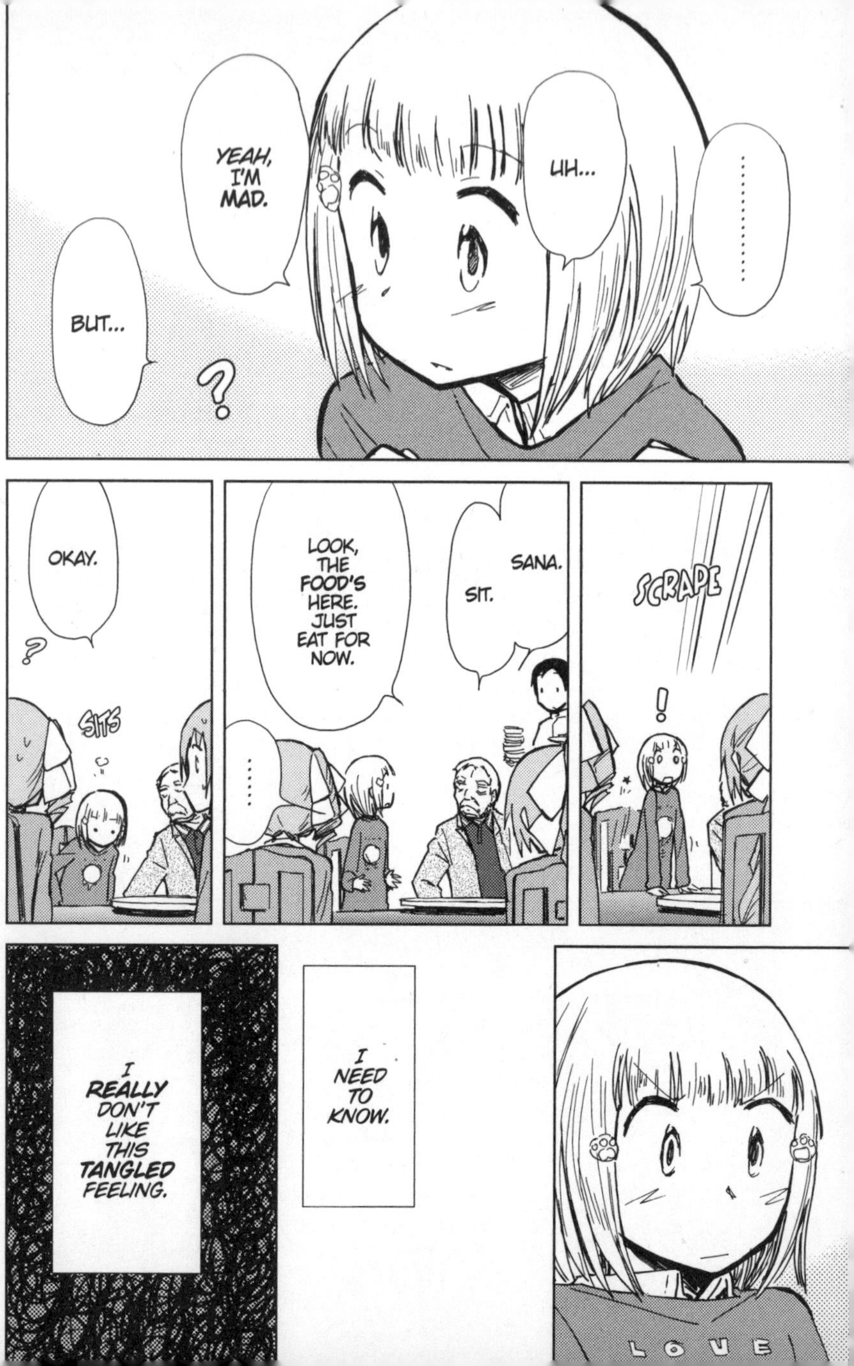
......
UH...
YEAH, I'M MAD.
BUT...
?
SCRAPE
!
SANA.
SIT.
LOOK, THE FOOD'S HERE. JUST EAT FOR NOW.
......
OKAY.
?
SITS
LOVE
I NEED TO KNOW.
I REALLY DON'T LIKE THIS TANGLED FEELING.

Alice & Zoroku

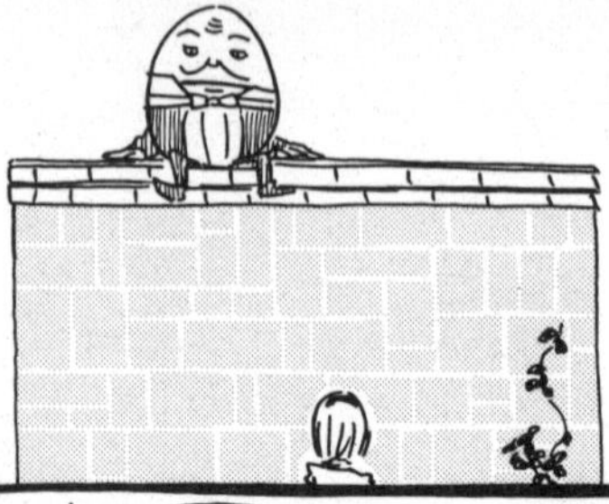

INTERLUDE

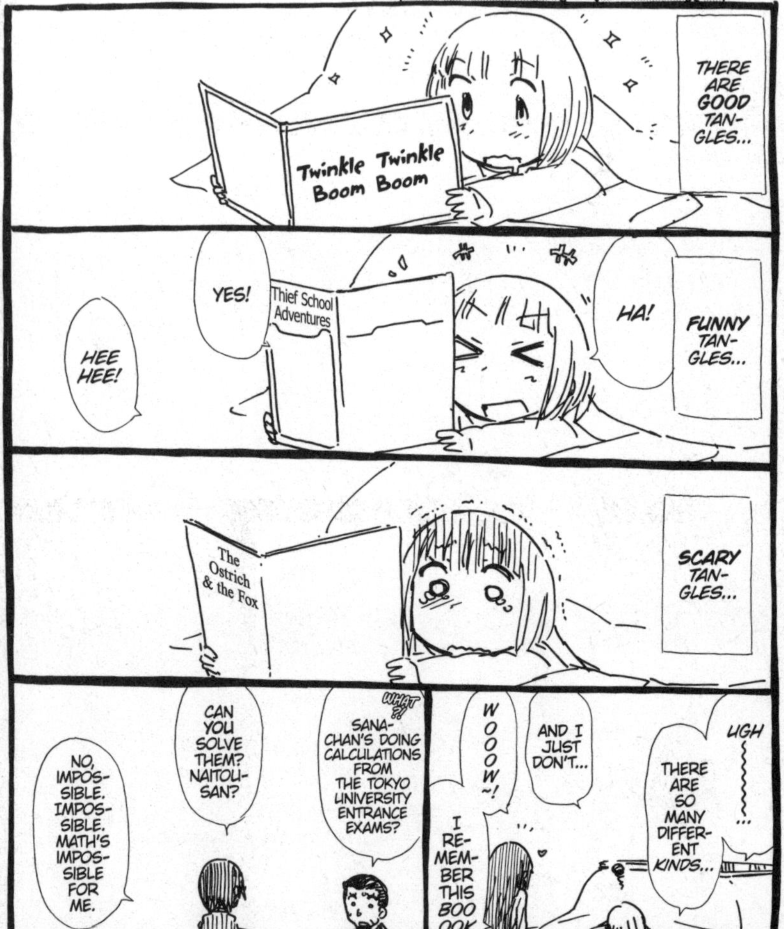

THERE ARE GOOD TAN-GLES...
Twinkle Twinkle Boom Boom
FUNNY TAN-GLES...
HA!
Thief School Adventures
YES!
HEE HEE!
SCARY TAN-GLES...
The Ostrich & the Fox
UGH~~~~~...
THERE ARE SO MANY DIFFER-ENT KINDS...
AND I JUST DON'T...
WOOOOW~!
I RE-MEM-BER THIS BOOOOK~!
WHAT?!
SANA-CHAN'S DOING CALCULATIONS FROM THE TOKYO UNIVERSITY ENTRANCE EXAMS?
Math Drills
CAN YOU SOLVE THEM? NAITOU-SAN?
NO, IMPOS-SIBLE. IMPOS-SIBLE. MATH'S IMPOS-SIBLE FOR ME.

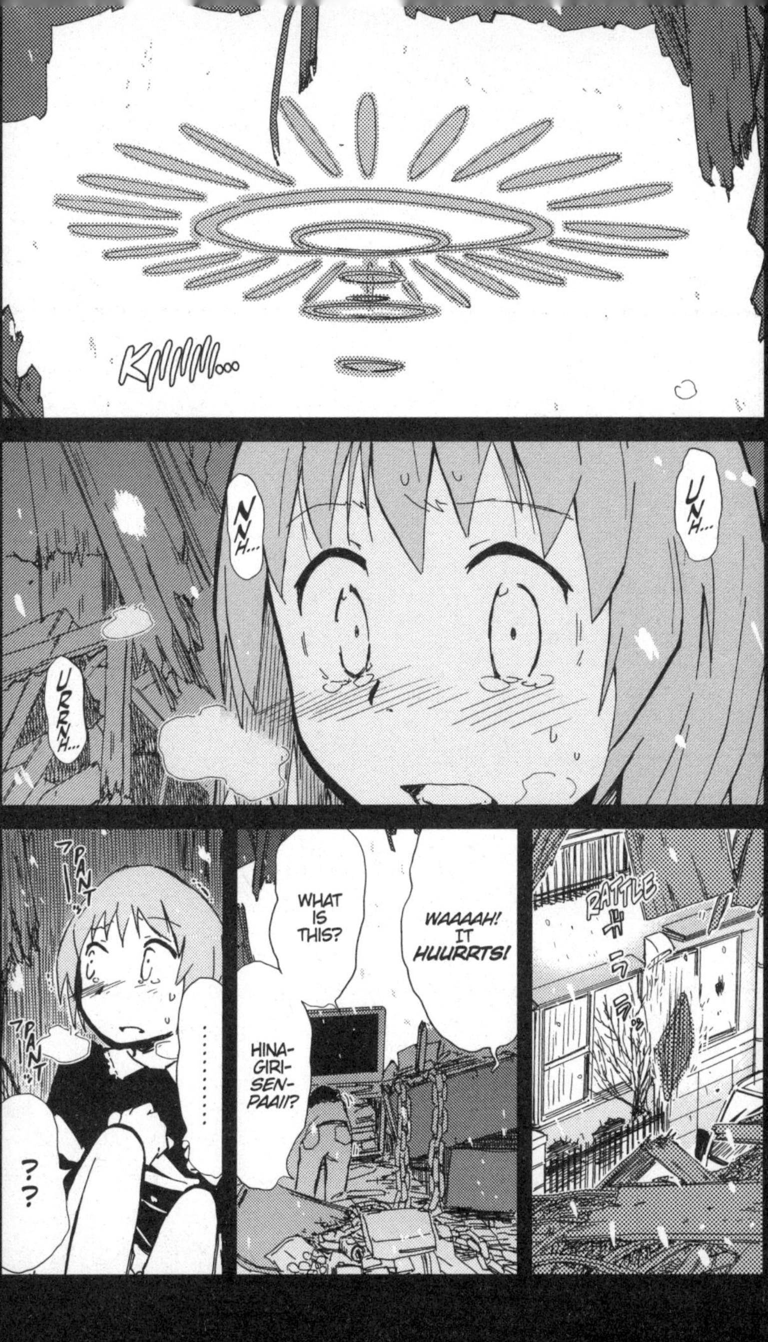

KMMM...
UNH...
NNH...
URRNH...
RATTLE
WAAAAH! IT HUURRTS!
WHAT IS THIS?
HINA-GIRI-SEN-PAAII?
PANT
PANT
......

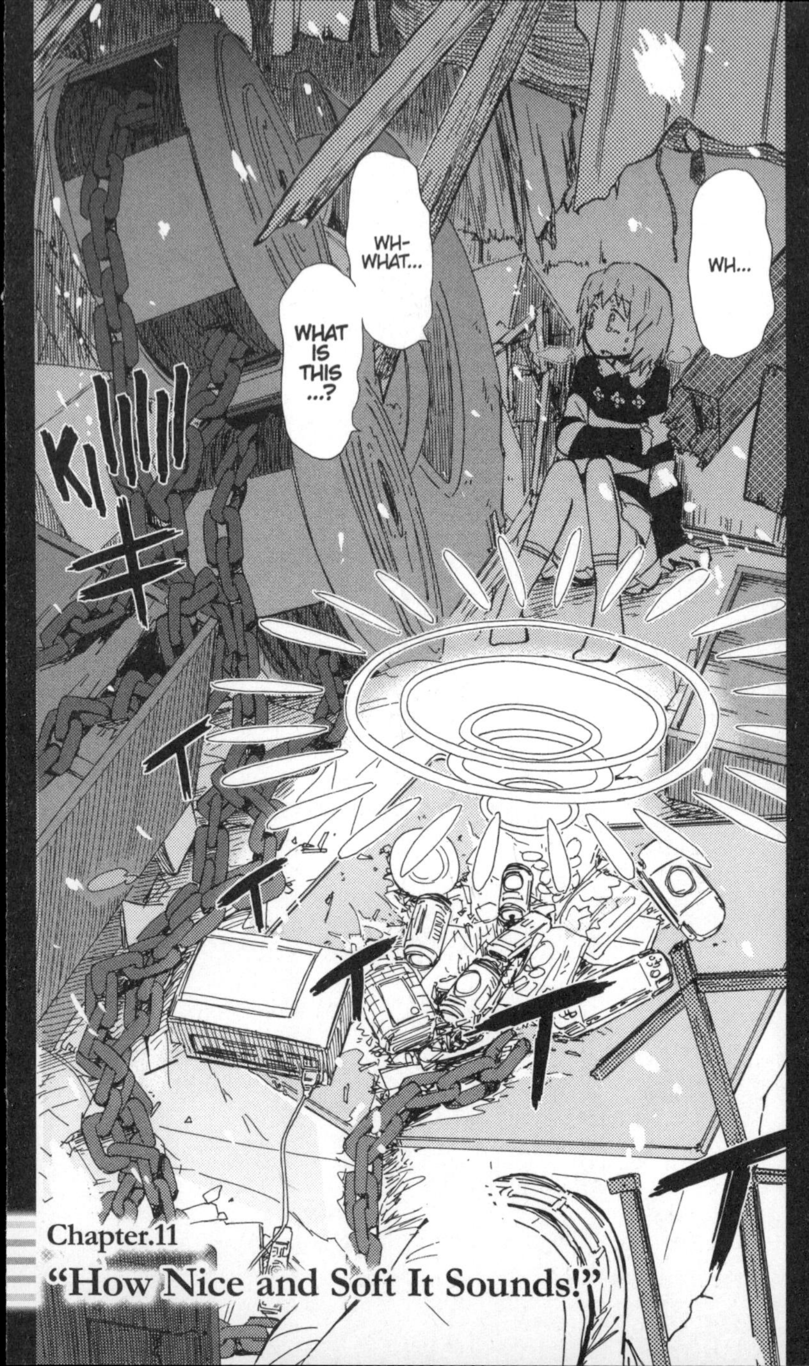
WH...
WH- WHAT...
WHAT IS THIS ...?
KI
キ
T
T
T
T
T

Chapter.11
"How Nice and Soft It Sounds!"

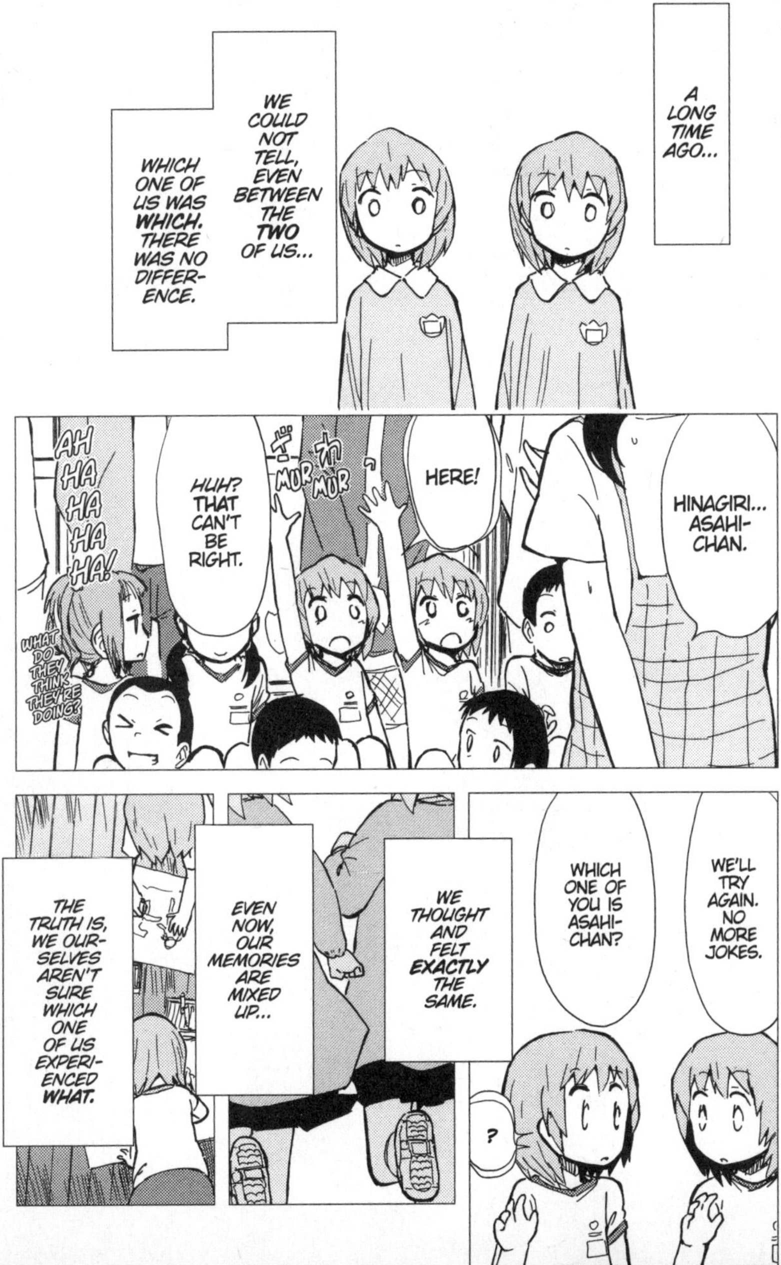
A LONG TIME AGO...
WE COULD NOT TELL, EVEN BETWEEN THE TWO OF US...
WHICH ONE OF US WAS WHICH. THERE WAS NO DIFFERENCE.
HINAGIRI... ASAHI-CHAN.
HERE!
MUR MUR
HUH? THAT CAN'T BE RIGHT.
AH HA HA HA HA!
WHAT DO THEY THINK THEY'RE DOING?
WE'LL TRY AGAIN. NO MORE JOKES.
WHICH ONE OF YOU IS ASAHI-CHAN?
?
WE THOUGHT AND FELT EXACTLY THE SAME.
EVEN NOW, OUR MEMORIES ARE MIXED UP...
THE TRUTH IS, WE OURSELVES AREN'T SURE WHICH ONE OF US EXPERIENCED WHAT.

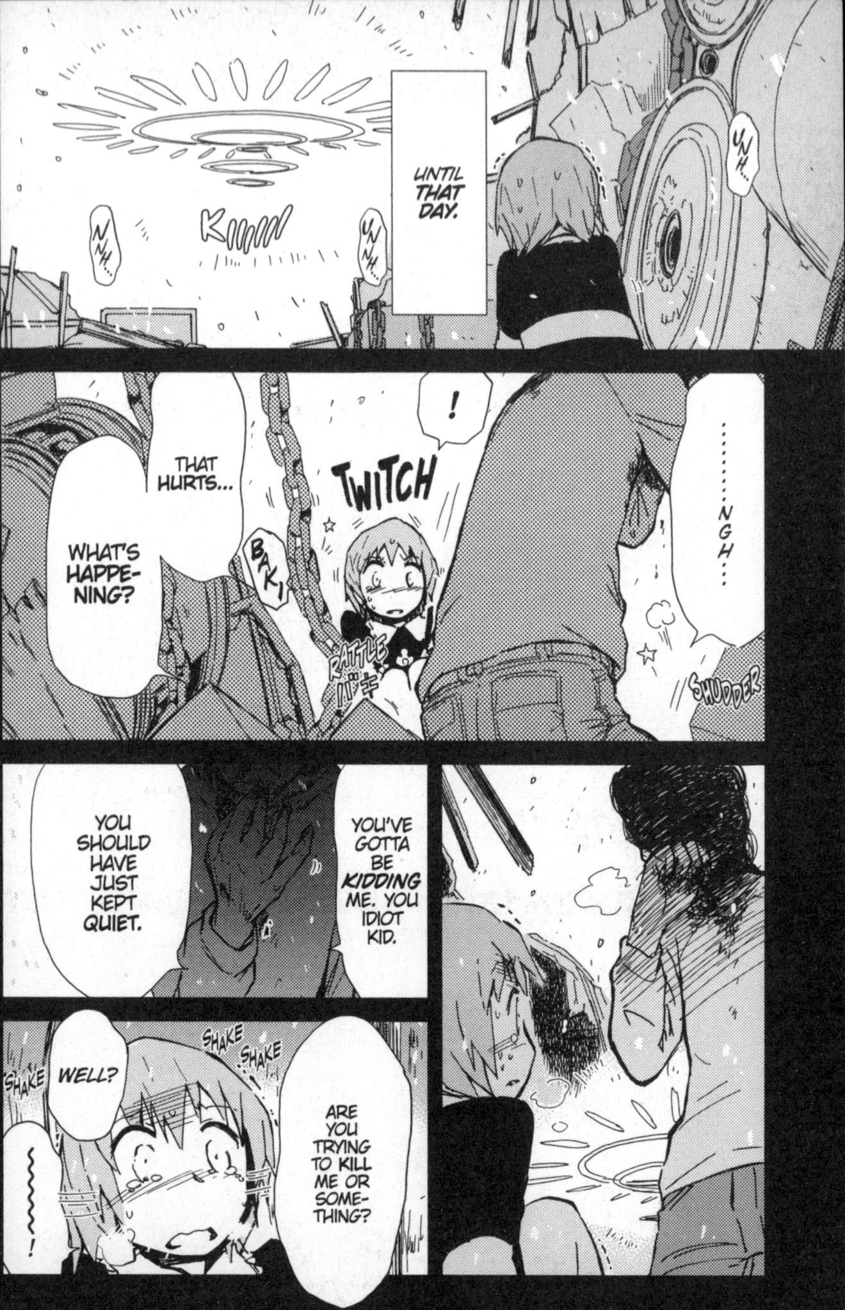
UNH...
UNTIL THAT DAY.
UNNH...
KIIIIIII
NNH...
......NGH...
SHUDDER
!
TWITCH
THAT HURTS...
WHAT'S HAPPE-NING?
BAKI
RATTLE
バキ
YOU'VE GOTTA BE *KIDDING* ME. YOU IDIOT KID.
YOU SHOULD HAVE JUST KEPT QUIET.
ARE YOU TRYING TO KILL ME OR SOME-THING?
SHAKE SHAKE
WELL?
SHAKE
~~~~!
~~~~

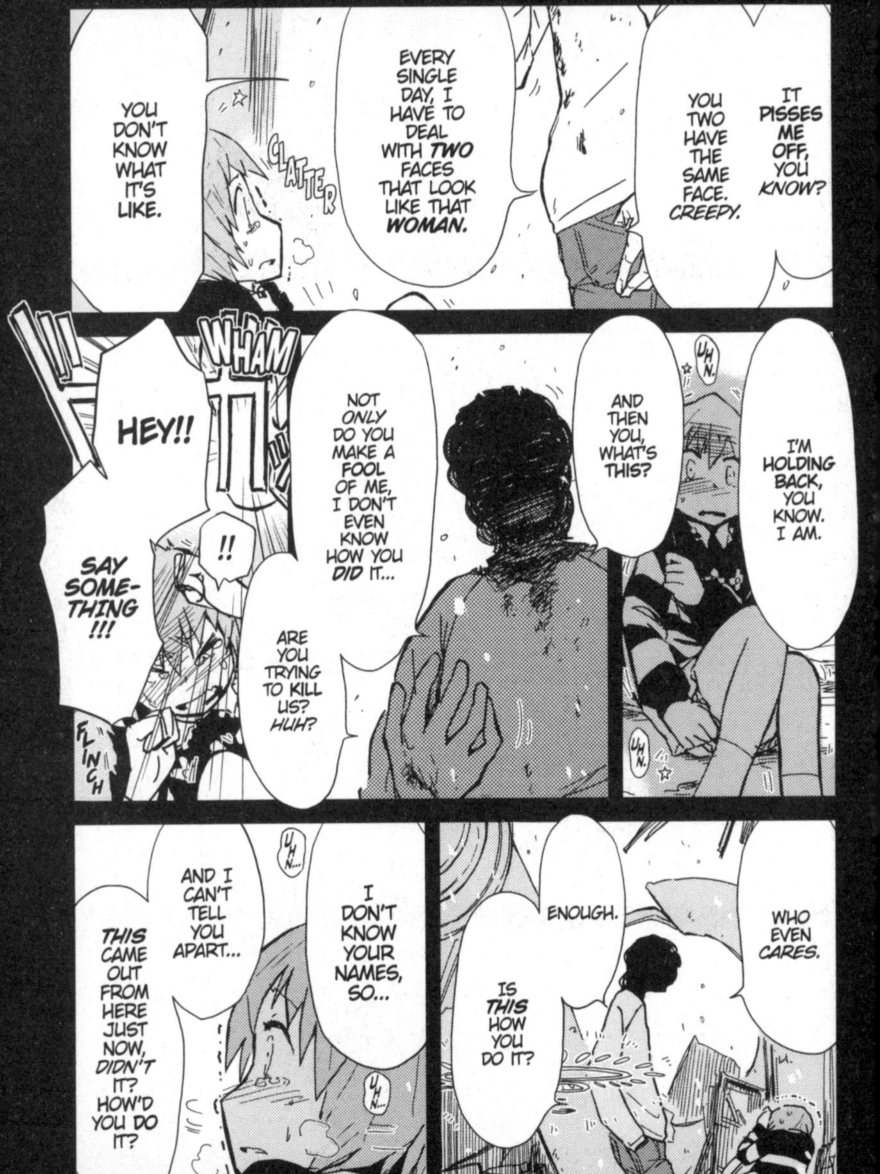
IT PISSES ME OFF, YOU *KNOW?*
YOU TWO HAVE THE SAME FACE. *CREEPY.*
EVERY SINGLE DAY, I HAVE TO DEAL WITH ***TWO*** FACES THAT LOOK LIKE THAT ***WOMAN.***
CLATTER
YOU DON'T KNOW WHAT IT'S LIKE.
I'M HOLDING BACK, YOU KNOW. I AM.
UHN.
AND THEN YOU, WHAT'S THIS?
UHN.
NOT *ONLY* DO YOU MAKE A **FOOL** OF ME, I DON'T EVEN KNOW HOW YOU *DID* IT...
ARE YOU TRYING TO KILL US? *HUH?*
WHAM
HEY!!
!!
SAY SOME-THING !!!
FLINCH
WHO EVEN *CARES.*
ENOUGH.
IS ***THIS*** HOW YOU DO IT?
I DON'T KNOW YOUR NAMES, SO...
UHN...
AND I CAN'T TELL YOU APART...
THIS CAME OUT FROM HERE JUST NOW, *DIDN'T* IT? HOW'D YOU DO IT?
UHN...

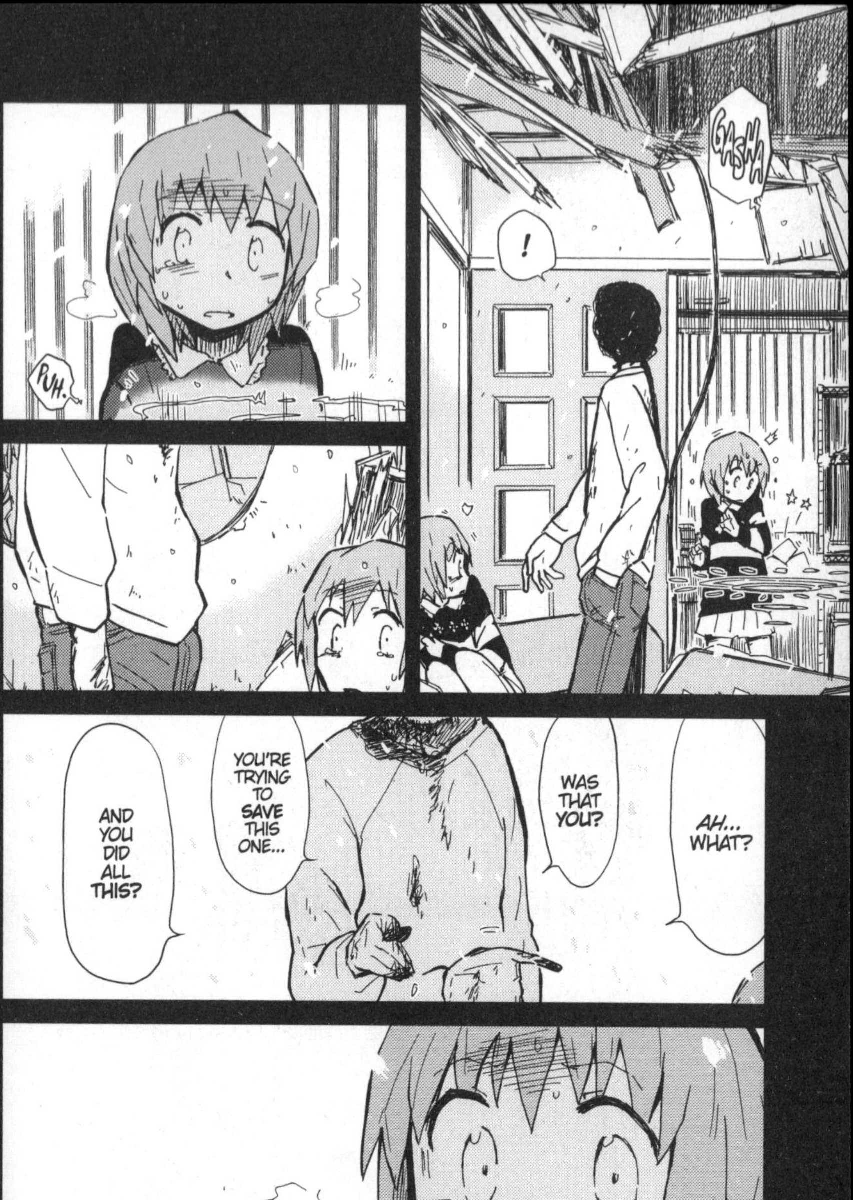
GASHA
!
PUH.
AH... WHAT?
WAS THAT YOU?
YOU'RE TRYING TO SAVE THIS ONE...
AND YOU DID ALL THIS?

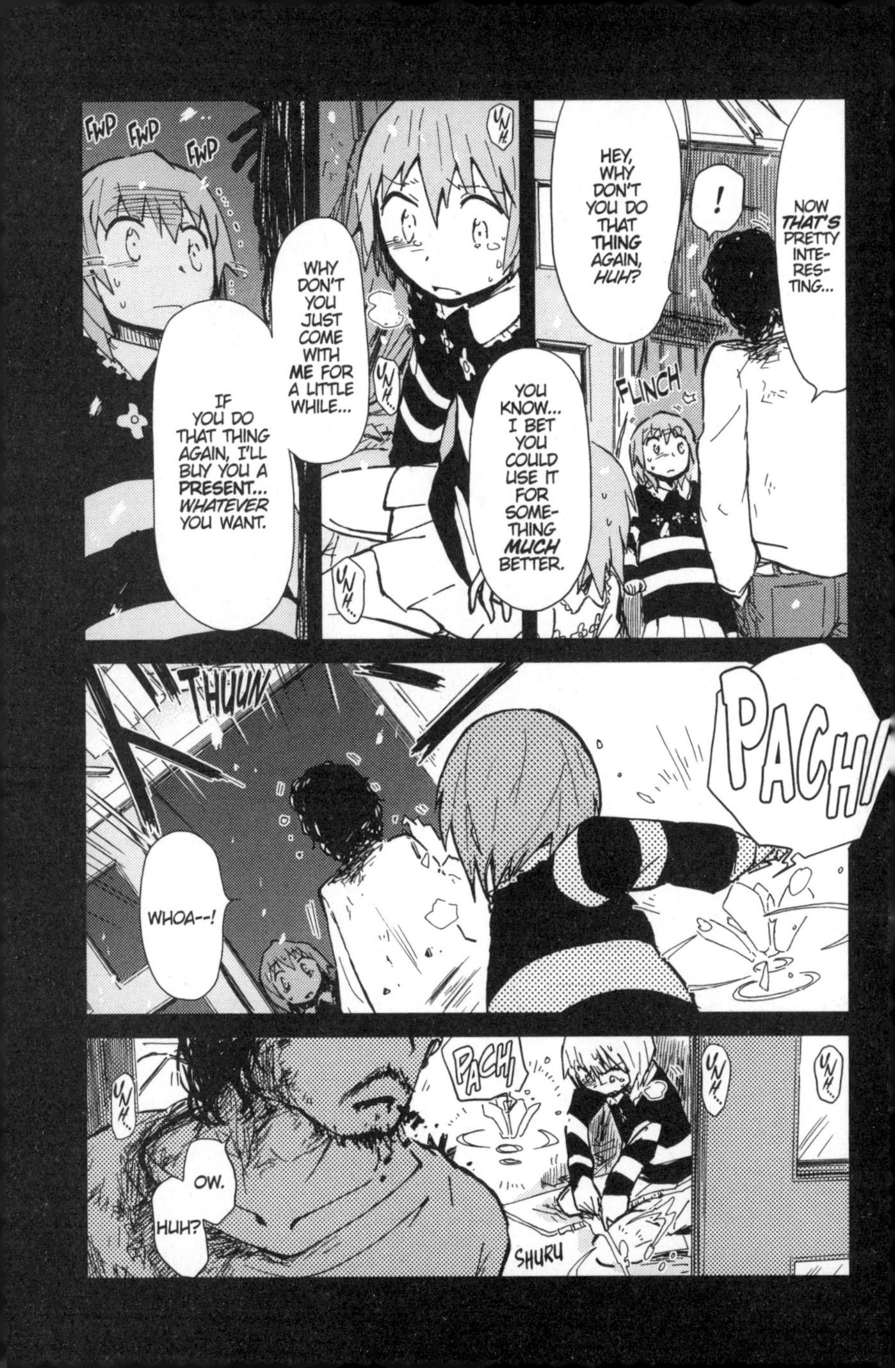
NOW THAT'S PRETTY INTERESTING...
!
HEY, WHY DON'T YOU DO THAT THING AGAIN, HUH?
FLINCH
YOU KNOW... I BET YOU COULD USE IT FOR SOMETHING MUCH BETTER.
UNH.
WHY DON'T YOU JUST COME WITH ME FOR A LITTLE WHILE...
UNH...
UNH...
FWP
FWP
FWP
IF YOU DO THAT THING AGAIN, I'LL BUY YOU A PRESENT... WHATEVER YOU WANT.
PACHI
THUUN
WHOA--!
UNH...
UNH...
PACH
SHURU
UNH...
OW.
HUH?

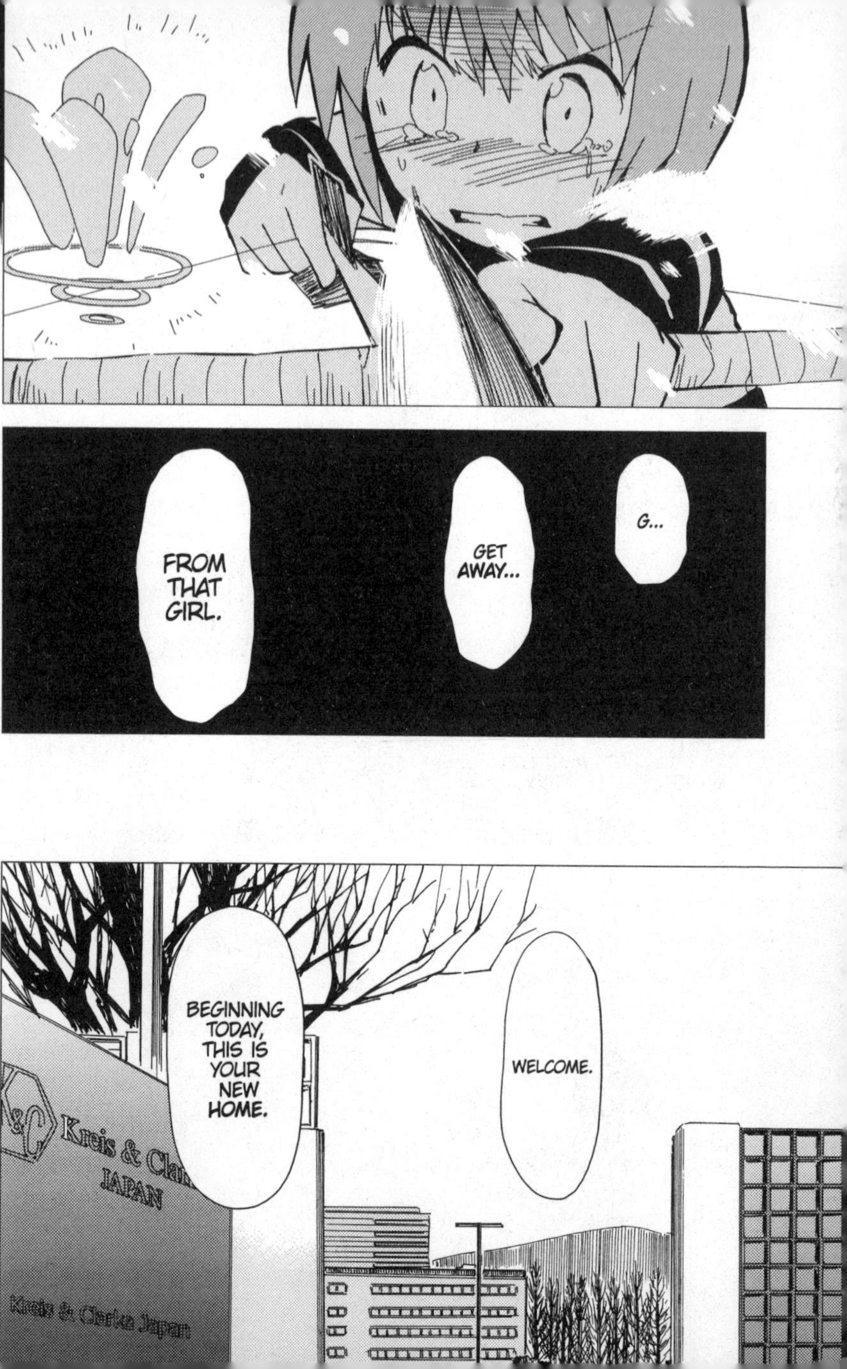
G...
GET AWAY...
FROM THAT GIRL.
WELCOME.
BEGINNING TODAY, THIS IS YOUR NEW HOME.
JAPAN
Kreis & Clarke Japan

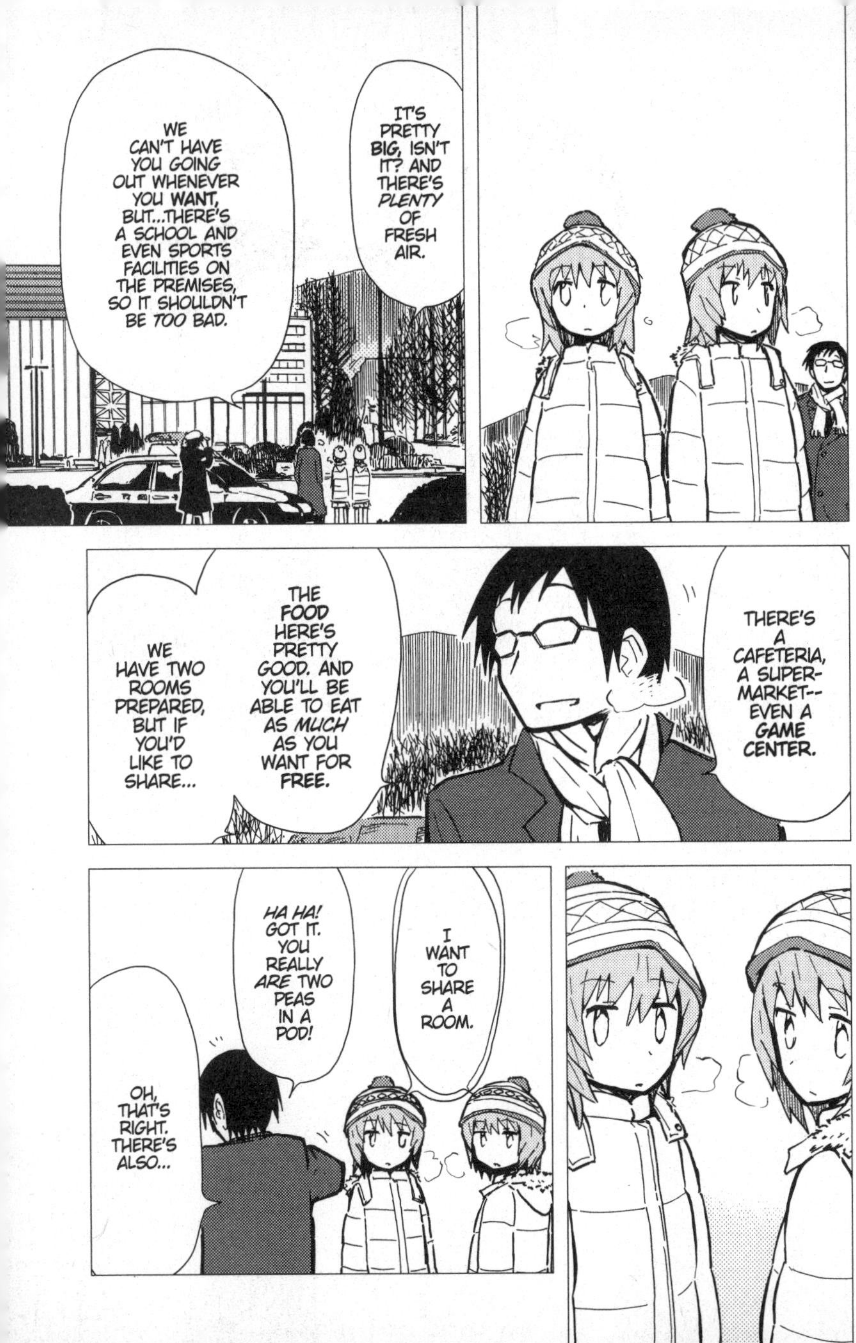
IT'S PRETTY BIG, ISN'T IT? AND THERE'S *PLENTY* OF FRESH AIR.
WE CAN'T HAVE YOU GOING OUT WHENEVER YOU WANT, BUT...THERE'S A SCHOOL AND EVEN SPORTS FACILITIES ON THE PREMISES, SO IT SHOULDN'T BE *TOO* BAD.
THERE'S A CAFETERIA, A SUPER-MARKET--EVEN A GAME CENTER.
THE FOOD HERE'S PRETTY GOOD. AND YOU'LL BE ABLE TO EAT AS *MUCH* AS YOU WANT FOR FREE.
WE HAVE TWO ROOMS PREPARED, BUT IF YOU'D LIKE TO SHARE...
I WANT TO SHARE A ROOM.
HA HA! GOT IT. YOU REALLY *ARE* TWO PEAS IN A POD!
OH, THAT'S RIGHT. THERE'S ALSO...

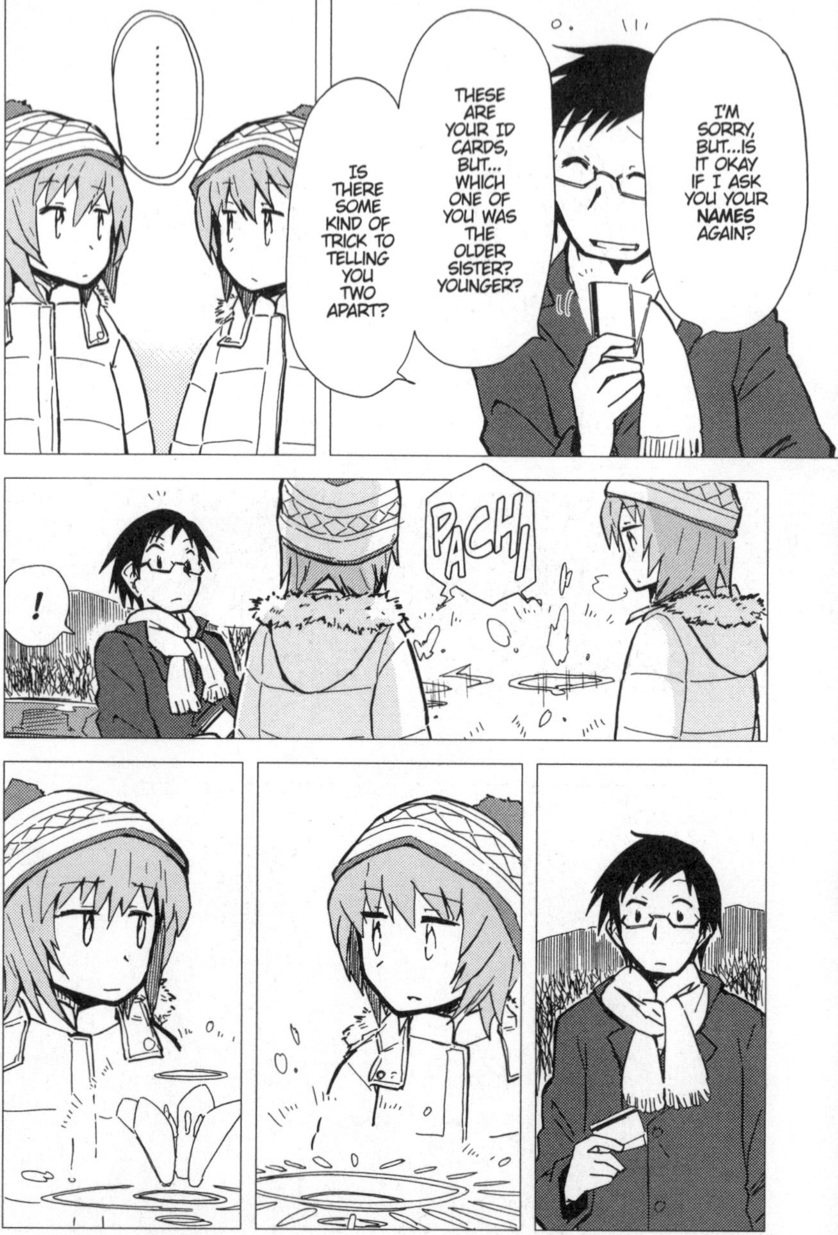
I'M SORRY, BUT...IS IT OKAY IF I ASK YOU YOUR NAMES AGAIN?
THESE ARE YOUR ID CARDS, BUT... WHICH ONE OF YOU WAS THE OLDER SISTER? YOUNGER?
IS THERE SOME KIND OF TRICK TO TELLING YOU TWO APART?
......
PACHI
!

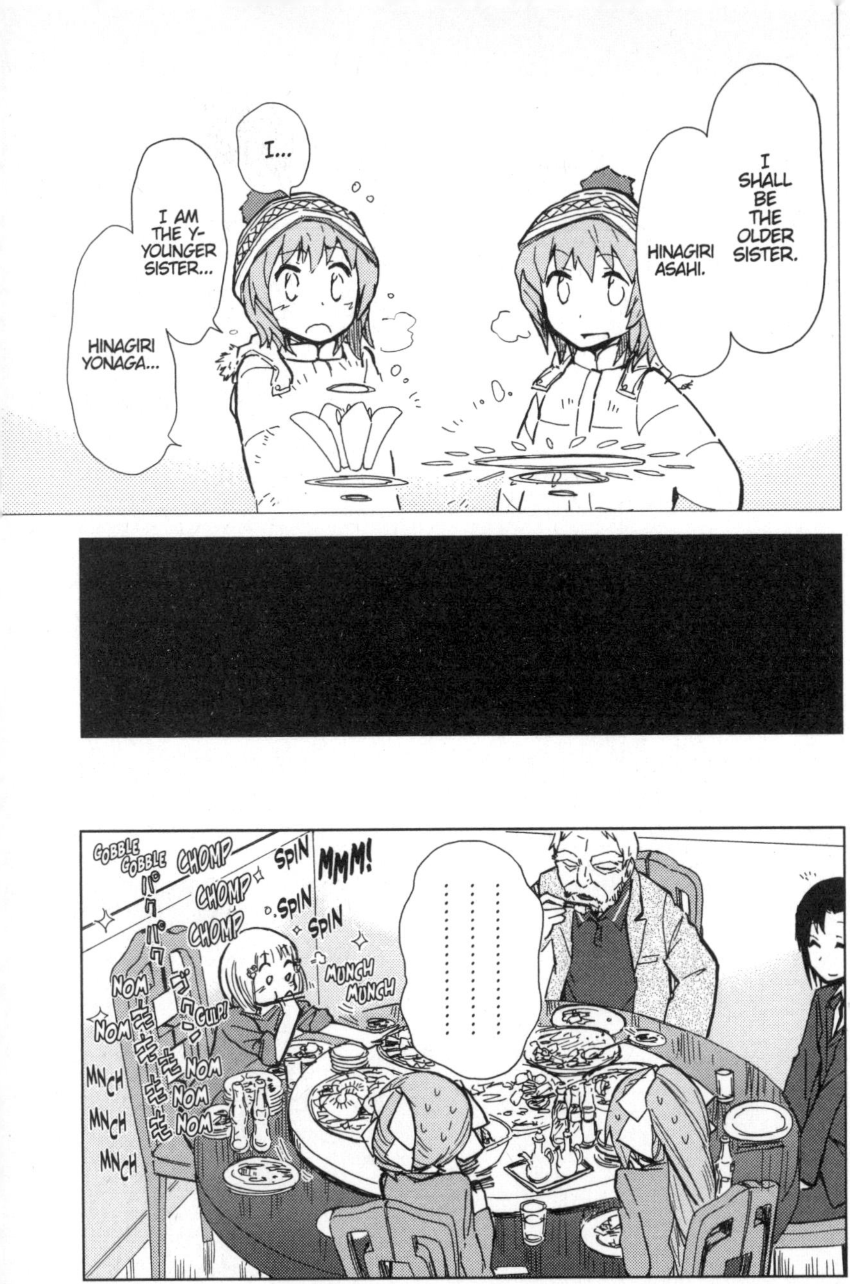
I SHALL BE THE OLDER SISTER.
HINAGIRI ASAHI.
I...
I AM THE Y-YOUNGER SISTER...
HINAGIRI YONAGA...
MMM!
......
SPIN
SPIN
SPIN
MUNCH MUNCH
CHOMP
CHOMP
CHOMP
GOBBLE GOBBLE
GULP!
NOM
NOM
NOM
NOM
NOM
MNCH
MNCH
MNCH

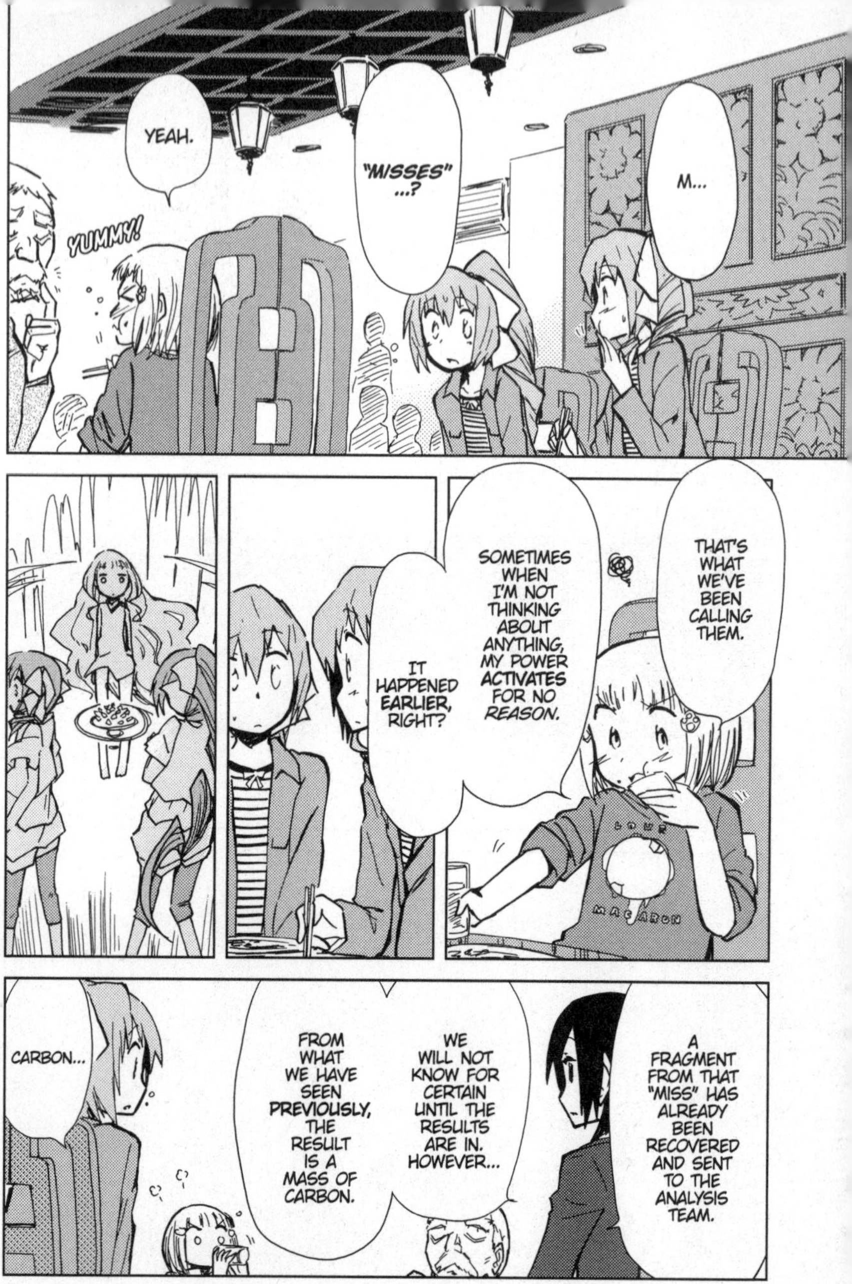
M...
"MISSES" ...?
YEAH.
YUMMY!
THAT'S WHAT WE'VE BEEN CALLING THEM.
SOMETIMES WHEN I'M NOT THINKING ABOUT ANYTHING, MY POWER ACTIVATES FOR NO REASON.
IT HAPPENED EARLIER, RIGHT?
A FRAGMENT FROM THAT "MISS" HAS ALREADY BEEN RECOVERED AND SENT TO THE ANALYSIS TEAM.
WE WILL NOT KNOW FOR CERTAIN UNTIL THE RESULTS ARE IN. HOWEVER...
FROM WHAT WE HAVE SEEN PREVIOUSLY, THE RESULT IS A MASS OF CARBON.
CARBON...

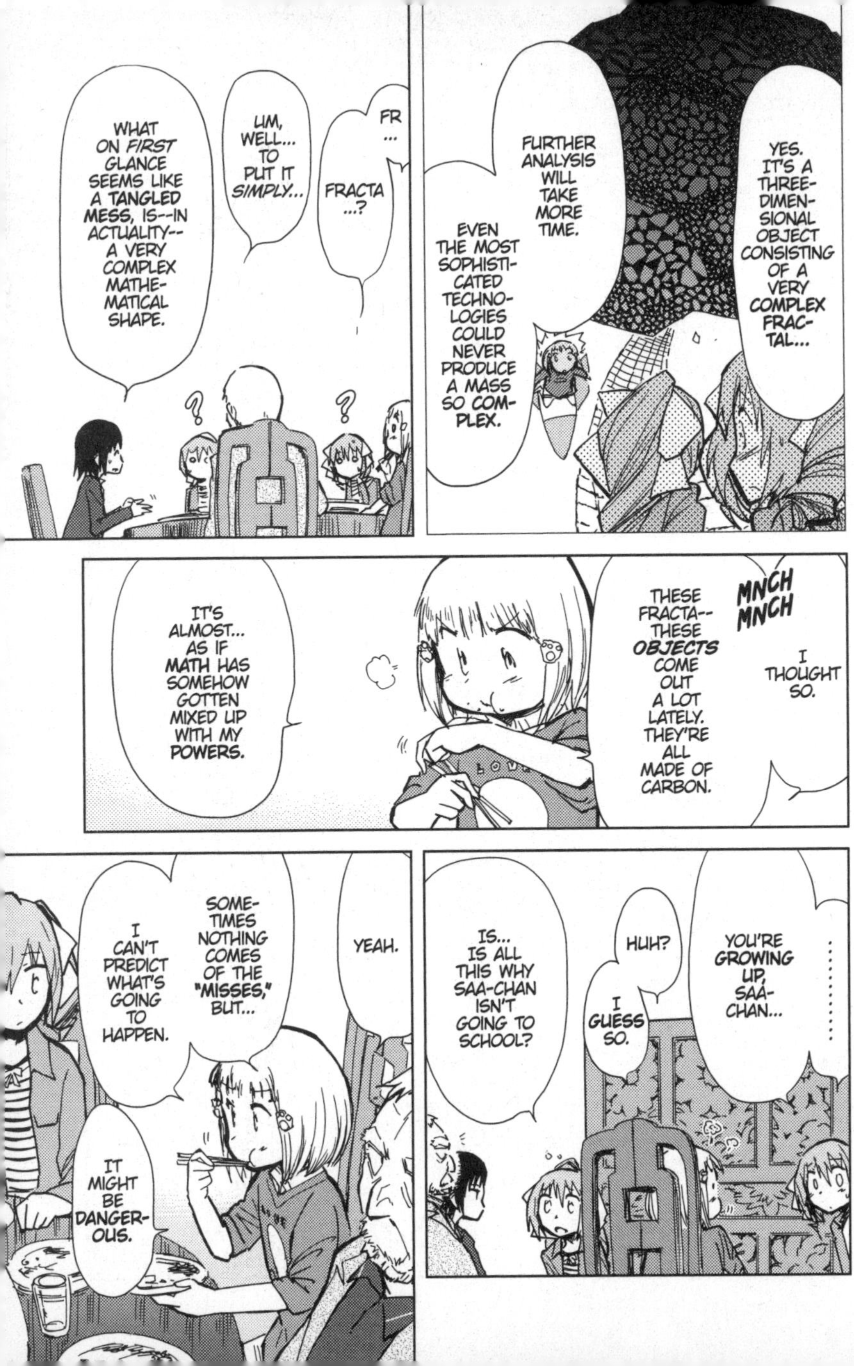
YES. IT'S A THREE-DIMENSIONAL OBJECT CONSISTING OF A VERY COMPLEX FRACTAL...
FURTHER ANALYSIS WILL TAKE MORE TIME.
EVEN THE MOST SOPHISTICATED TECHNOLOGIES COULD NEVER PRODUCE A MASS SO COMPLEX.
FR...
FRACTA...?
UM, WELL... TO PUT IT SIMPLY...
WHAT ON FIRST GLANCE SEEMS LIKE A TANGLED MESS, IS--IN ACTUALITY--A VERY COMPLEX MATHEMATICAL SHAPE.
MNCH MNCH
I THOUGHT SO.
THESE FRACTA--THESE OBJECTS COME OUT A LOT LATELY. THEY'RE ALL MADE OF CARBON.
IT'S ALMOST... AS IF MATH HAS SOMEHOW GOTTEN MIXED UP WITH MY POWERS.
......
YOU'RE GROWING UP, SAA-CHAN...
HUH?
I GUESS SO.
IS... IS ALL THIS WHY SAA-CHAN ISN'T GOING TO SCHOOL?
YEAH.
SOMETIMES NOTHING COMES OF THE "MISSES," BUT...
I CAN'T PREDICT WHAT'S GOING TO HAPPEN.
IT MIGHT BE DANGEROUS.

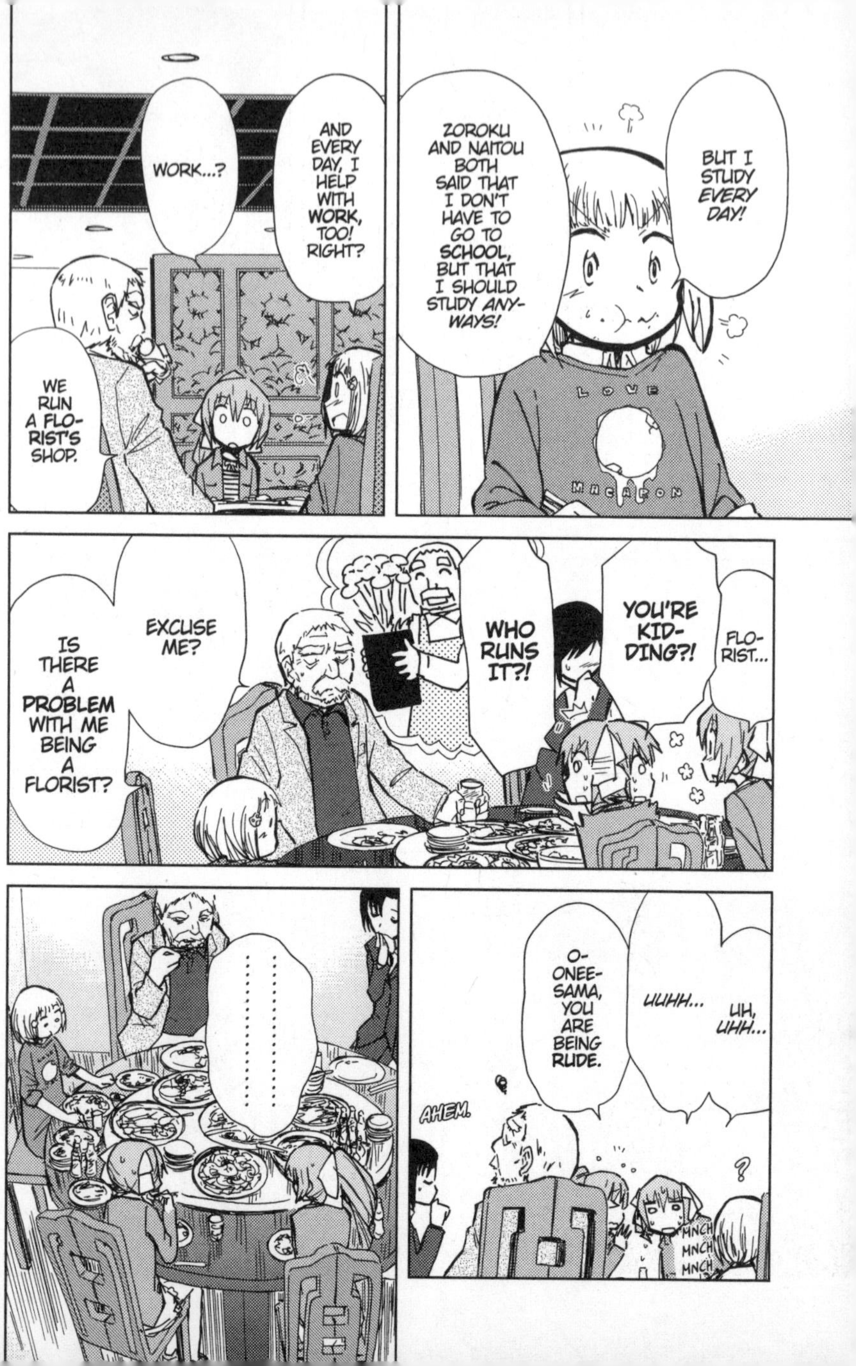
BUT I STUDY EVERY DAY!
ZOROKU AND NAITOU BOTH SAID THAT I DON'T HAVE TO GO TO SCHOOL, BUT THAT I SHOULD STUDY ANYWAYS!
AND EVERY DAY, I HELP WITH WORK, TOO! RIGHT?
WORK...?
WE RUN A FLORIST'S SHOP.
FLORIST...
YOU'RE KIDDING?!
WHO RUNS IT?!
EXCUSE ME?
IS THERE A PROBLEM WITH ME BEING A FLORIST?
UH, UHH...
UUHH...
O-ONEE-SAMA, YOU ARE BEING RUDE.
AHEM.
MNCH MNCH MNCH
......

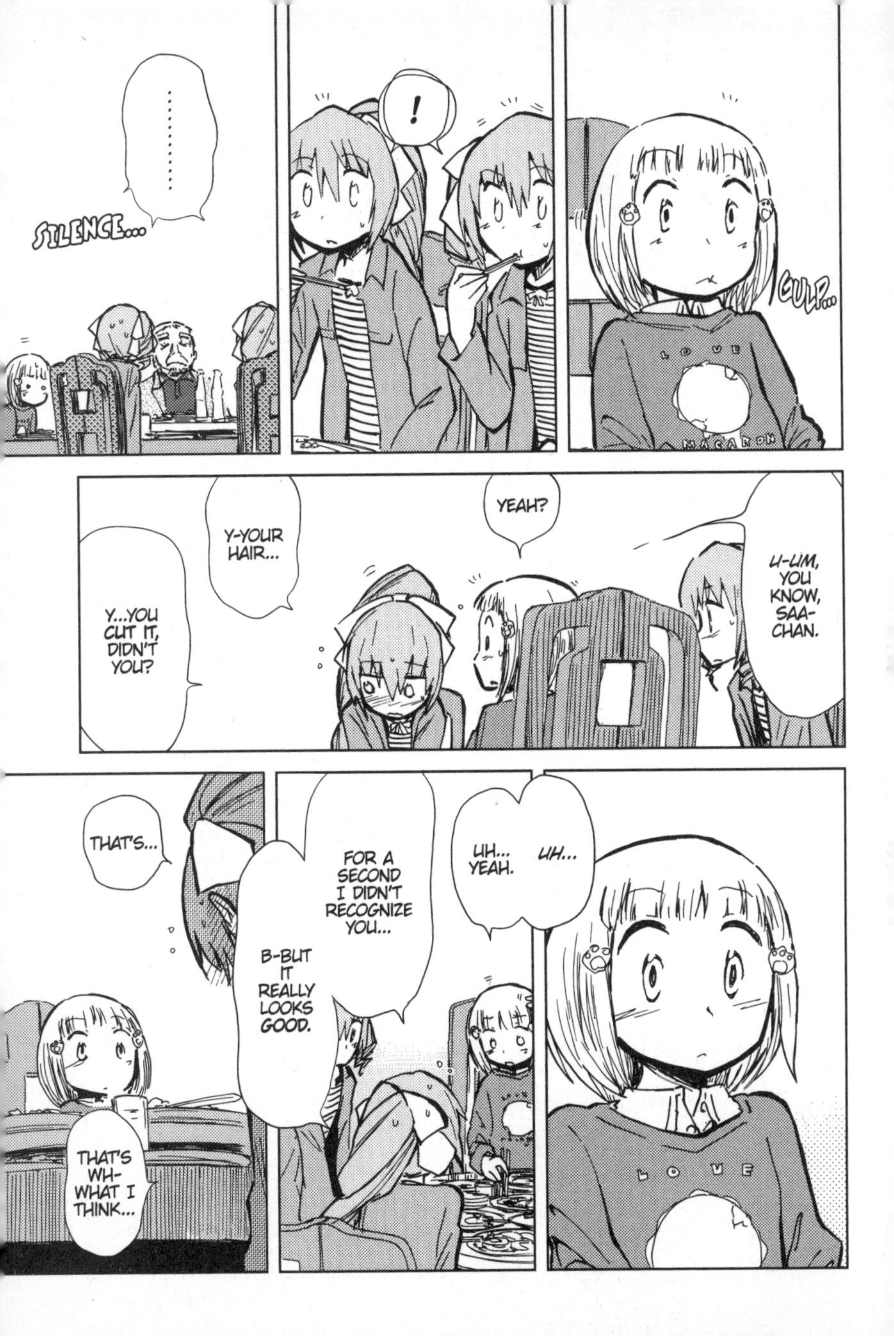
GULP...
!
......
SILENCE...
U-UM, YOU KNOW, SAA-CHAN.
YEAH?
Y-YOUR HAIR...
Y...YOU CUT IT, DIDN'T YOU?
UH...
UH... YEAH.
FOR A SECOND I DIDN'T RECOGNIZE YOU...
B-BUT IT REALLY LOOKS GOOD.
THAT'S...
THAT'S WH-WHAT I THINK...

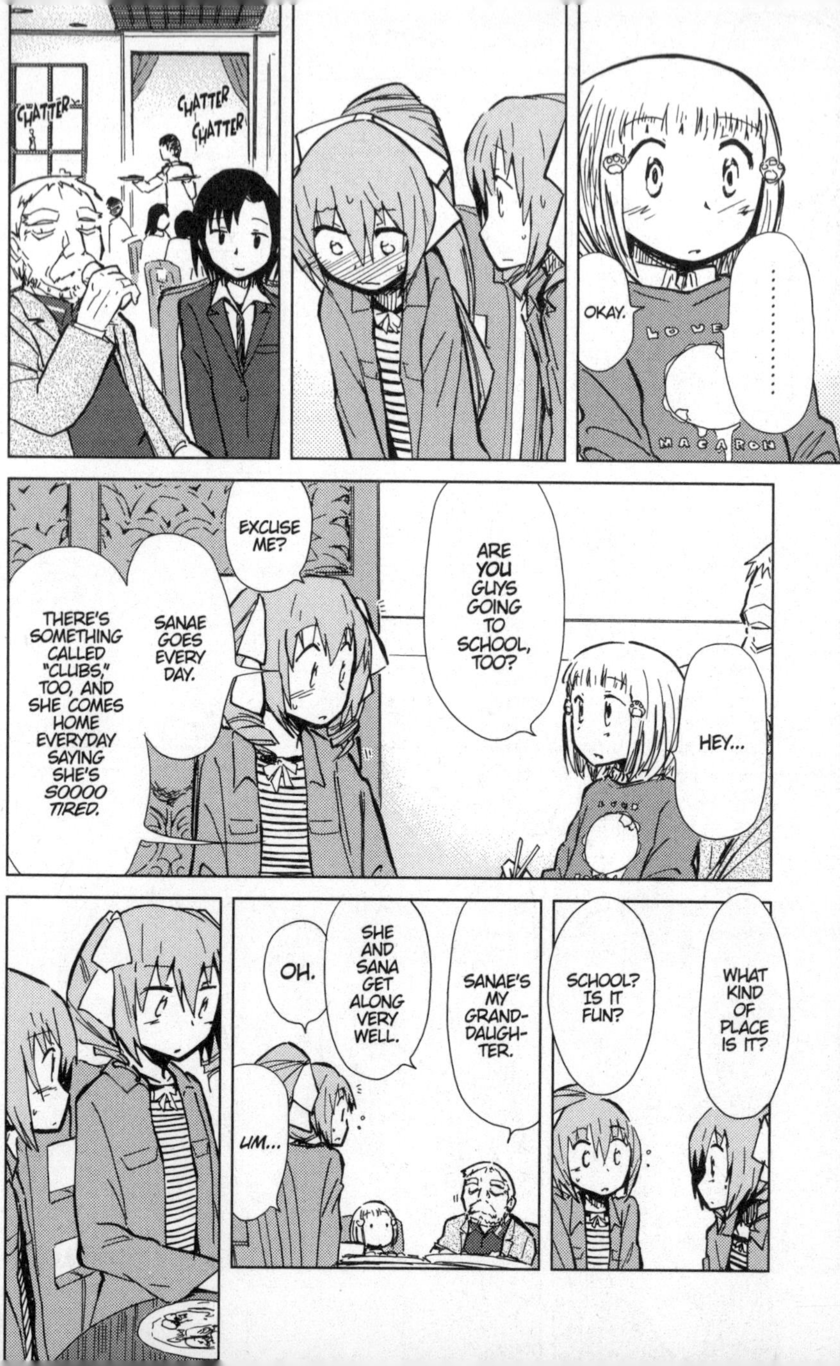
......
OKAY.
MACARON
CHATTER CHATTER
CHATTER
HEY...
ARE YOU GUYS GOING TO SCHOOL, TOO?
EXCUSE ME?
SANAE GOES EVERY DAY.
THERE'S SOMETHING CALLED "CLUBS," TOO, AND SHE COMES HOME EVERYDAY SAYING SHE'S SOOOO TIRED.
WHAT KIND OF PLACE IS IT?
SCHOOL? IS IT FUN?
SANAE'S MY GRAND-DAUGH-TER.
SHE AND SANA GET ALONG VERY WELL.
OH.
UM...

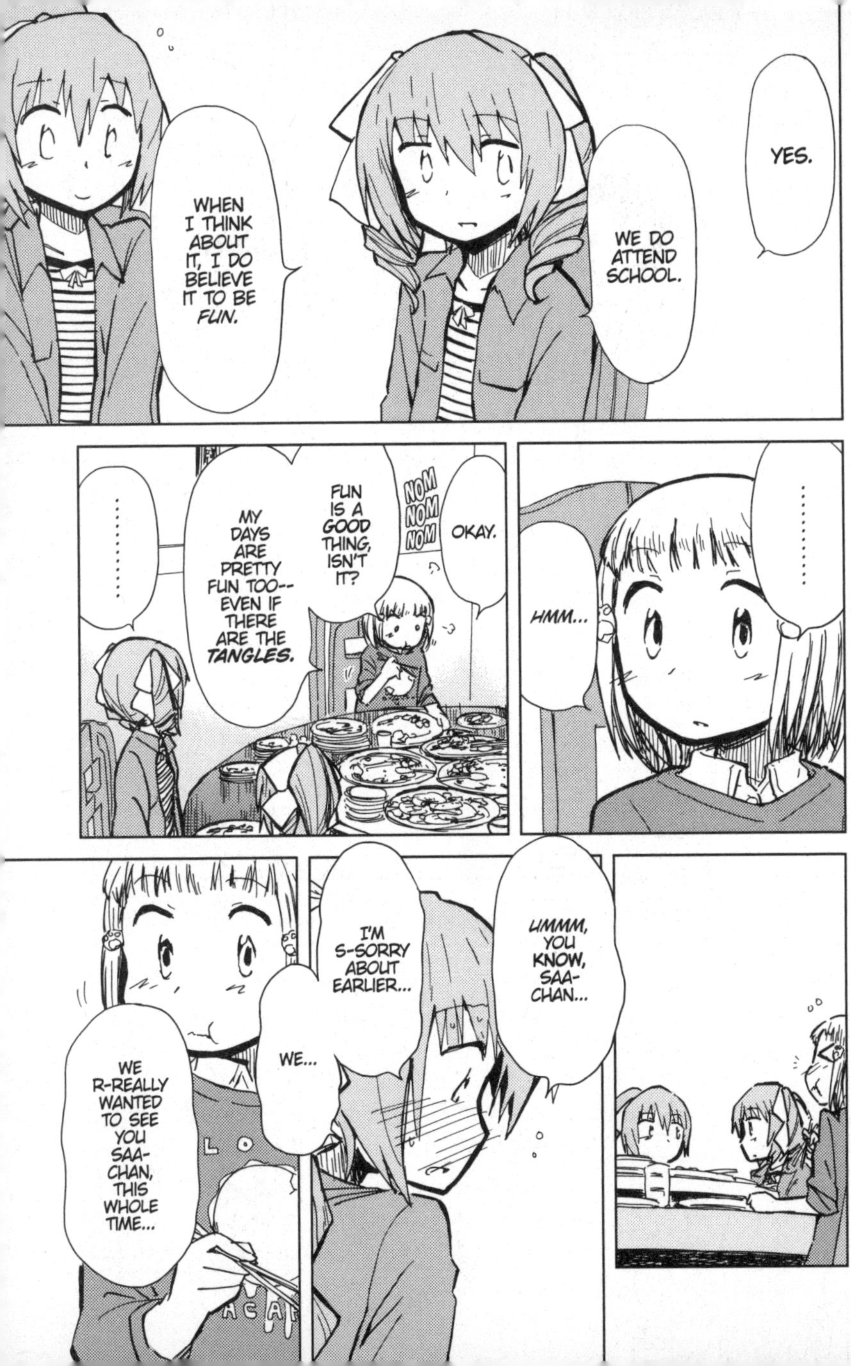
YES.
WE DO ATTEND SCHOOL.
WHEN I THINK ABOUT IT, I DO BELIEVE IT TO BE *FUN.*
....
HMM...
OKAY.
NOM NOM NOM
FUN IS A GOOD THING, ISN'T IT?
MY DAYS ARE PRETTY FUN TOO--EVEN IF THERE ARE THE *TANGLES.*
....
UMMM, YOU KNOW, SAA-CHAN...
I'M S-SORRY ABOUT EARLIER...
WE...
WE R-REALLY WANTED TO SEE YOU SAA-CHAN, THIS WHOLE TIME...

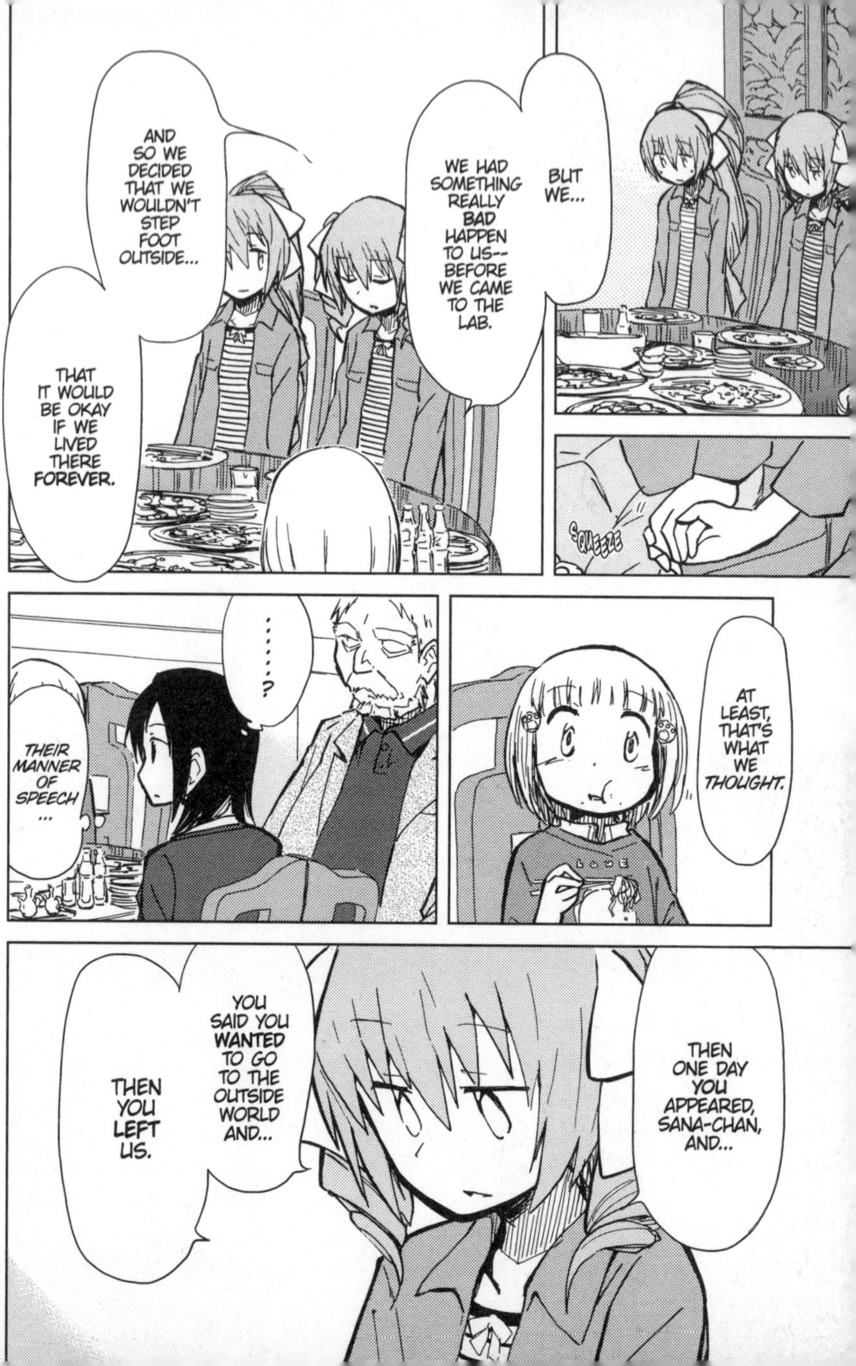
SQUEEZE
BUT WE...
WE HAD SOMETHING REALLY BAD HAPPEN TO US-- BEFORE WE CAME TO THE LAB.
AND SO WE DECIDED THAT WE WOULDN'T STEP FOOT OUTSIDE...
THAT IT WOULD BE OKAY IF WE LIVED THERE FOREVER.
AT LEAST, THAT'S WHAT WE *THOUGHT.*
......?
THEIR MANNER OF SPEECH ...
THEN ONE DAY **YOU** APPEARED, SANA-CHAN, AND...
YOU SAID YOU **WANTED** TO GO TO THE OUTSIDE WORLD AND...
THEN YOU **LEFT** US.

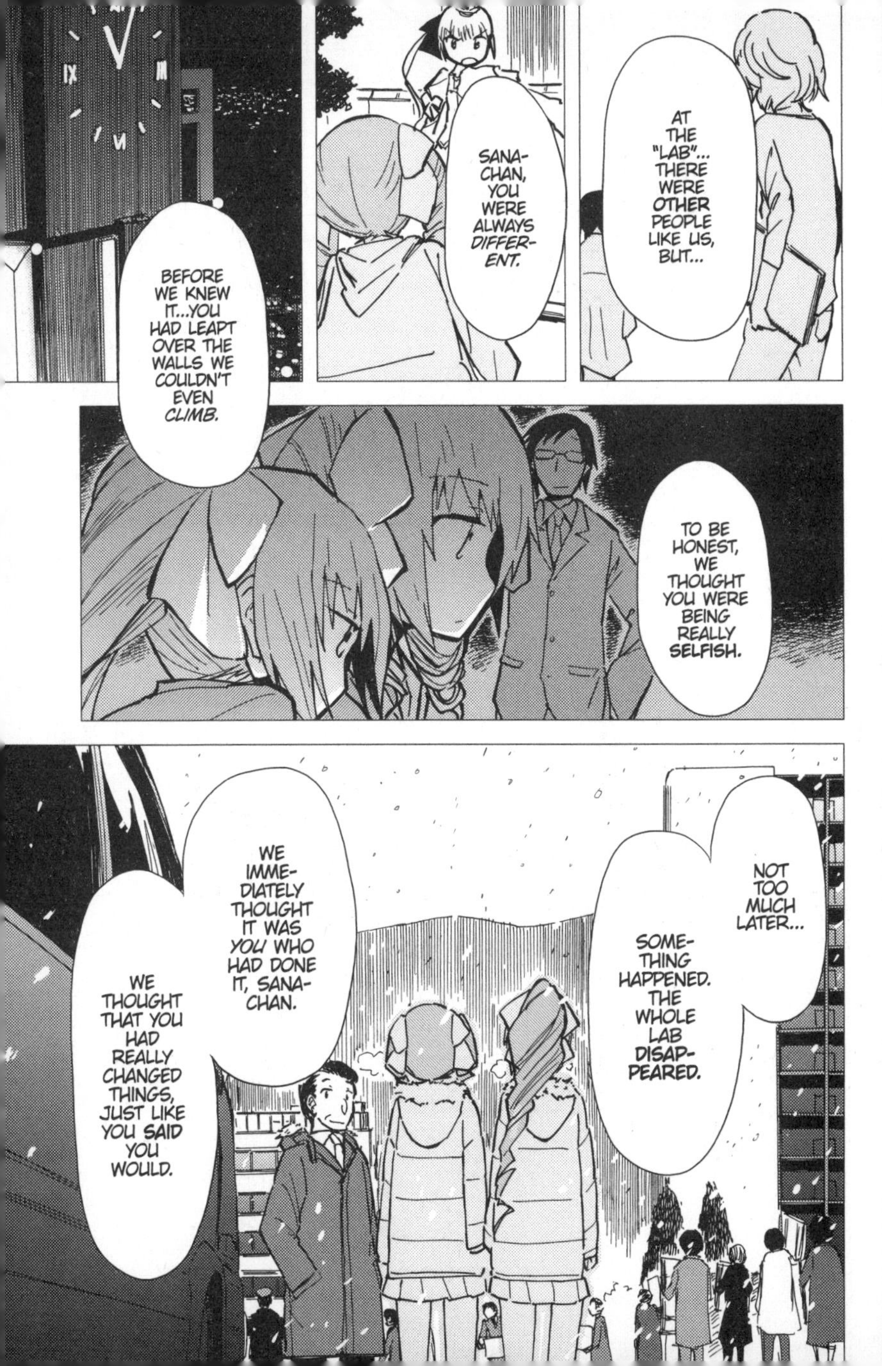
AT THE "LAB"... THERE WERE OTHER PEOPLE LIKE US, BUT...
SANA-CHAN, YOU WERE ALWAYS DIFFERENT.
BEFORE WE KNEW IT...YOU HAD LEAPT OVER THE WALLS WE COULDN'T EVEN CLIMB.
TO BE HONEST, WE THOUGHT YOU WERE BEING REALLY SELFISH.
NOT TOO MUCH LATER...
SOMETHING HAPPENED. THE WHOLE LAB DISAPPEARED.
WE IMMEDIATELY THOUGHT IT WAS YOU WHO HAD DONE IT, SANA-CHAN.
WE THOUGHT THAT YOU HAD REALLY CHANGED THINGS, JUST LIKE YOU SAID YOU WOULD.

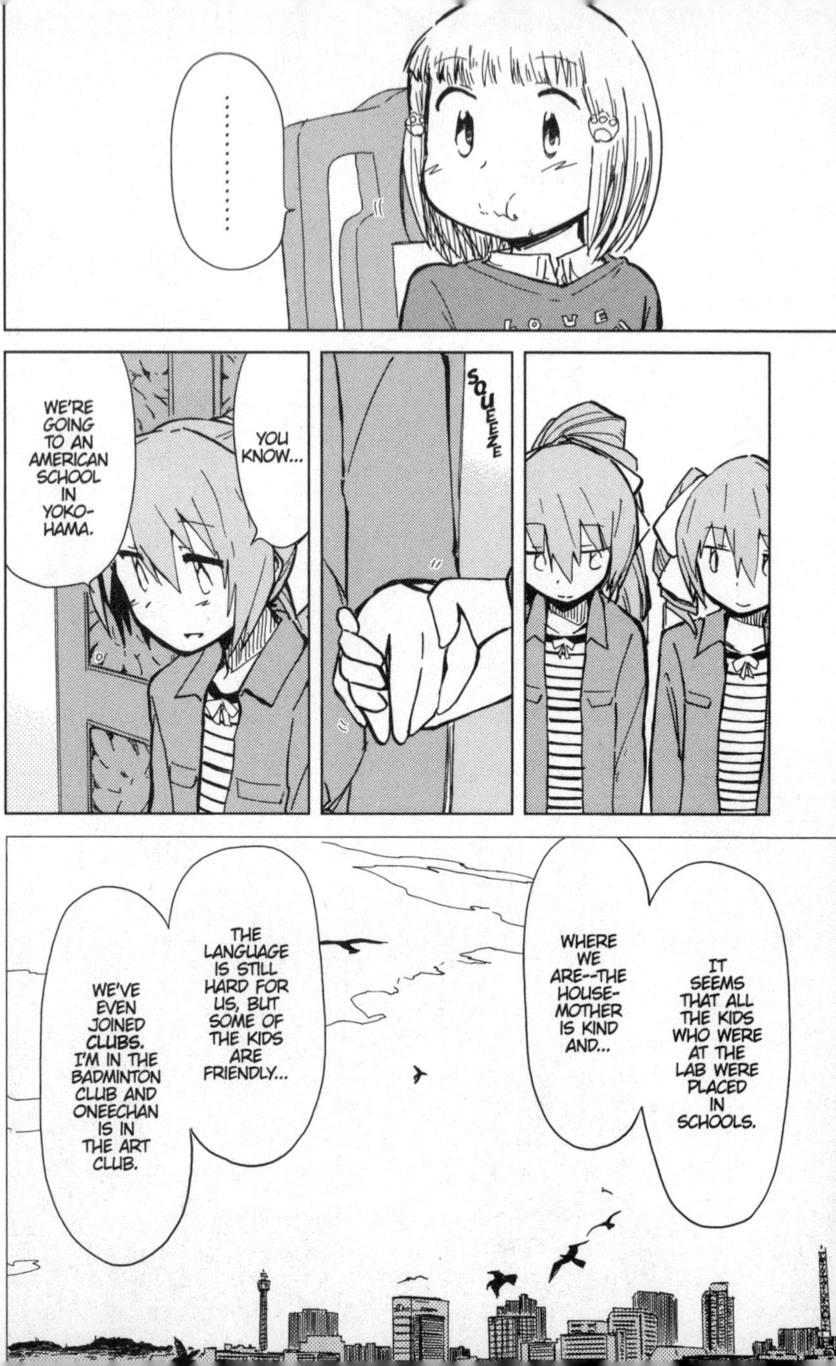
......
SQUEEZE
YOU KNOW...
WE'RE GOING TO AN AMERICAN SCHOOL IN YOKOHAMA.
IT SEEMS THAT ALL THE KIDS WHO WERE AT THE LAB WERE PLACED IN SCHOOLS.
WHERE WE ARE--THE HOUSEMOTHER IS KIND AND...
THE LANGUAGE IS STILL HARD FOR US, BUT SOME OF THE KIDS ARE FRIENDLY...
WE'VE EVEN JOINED CLUBS. I'M IN THE BADMINTON CLUB AND ONEECHAN IS IN THE ART CLUB.

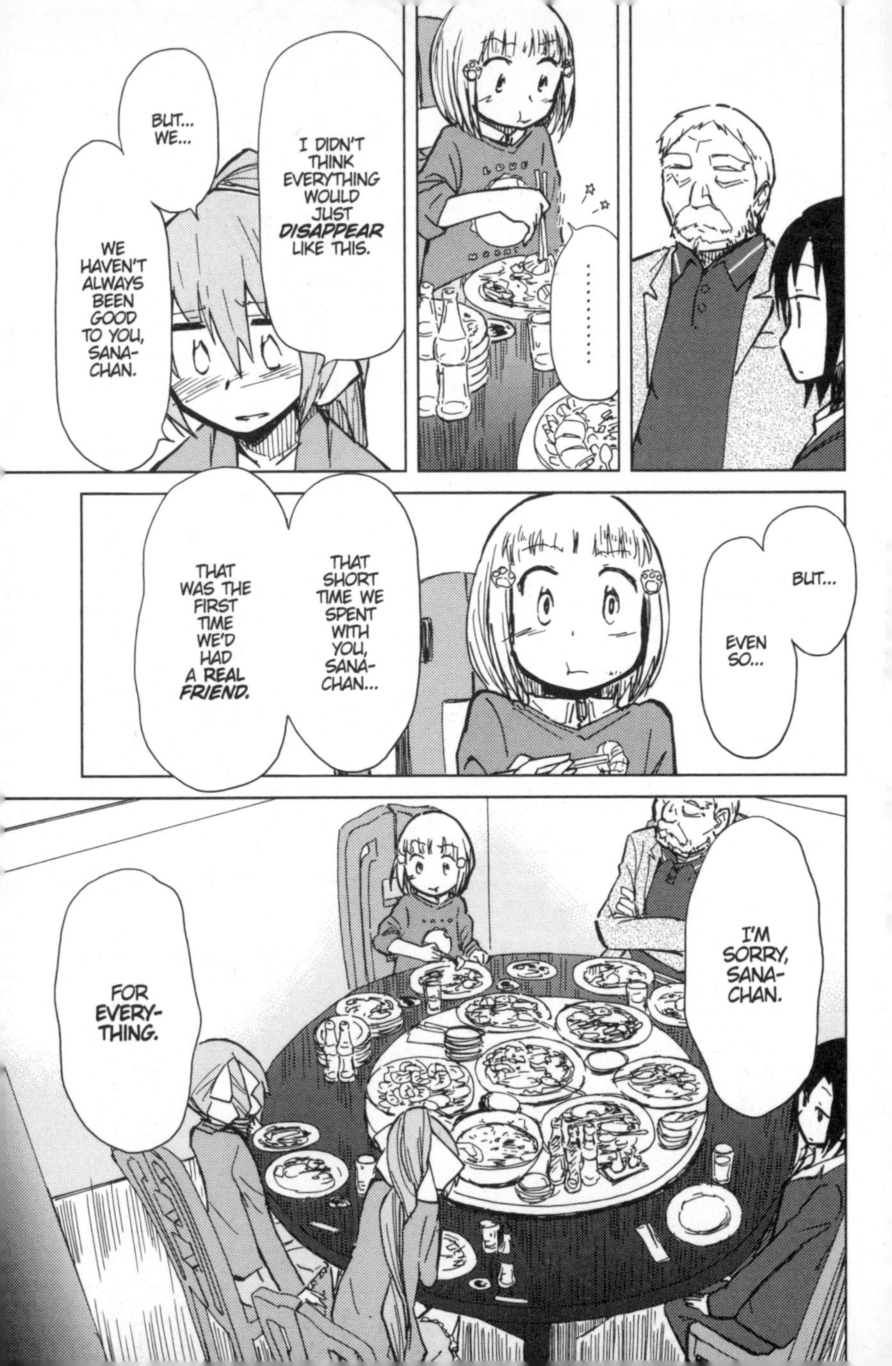
......
I DIDN'T THINK EVERYTHING WOULD JUST ***DISAPPEAR*** LIKE THIS.
BUT... WE...
WE HAVEN'T ALWAYS BEEN GOOD TO YOU, SANA-CHAN.
BUT...
EVEN SO...
THAT SHORT TIME WE SPENT WITH YOU, SANA-CHAN...
THAT WAS THE FIRST TIME WE'D HAD A REAL ***FRIEND.***
I'M SORRY, SANA-CHAN.
FOR EVERYTHING.

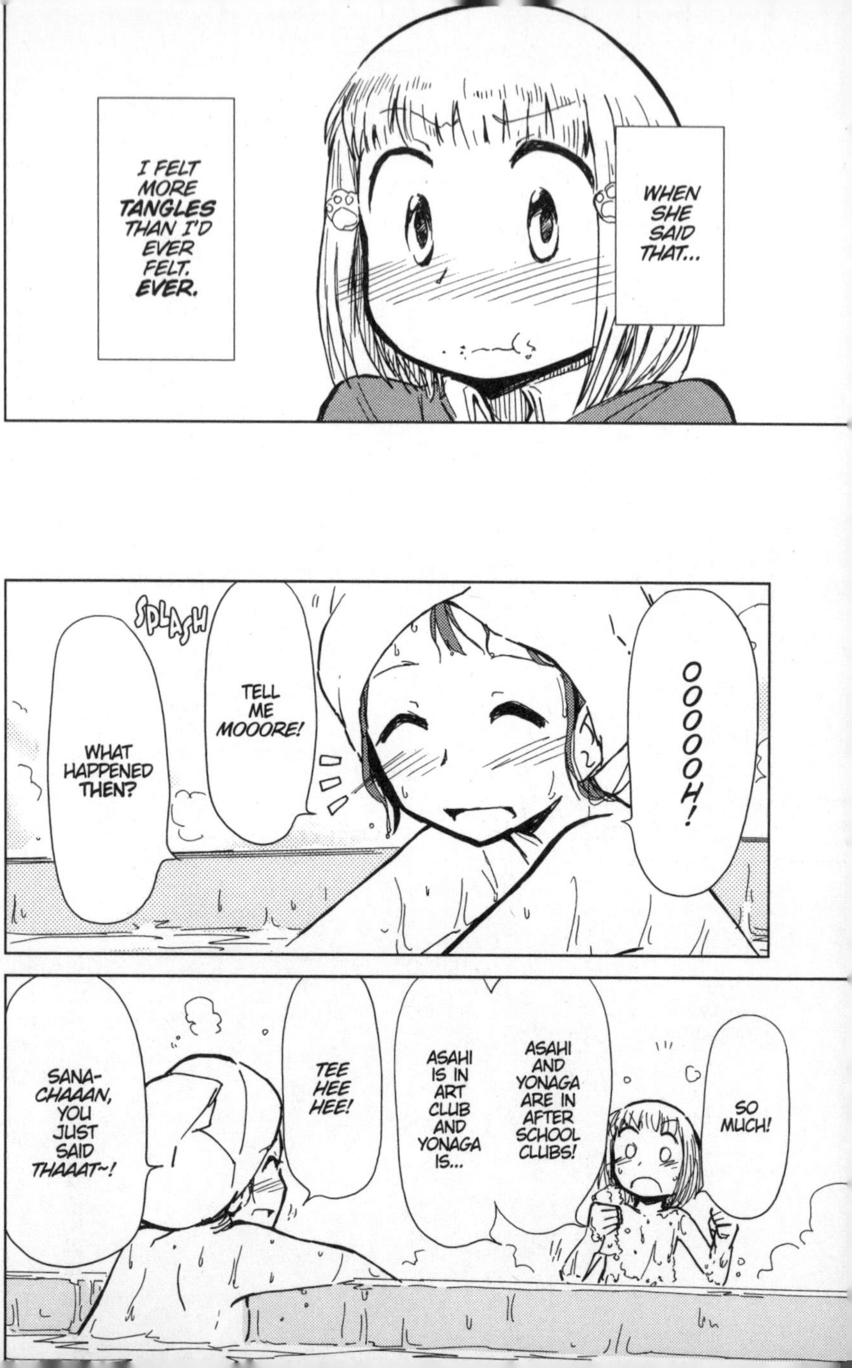
WHEN SHE SAID THAT...
I FELT MORE TANGLES THAN I'D EVER FELT. EVER.
OOOOOOH!
TELL ME MOOORE!
SPLASH
WHAT HAPPENED THEN?
SO MUCH!
ASAHI AND YONAGA ARE IN AFTER SCHOOL CLUBS!
ASAHI IS IN ART CLUB AND YONAGA IS...
TEE HEE HEE!
SANA-CHAAAN, YOU JUST SAID THAAAT~!

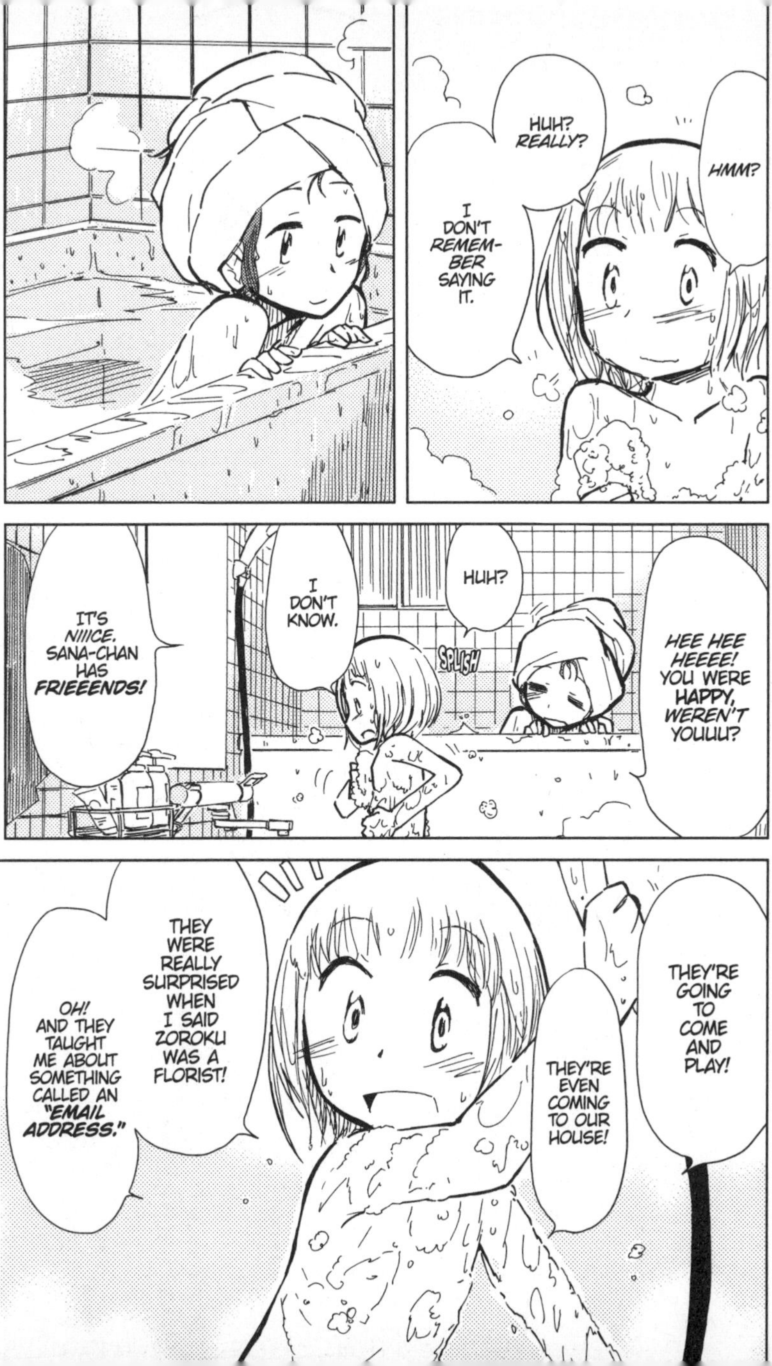
HMM?
HUH? REALLY?
I DON'T REMEMBER SAYING IT.
HEE HEE HEEEE! YOU WERE HAPPY, WEREN'T YOUUU?
HUH?
SPLISH
I DON'T KNOW.
IT'S NIIICE. SANA-CHAN HAS FRIEEENDS!
THEY'RE GOING TO COME AND PLAY!
THEY'RE EVEN COMING TO OUR HOUSE!
THEY WERE REALLY SURPRISED WHEN I SAID ZOROKU WAS A FLORIST!
OH! AND THEY TAUGHT ME ABOUT SOMETHING CALLED AN "EMAIL ADDRESS."

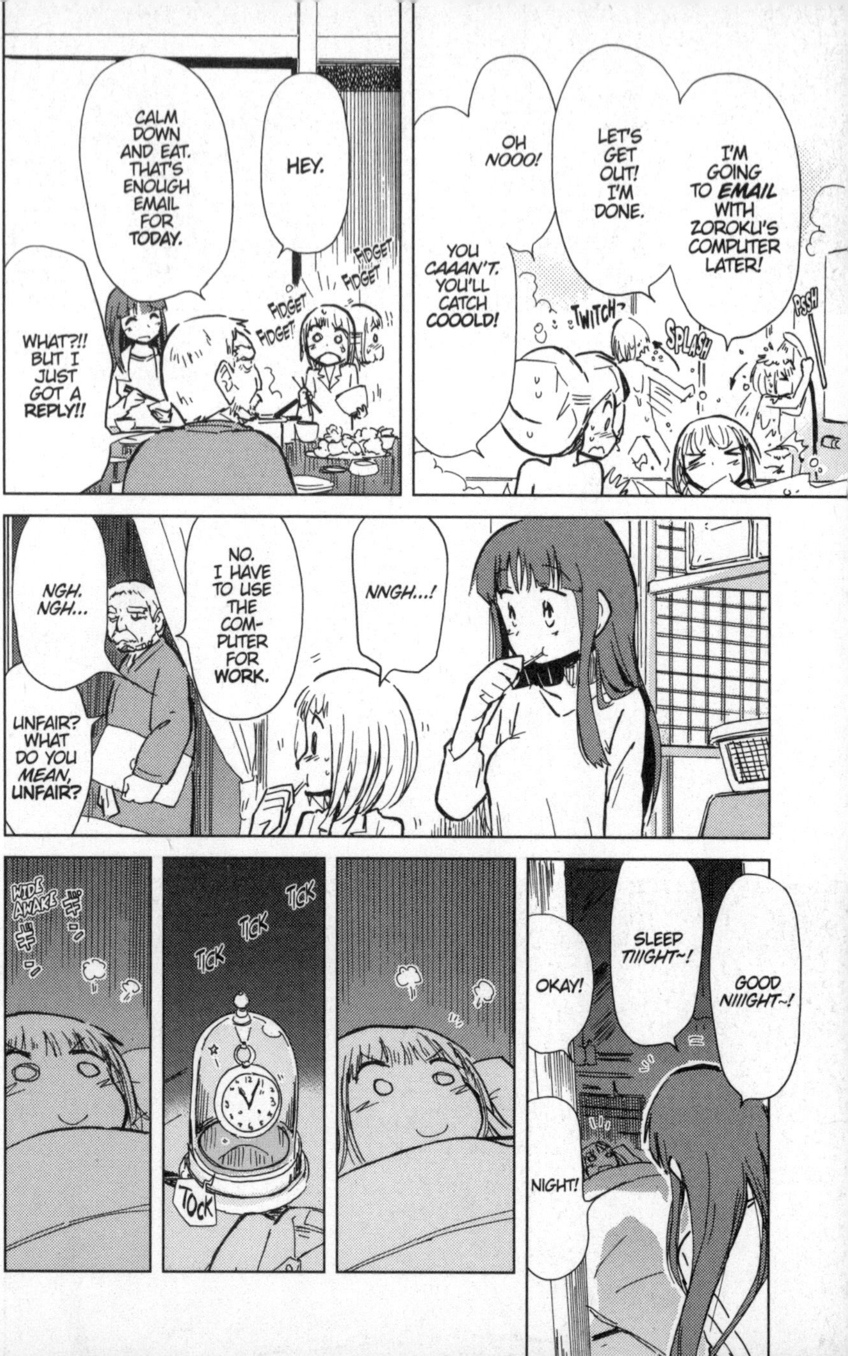
I'M GOING TO EMAIL WITH ZOROKU'S COMPUTER LATER!
LET'S GET OUT! I'M DONE.
OH NOOO!
YOU CAAAN'T. YOU'LL CATCH COOOLD!
PSSH
SPLASH
TWITCH
HEY.
CALM DOWN AND EAT. THAT'S ENOUGH EMAIL FOR TODAY.
FIDGET FIDGET
FIDGET FIDGET
WHAT?!! BUT I JUST GOT A REPLY!!
NNGH...!
NO. I HAVE TO USE THE COMPUTER FOR WORK.
NGH. NGH...
UNFAIR? WHAT DO YOU MEAN, UNFAIR?
GOOD NIIIGHT~!
SLEEP TIIIGHT~!
OKAY!
NIGHT!
TICK
TICK
TICK
TOCK
WIDE AWAKE

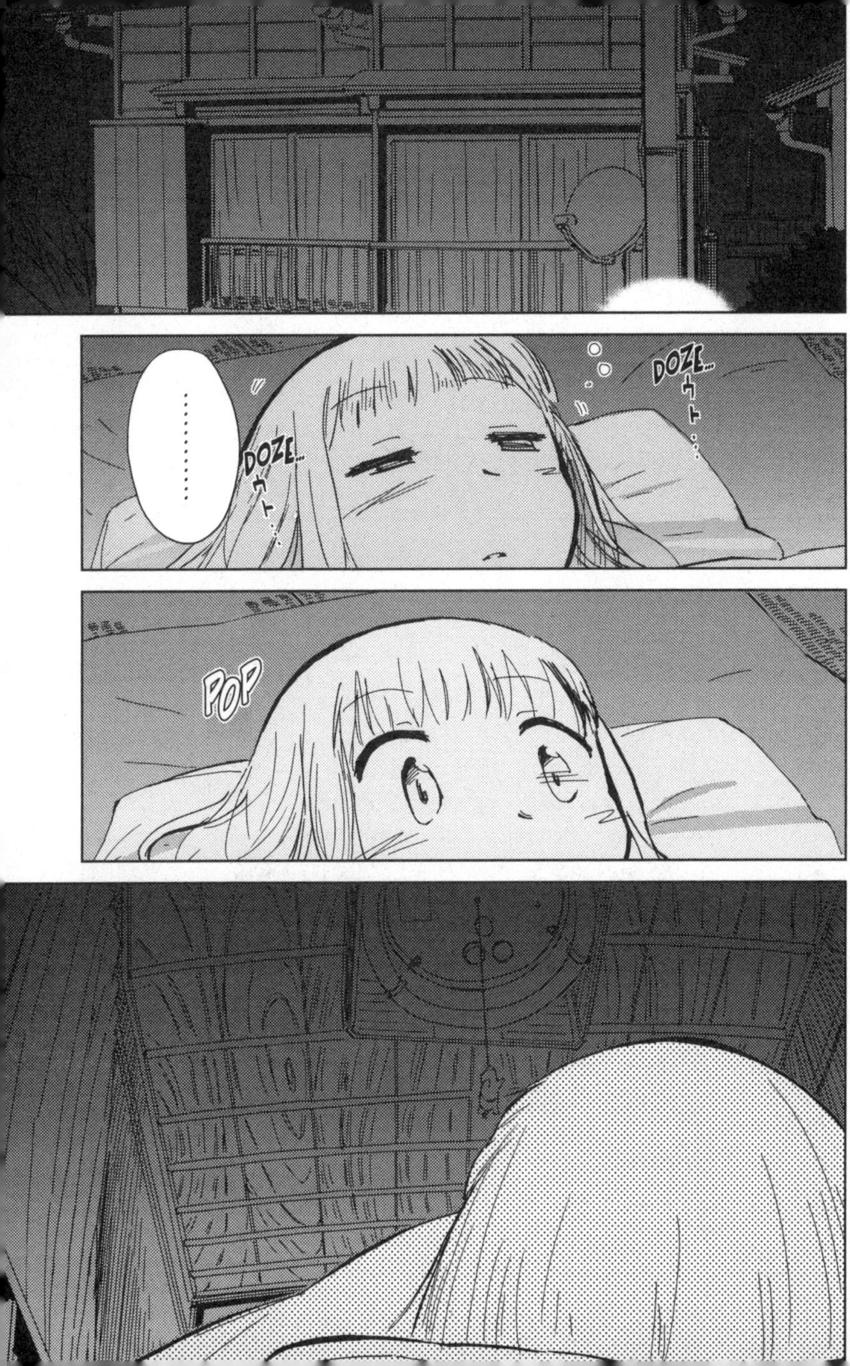
DOZE...
ウト...
DOZE...
ウト...
......
POP

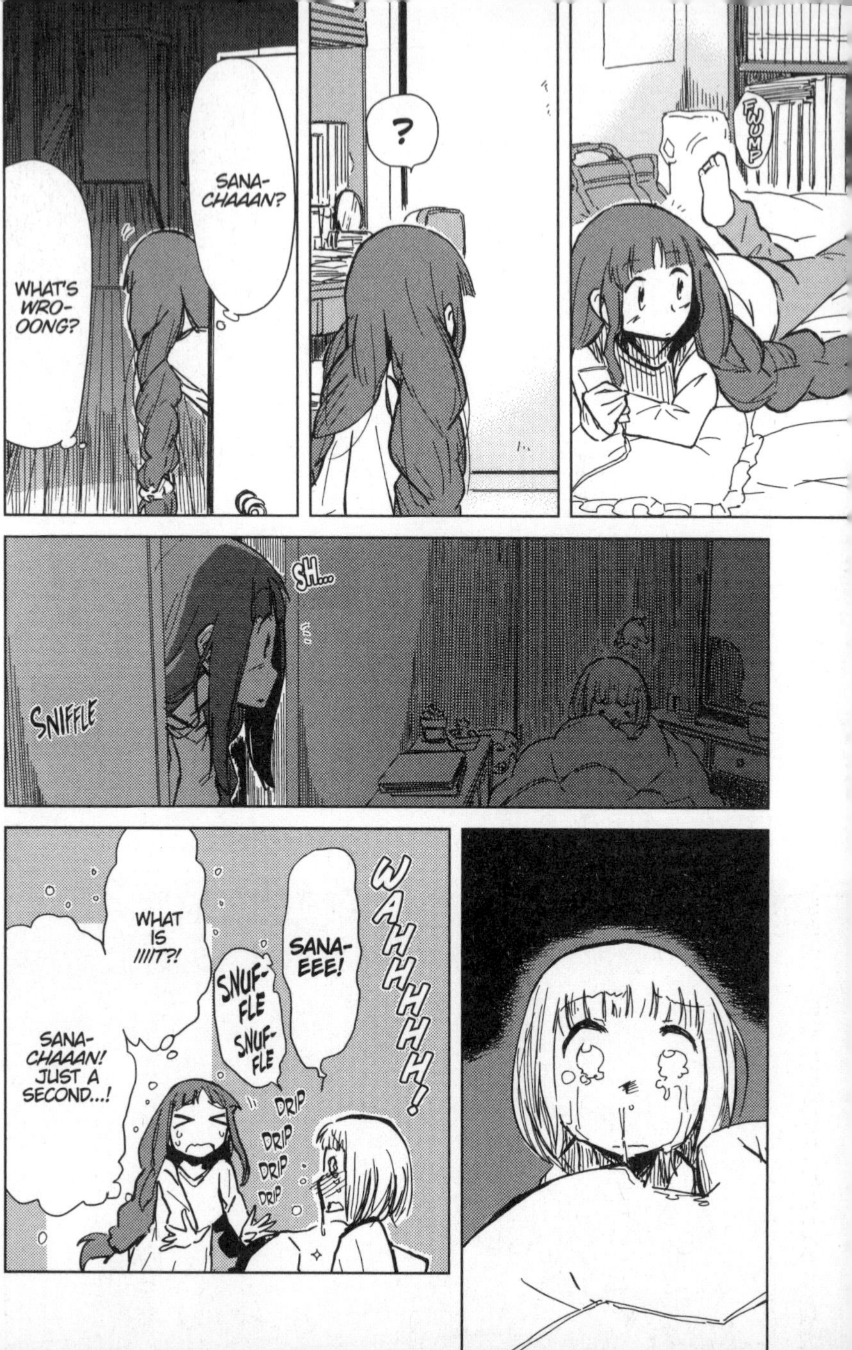
FWUMP
?
SANA-CHAAAN?
WHAT'S WRO-OONG?
SH...
SNIFFLE
WAHHHHHH!
SANA-EEE!
SNUF-FLE SNUF-FLE
DRIP DRIP DRIP DRIP
WHAT IS IIIIT?!
SANA-CHAAAN! JUST A SECOND...!

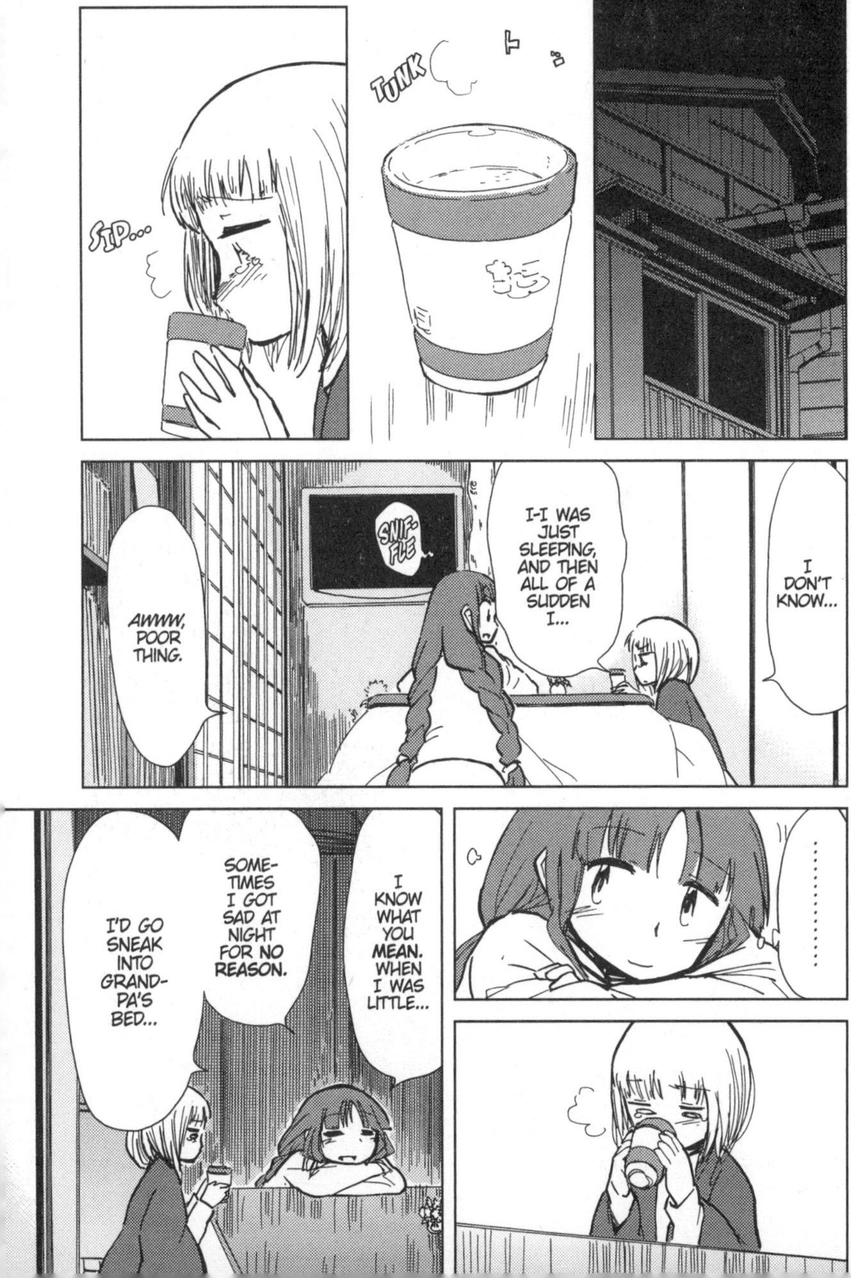
TUNK
SIP...
I DON'T KNOW...
I-I WAS JUST SLEEPING, AND THEN ALL OF A SUDDEN I...
SNIF-FLE
AWWW, POOR THING.
......
I KNOW WHAT YOU MEAN. WHEN I WAS LITTLE...
SOME-TIMES I GOT SAD AT NIGHT FOR NO REASON.
I'D GO SNEAK INTO GRAND-PA'S BED...

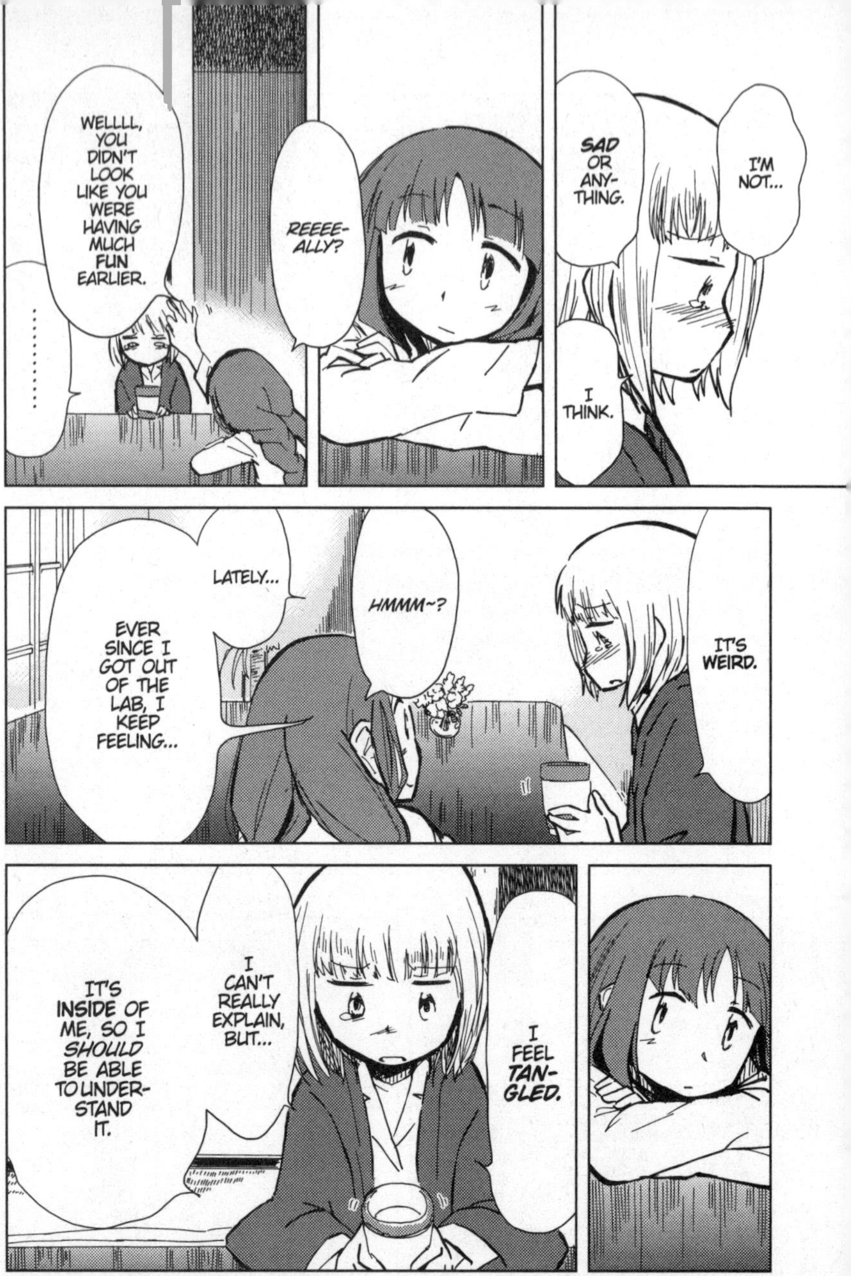
I'M NOT...
SAD OR ANY-THING.
I THINK.
REEEE-ALLY?
WELLLL, YOU DIDN'T LOOK LIKE YOU WERE HAVING MUCH FUN EARLIER.
......
IT'S WEIRD.
HMMM~?
LATELY...
EVER SINCE I GOT OUT OF THE LAB, I KEEP FEELING...
I FEEL TANGLED.
I CAN'T REALLY EXPLAIN, BUT...
IT'S INSIDE OF ME, SO I SHOULD BE ABLE TO UNDERSTAND IT.

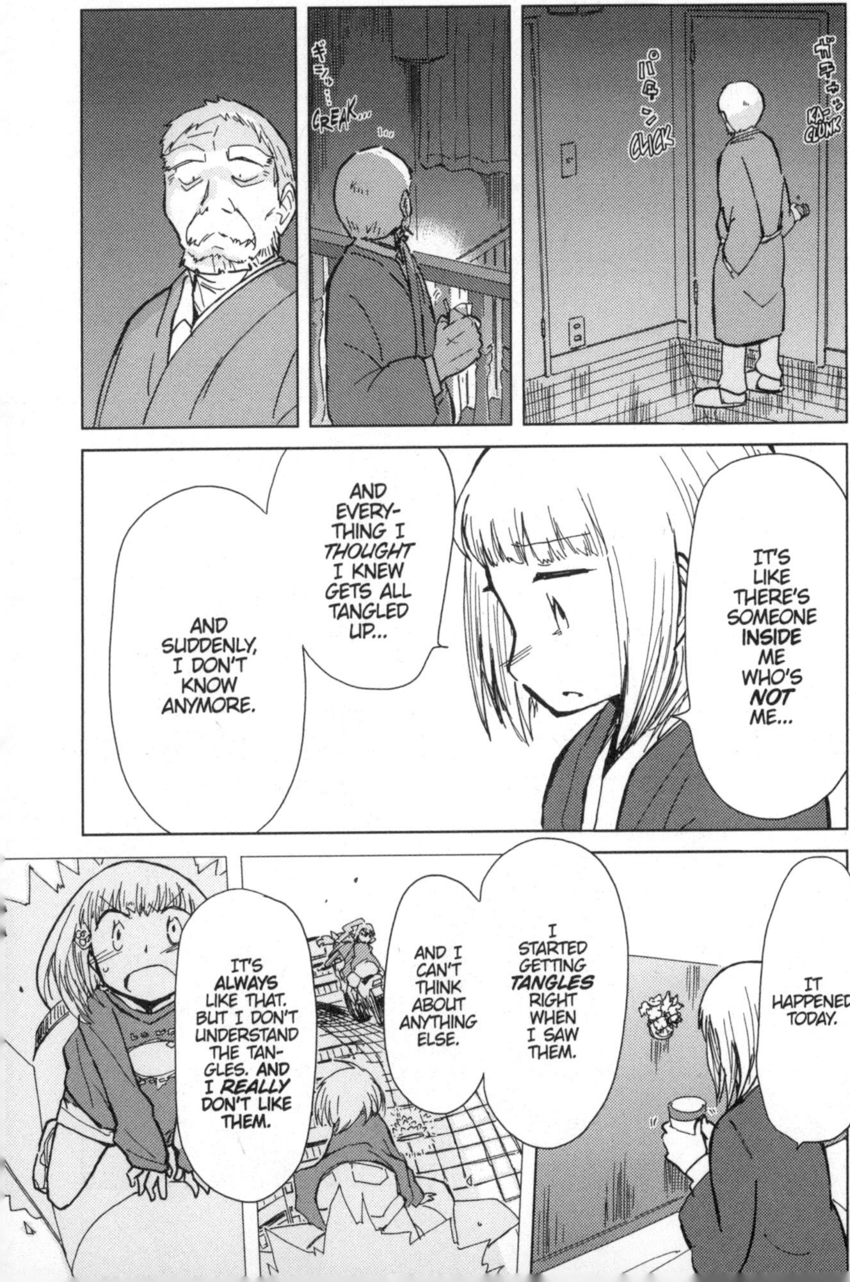

KA-CLUNK
CLICK
CREAK...
IT'S LIKE THERE'S SOMEONE INSIDE ME WHO'S NOT ME...
AND EVERYTHING I THOUGHT I KNEW GETS ALL TANGLED UP...
AND SUDDENLY, I DON'T KNOW ANYMORE.
IT HAPPENED TODAY.
I STARTED GETTING TANGLES RIGHT WHEN I SAW THEM.
AND I CAN'T THINK ABOUT ANYTHING ELSE.
IT'S ALWAYS LIKE THAT. BUT I DON'T UNDERSTAND THE TANGLES. AND I REALLY DON'T LIKE THEM.

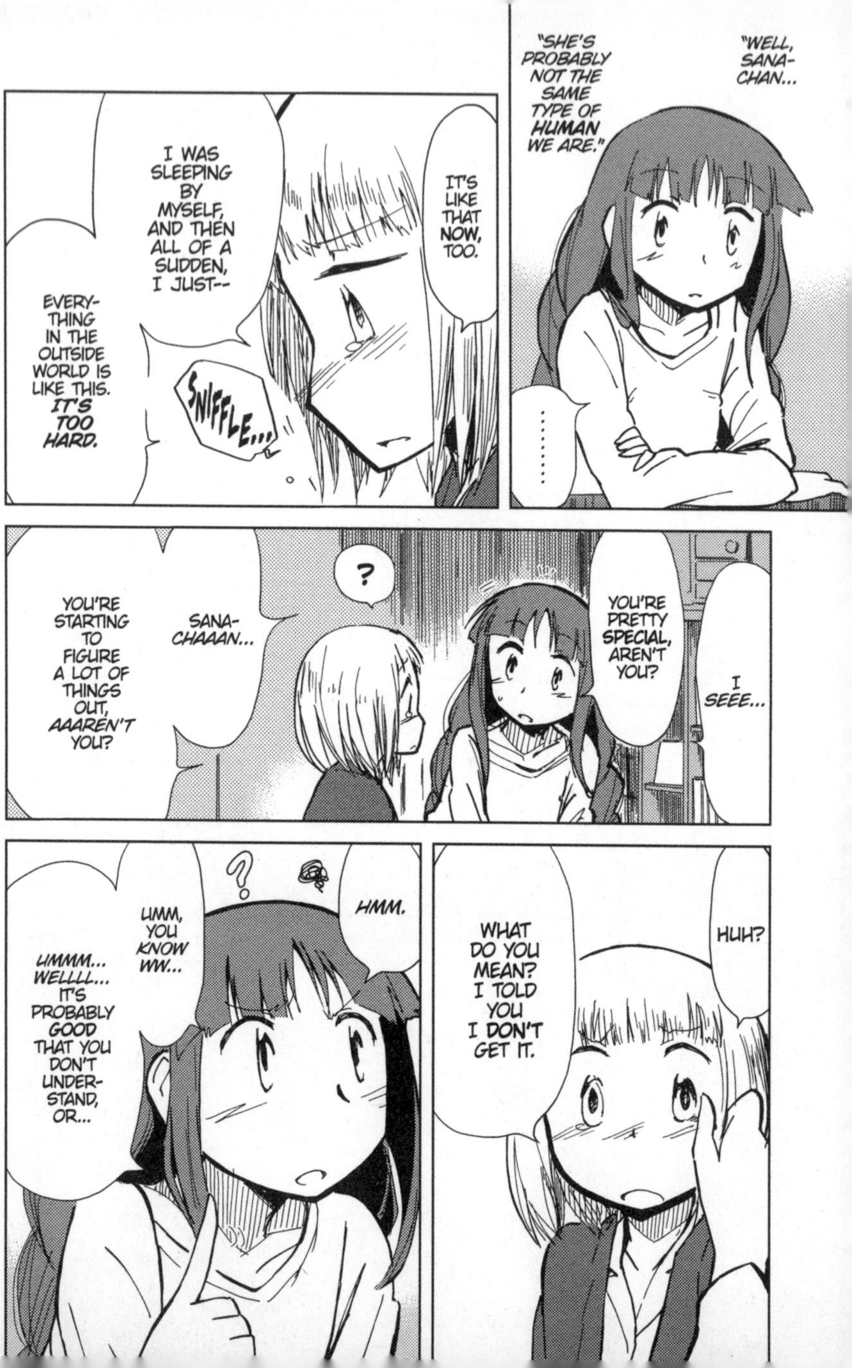
"WELL, SANA-CHAN...
"SHE'S PROBABLY NOT THE SAME TYPE OF HUMAN WE ARE."
......
IT'S LIKE THAT NOW, TOO.
I WAS SLEEPING BY MYSELF, AND THEN ALL OF A SUDDEN, I JUST--
SNIFFLE...
EVERYTHING IN THE OUTSIDE WORLD IS LIKE THIS. IT'S TOO HARD.
I SEEE...
YOU'RE PRETTY SPECIAL, AREN'T YOU?
?
SANA-CHAAAN...
YOU'RE STARTING TO FIGURE A LOT OF THINGS OUT, AAAREN'T YOU?
HUH?
WHAT DO YOU MEAN? I TOLD YOU I DON'T GET IT.
HMM.
UMM, YOU KNOWWW...
UMMM... WELLLL... IT'S PROBABLY GOOD THAT YOU DON'T UNDERSTAND, OR...

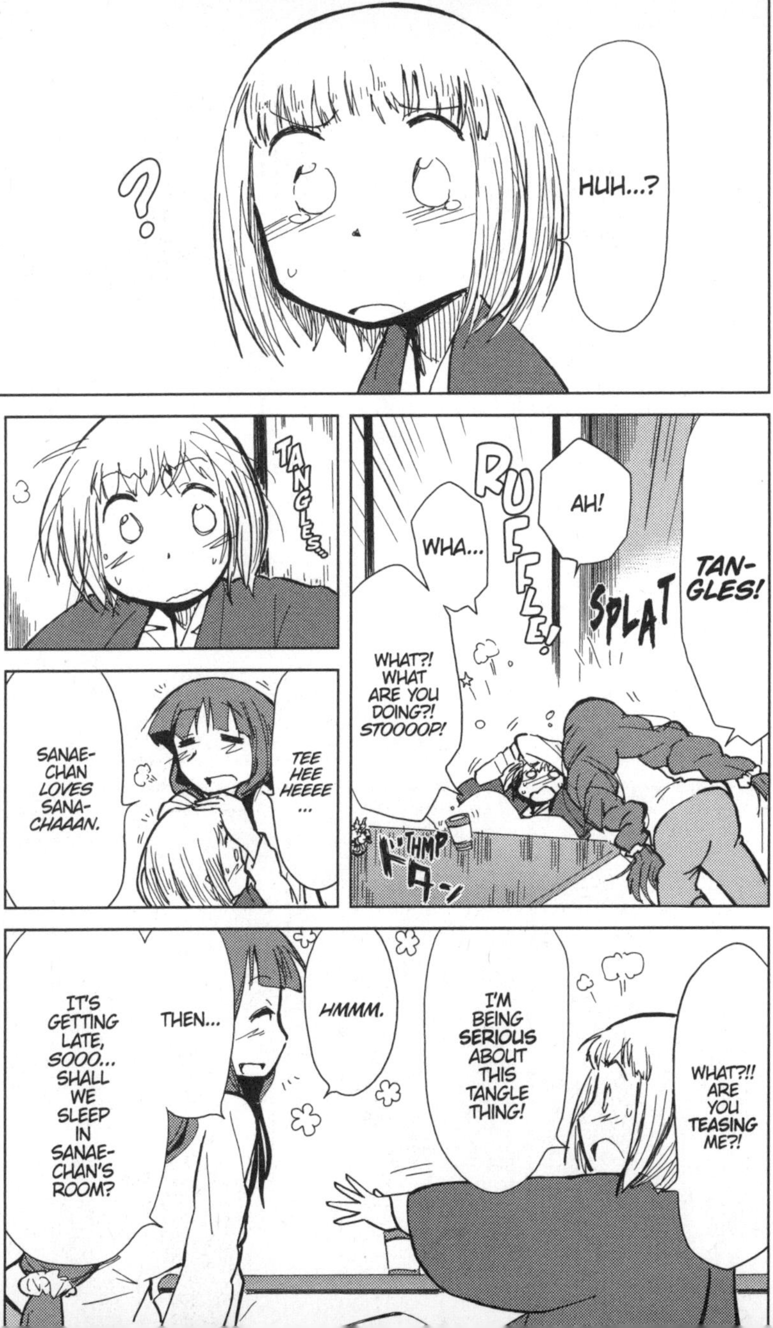
HUH...?
TAN-GLES!
SPLAT
AH!
RUFFLE!
WHA...
WHAT?! WHAT ARE YOU DOING?! STOOOOP!
THMP
ドタン
TANGLES...
TEE HEE HEEEE ...
SANAE-CHAN LOVES SANA-CHAAAN.
WHAT?!! ARE YOU TEASING ME?!
I'M BEING SERIOUS ABOUT THIS TANGLE THING!
HMMM.
THEN...
IT'S GETTING LATE, SOOO... SHALL WE SLEEP IN SANAE-CHAN'S ROOM?

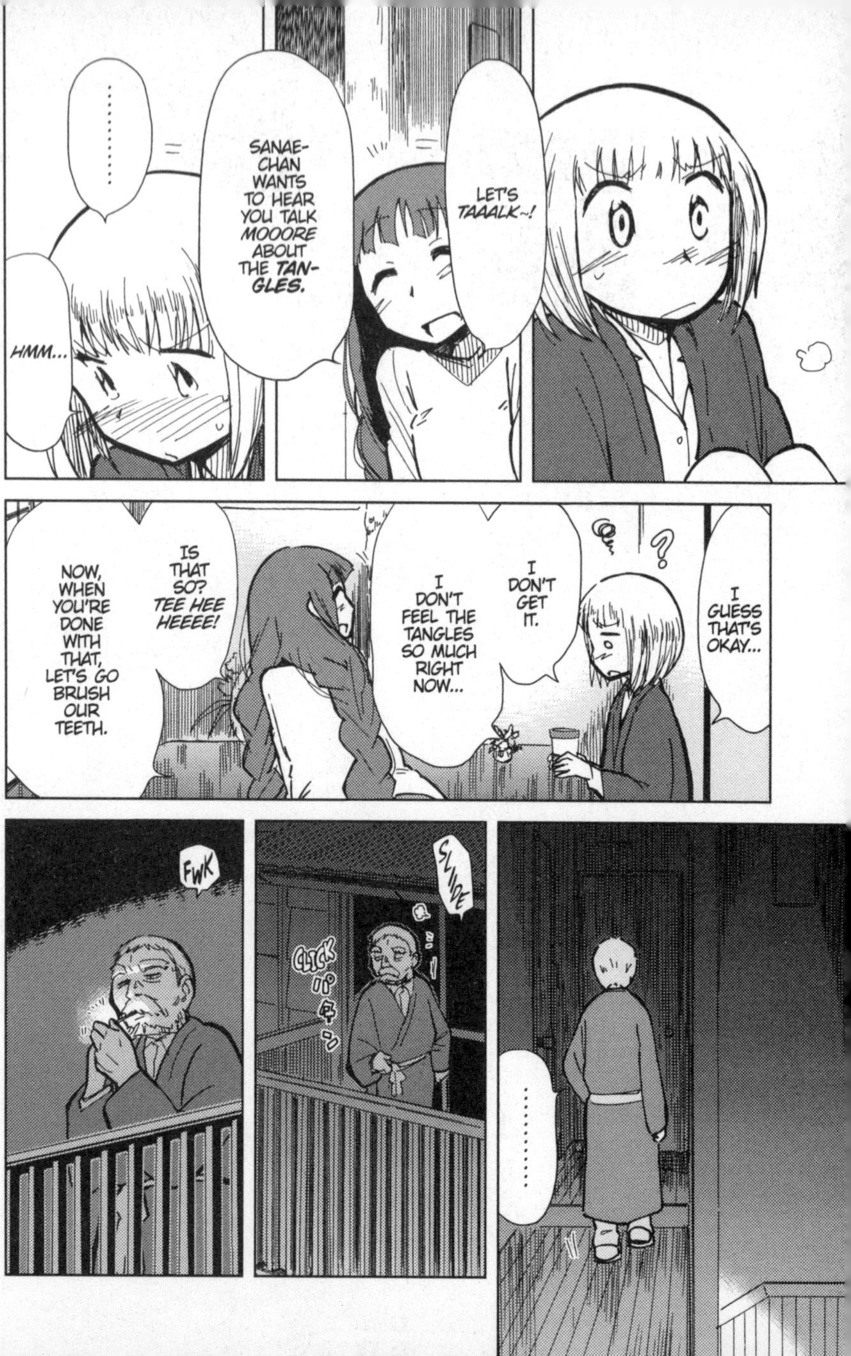
LET'S TAAALK~!
SANAE-CHAN WANTS TO HEAR YOU TALK MOOORE ABOUT THE TANGLES.
......
HMM...
I GUESS THAT'S OKAY...
I DON'T GET IT.
I DON'T FEEL THE TANGLES SO MUCH RIGHT NOW...
IS THAT SO? TEE HEE HEEEE!
NOW, WHEN YOU'RE DONE WITH THAT, LET'S GO BRUSH OUR TEETH.
......
SLIDE
CLICK
FWK

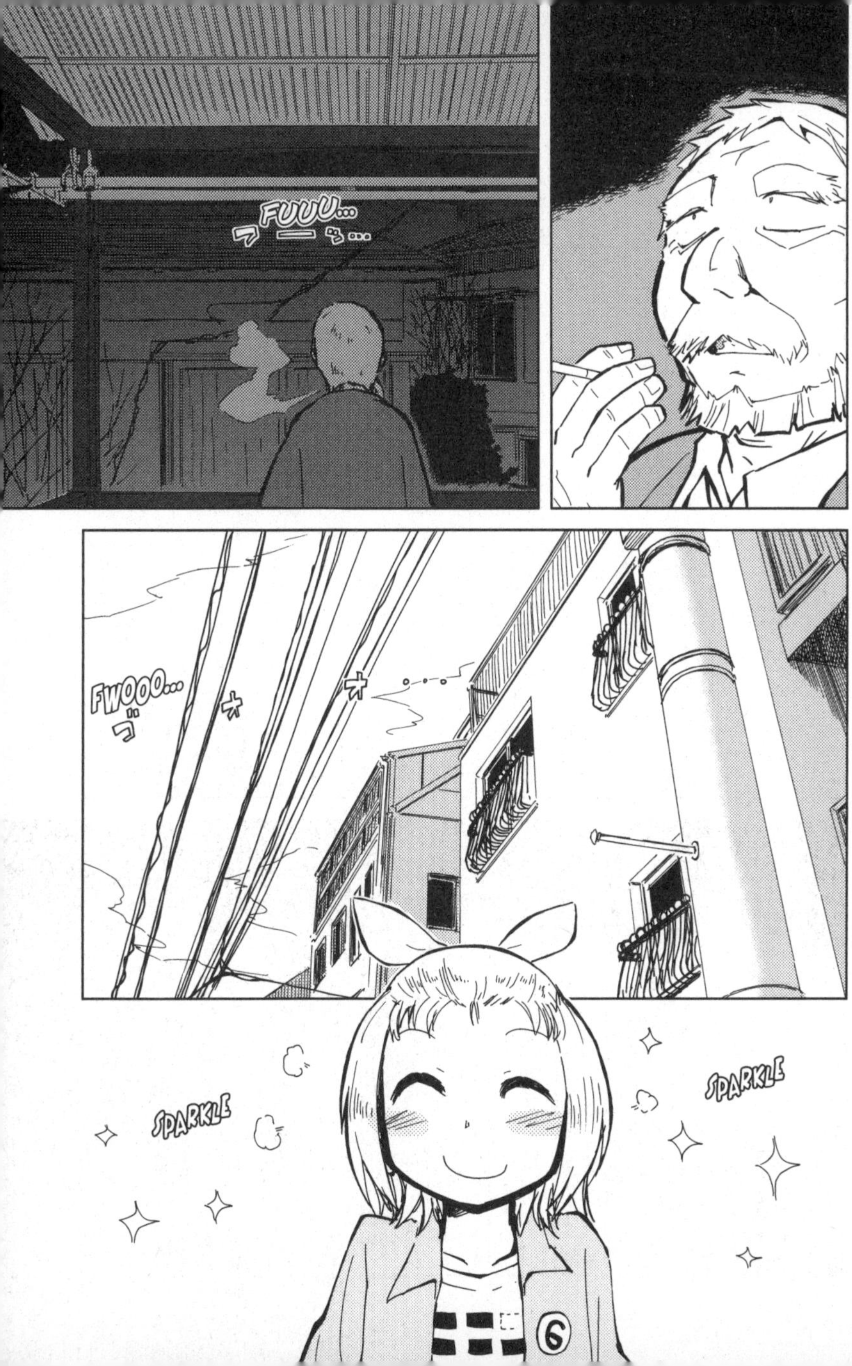
FUUU...
フーッ...
FWOOO...
ゴオオ
SPARKLE
SPARKLE

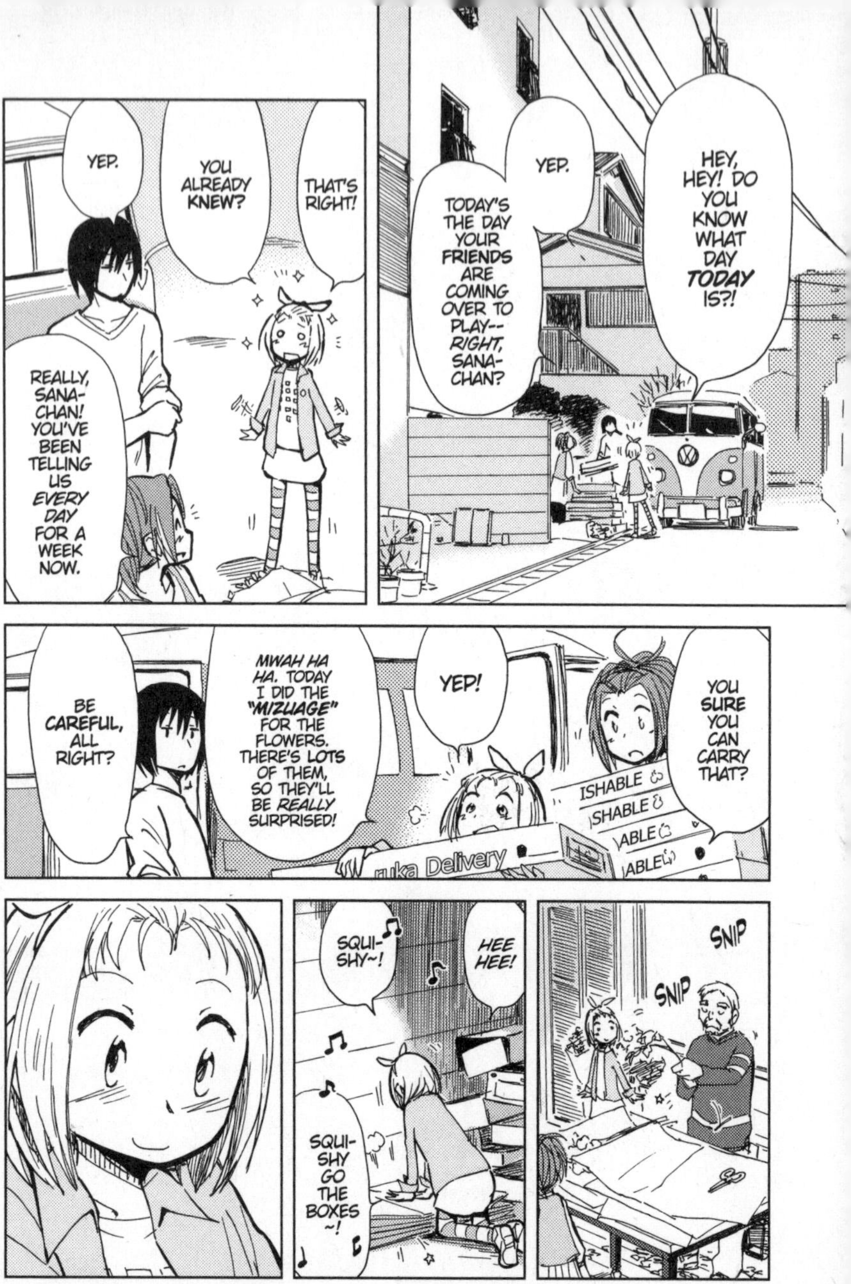
HEY, HEY! DO YOU KNOW WHAT DAY TODAY IS?!
YEP.
TODAY'S THE DAY YOUR FRIENDS ARE COMING OVER TO PLAY-- RIGHT, SANA-CHAN?
THAT'S RIGHT!
YOU ALREADY KNEW?
YEP.
REALLY, SANA-CHAN! YOU'VE BEEN TELLING US EVERY DAY FOR A WEEK NOW.
YOU SURE YOU CAN CARRY THAT?
YEP!
ISHABLE
SHABLE
ABLE
ABLE
ruka Delivery
MWAH HA HA. TODAY I DID THE "MIZUAGE" FOR THE FLOWERS. THERE'S LOTS OF THEM, SO THEY'LL BE REALLY SURPRISED!
BE CAREFUL, ALL RIGHT?
SNIP
SNIP
HEE HEE!
SQUI-SHY~!
SQUI-SHY GO THE BOXES ~!

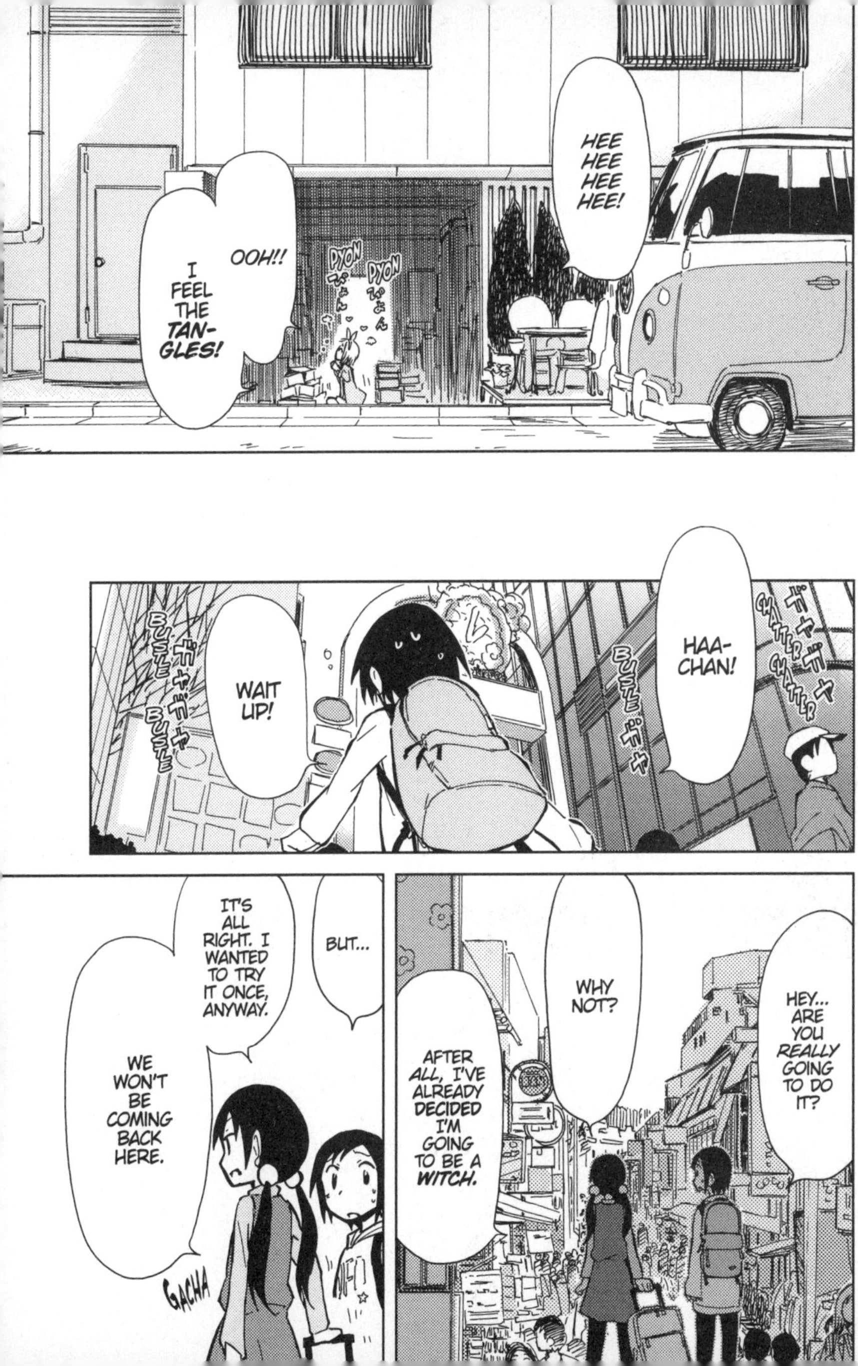
HEE HEE HEE HEE!
PYON PYON
OOH!! I FEEL THE TAN-GLES!
HAA-CHAN!
CHATTER CHATTER
BUSTLE
WAIT UP!
BUSTLE BUSTLE
HEY... ARE YOU REALLY GOING TO DO IT?
WHY NOT?
AFTER ALL, I'VE ALREADY DECIDED I'M GOING TO BE A WITCH.
BUT...
IT'S ALL RIGHT. I WANTED TO TRY IT ONCE, ANYWAY.
WE WON'T BE COMING BACK HERE.
GACHA

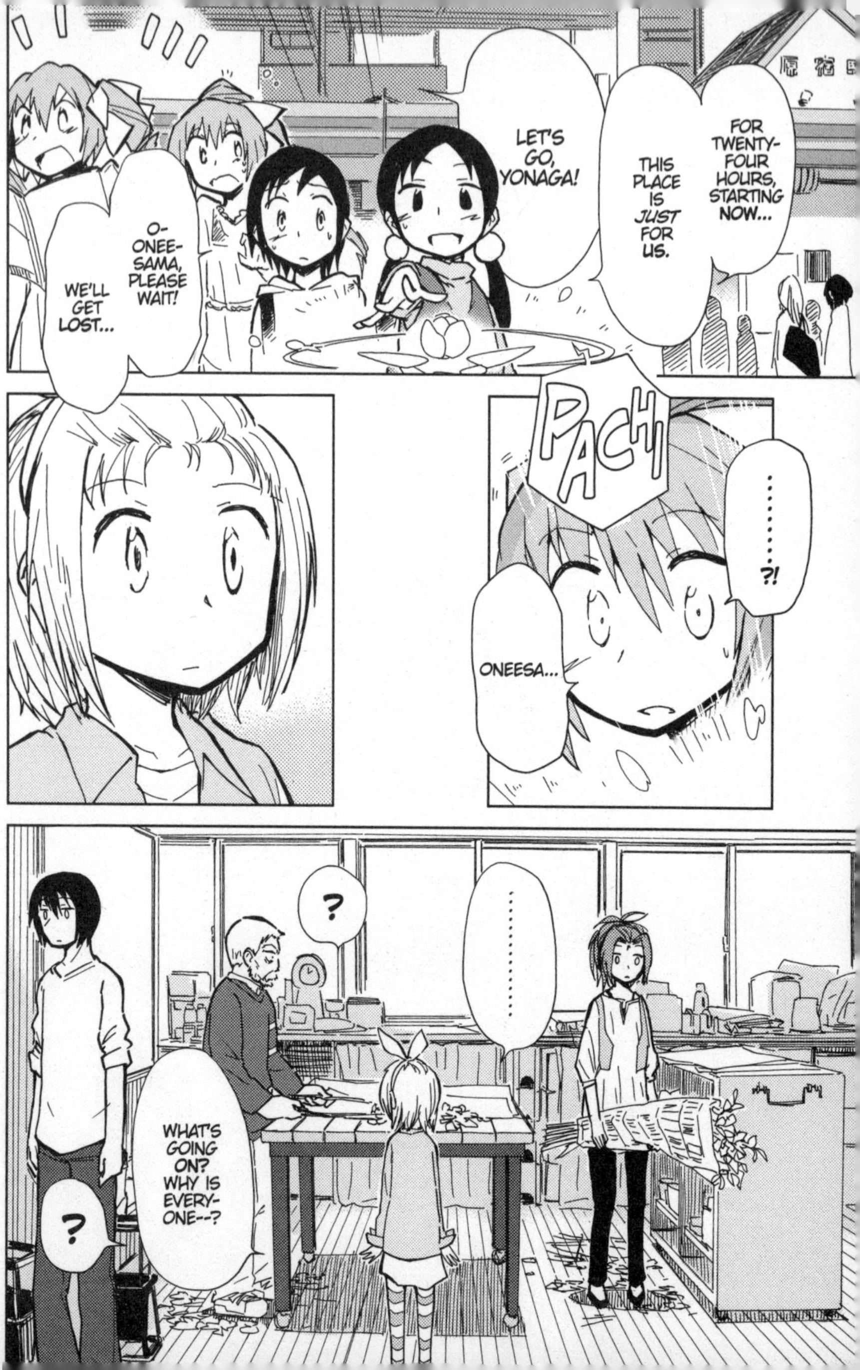
FOR TWENTY-FOUR HOURS, STARTING NOW...
THIS PLACE IS JUST FOR US.
LET'S GO, YONAGA!
O-ONEE-SAMA, PLEASE WAIT!
WE'LL GET LOST...
PACHI
......?!
ONEESA...
....
?
WHAT'S GOING ON? WHY IS EVERY-ONE--?
?

Alice & Zoroku

INTERLUDE

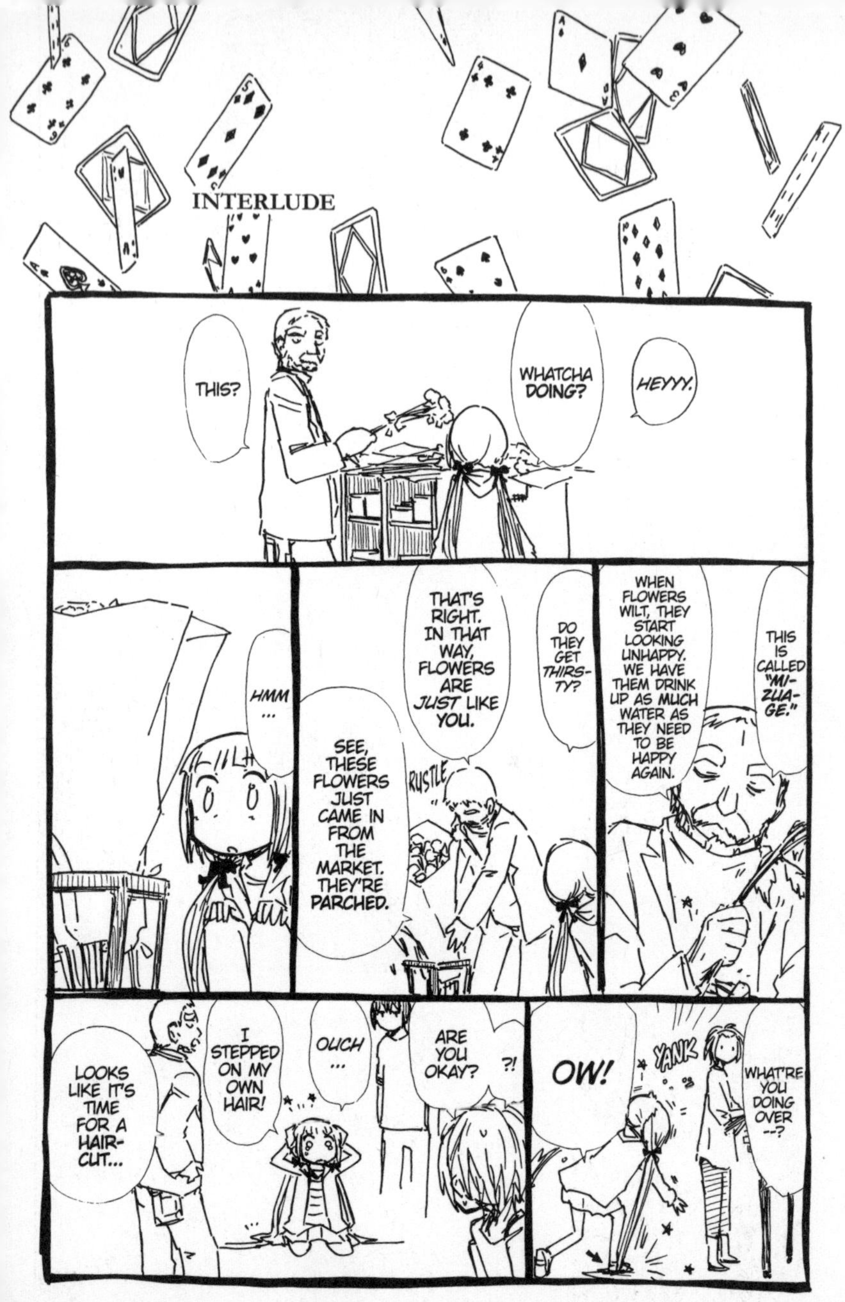
HEYYY.
WHATCHA DOING?
THIS?
THIS IS CALLED "MIZUAGE."
WHEN FLOWERS WILT, THEY START LOOKING UNHAPPY. WE HAVE THEM DRINK UP AS MUCH WATER AS THEY NEED TO BE HAPPY AGAIN.
DO THEY GET THIRSTY?
THAT'S RIGHT. IN THAT WAY, FLOWERS ARE JUST LIKE YOU.
RUSTLE
SEE, THESE FLOWERS JUST CAME IN FROM THE MARKET. THEY'RE PARCHED.
HMM ...
WHAT'RE YOU DOING OVER --?
YANK
OW!
?!
ARE YOU OKAY?
OUCH ...
I STEPPED ON MY OWN HAIR!
LOOKS LIKE IT'S TIME FOR A HAIR-CUT...

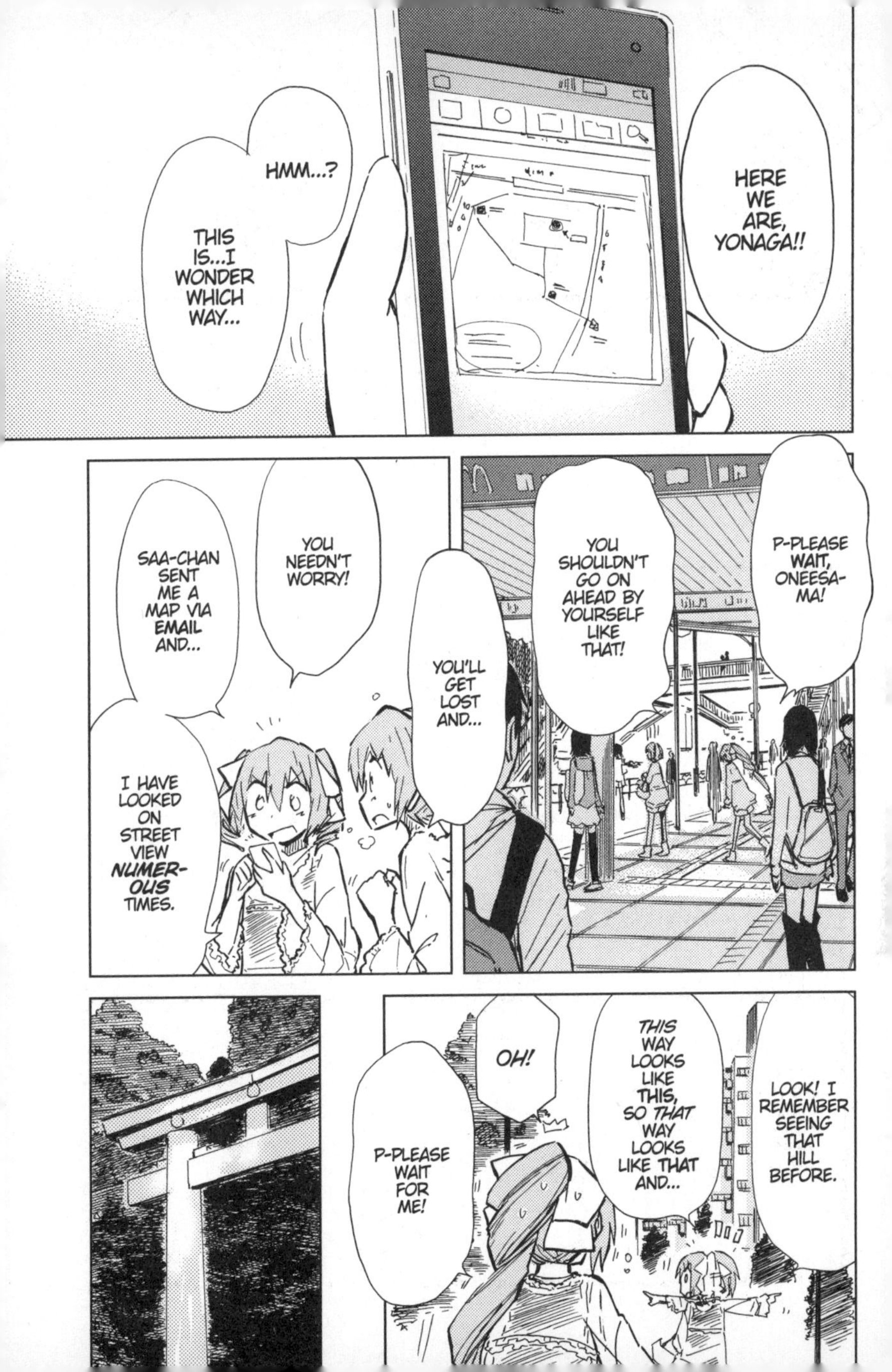
HERE WE ARE, YONAGA!!
HMM...?
THIS IS...I WONDER WHICH WAY...
P-PLEASE WAIT, ONEESAMA!
YOU SHOULDN'T GO ON AHEAD BY YOURSELF LIKE THAT!
YOU'LL GET LOST AND...
YOU NEEDN'T WORRY!
SAA-CHAN SENT ME A MAP VIA EMAIL AND...
I HAVE LOOKED ON STREET VIEW *NUMEROUS* TIMES.
LOOK! I REMEMBER SEEING THAT HILL BEFORE.
THIS WAY LOOKS LIKE **THIS**, SO *THAT* WAY LOOKS LIKE **THAT** AND...
OH!
P-PLEASE WAIT FOR ME!

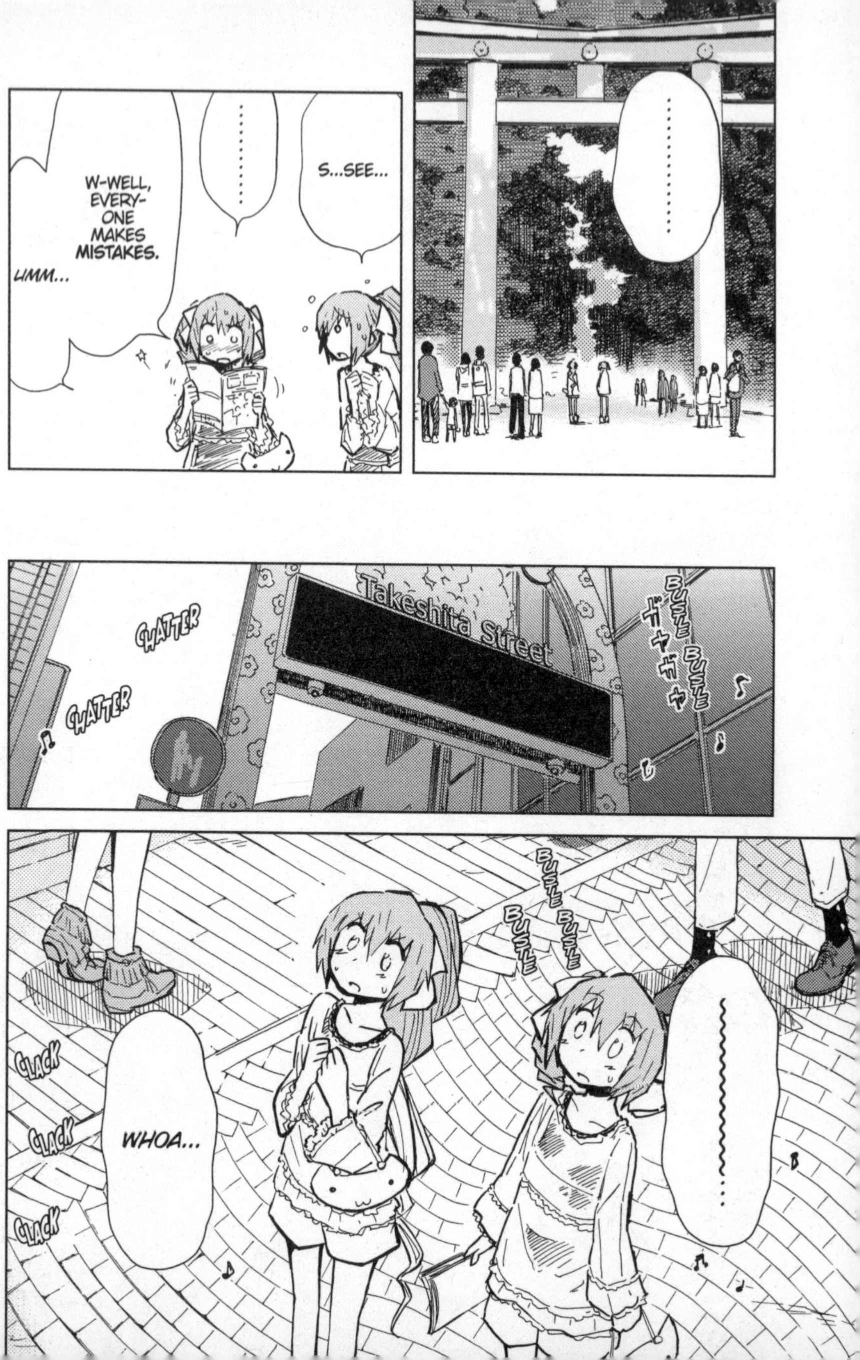
......
S...SEE...
......
W-WELL, EVERYONE MAKES MISTAKES.
UMM...
Takeshita Street
BUSTLE BUSTLE
ガヤガヤ
CHATTER
CHATTER
......
BUSTLE BUSTLE
BUSTLE
WHOA...
CLACK
CLACK
CLACK

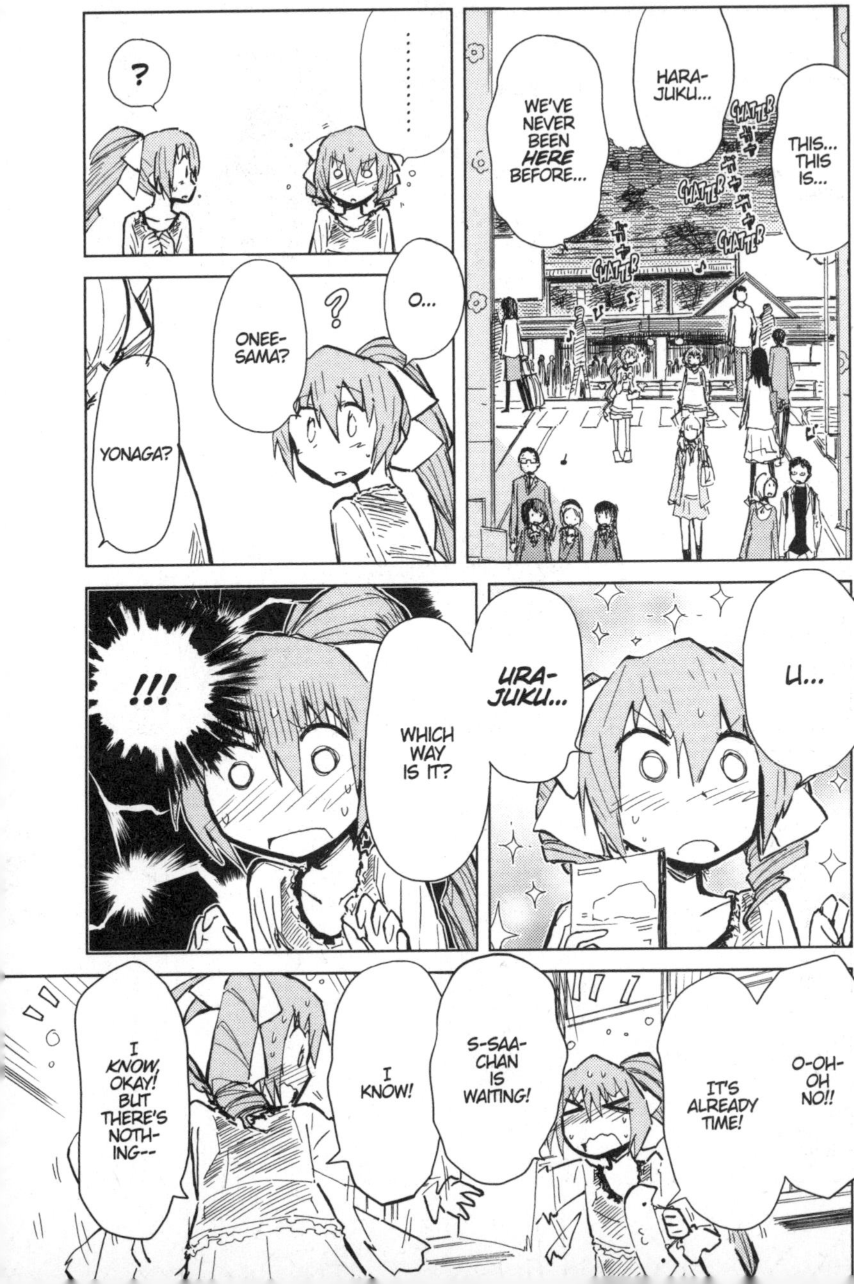
THIS... THIS IS...
HARA-JUKU...
CHATTER CHATTER CHATTER CHATTER
WE'VE NEVER BEEN HERE BEFORE...
......
?
O...
ONEE-SAMA?
?
YONAGA?
U...
URA-JUKU...
WHICH WAY IS IT?
!!!
O-OH-OH NO!!
IT'S ALREADY TIME!
S-SAA-CHAN IS WAITING!
I KNOW!
I KNOW, OKAY! BUT THERE'S NOTHING--

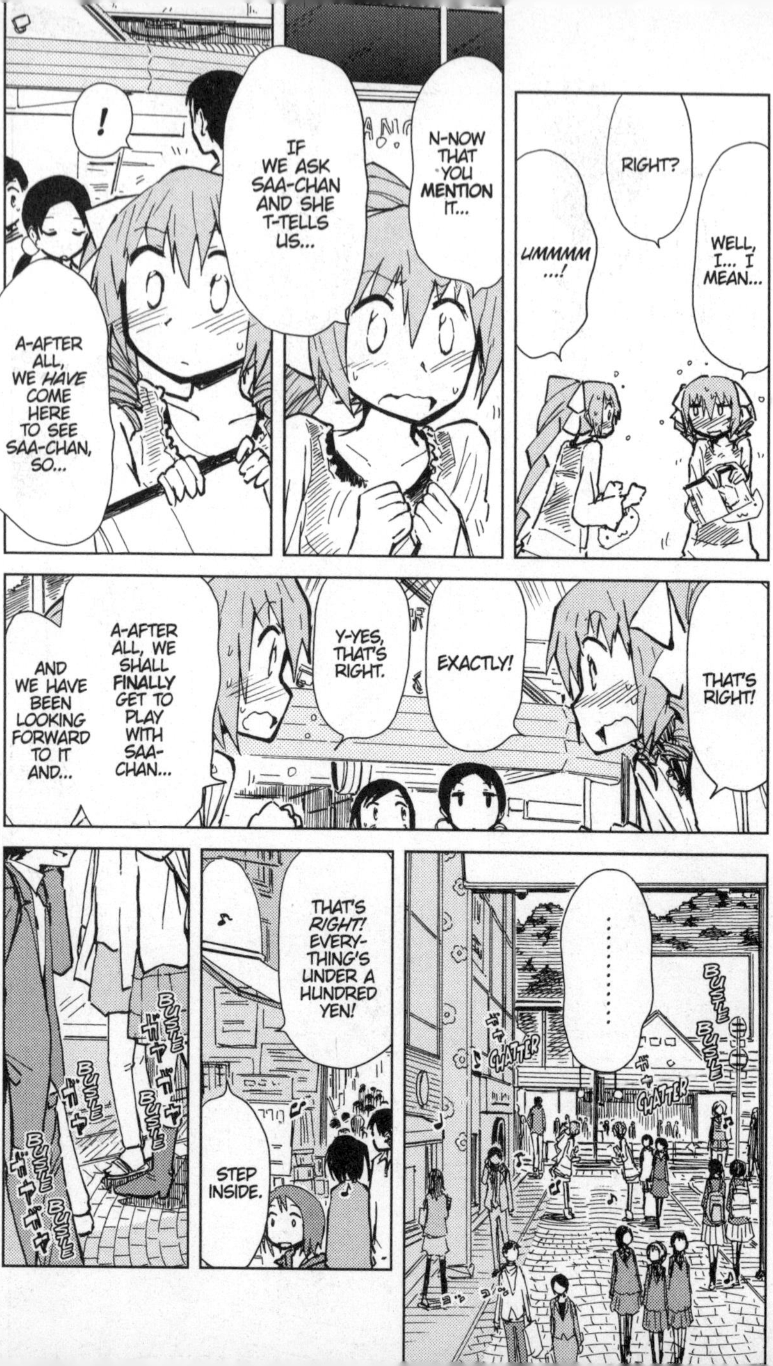
RIGHT?
WELL, I... I MEAN...
UMMMM ...!
N-NOW THAT YOU MENTION IT...
IF WE ASK SAA-CHAN AND SHE T-TELLS US...
!
A-AFTER ALL, WE *HAVE* COME HERE TO SEE SAA-CHAN, SO...
THAT'S RIGHT!
EXACTLY!
Y-YES, THAT'S RIGHT.
A-AFTER ALL, WE SHALL FINALLY GET TO PLAY WITH SAA-CHAN...
AND WE HAVE BEEN LOOKING FORWARD TO IT AND...
....
BUSTLE BUSTLE
ガヤ CHATTER
ガヤ CHATTER
THAT'S *RIGHT!* EVERY-THING'S UNDER A HUNDRED YEN!
STEP INSIDE.
BUSTLE ガヤ
BUSTLE ガヤ
BUSTLE ガヤ
BUSTLE BUSTLE ガヤ

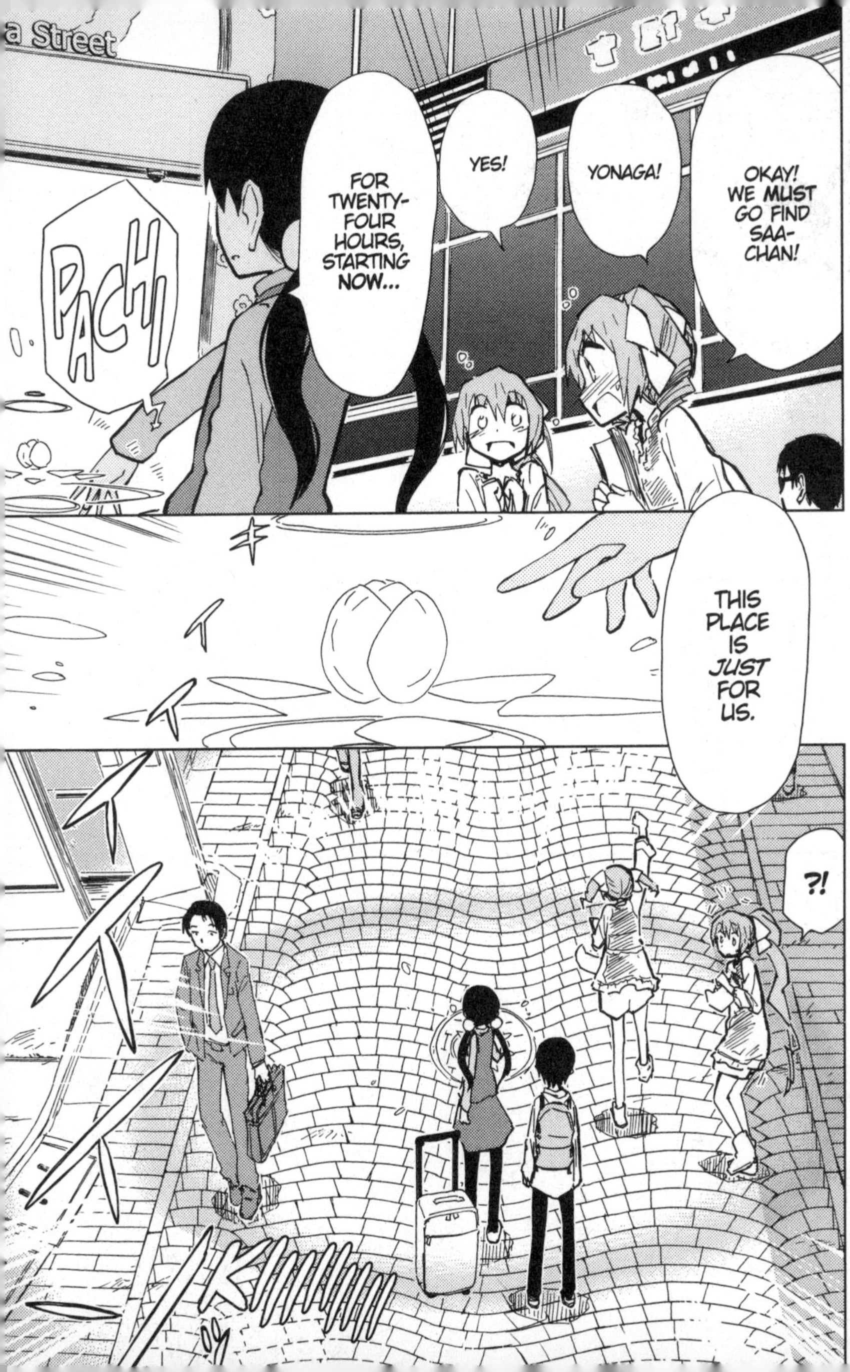
OKAY! WE MUST GO FIND SAA-CHAN!
YONAGA!
YES!
FOR TWENTY-FOUR HOURS, STARTING NOW...
a Street
PACHI
THIS PLACE IS JUST FOR US.
?!
KIIIIII

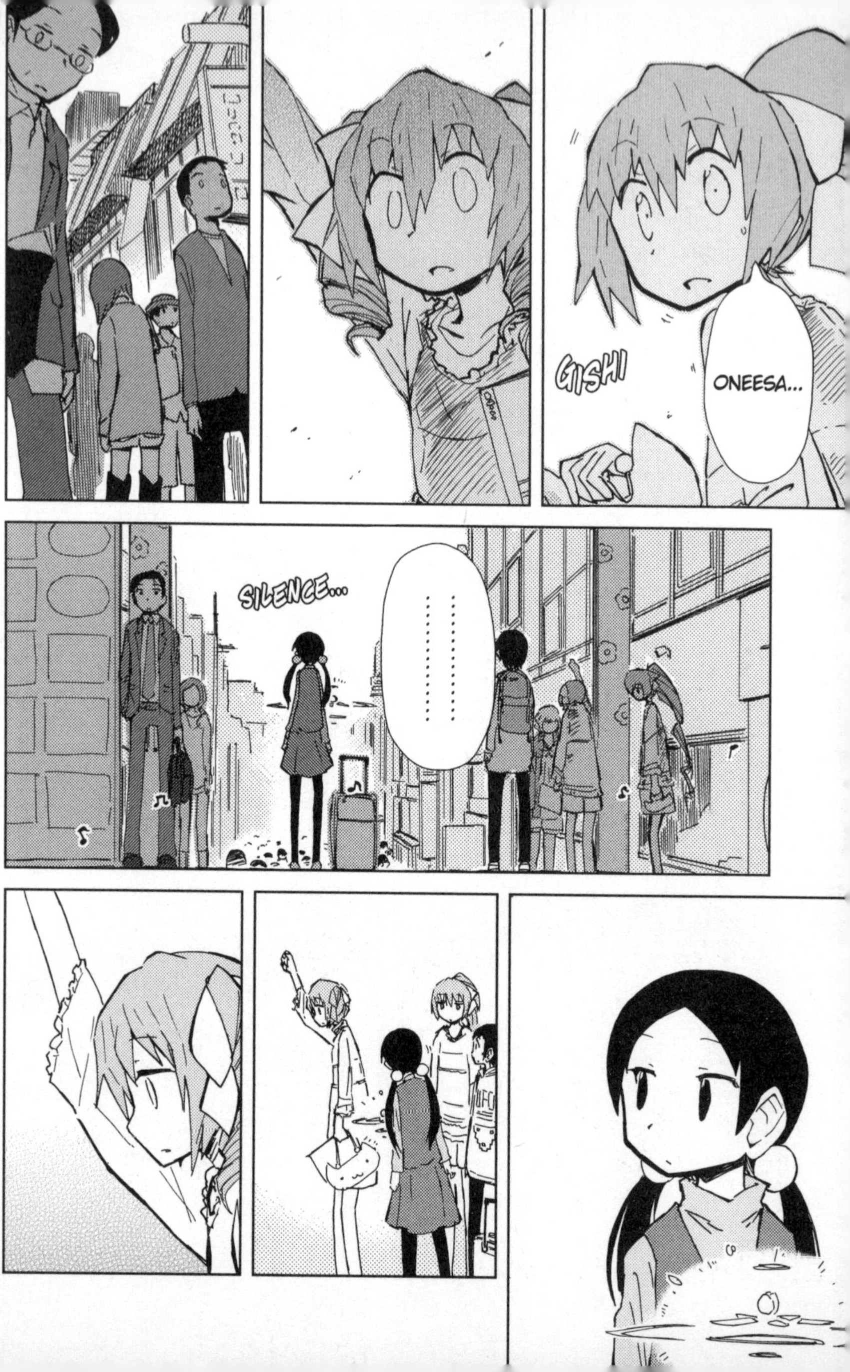
ONEESA...
GISHI
......
SILENCE...

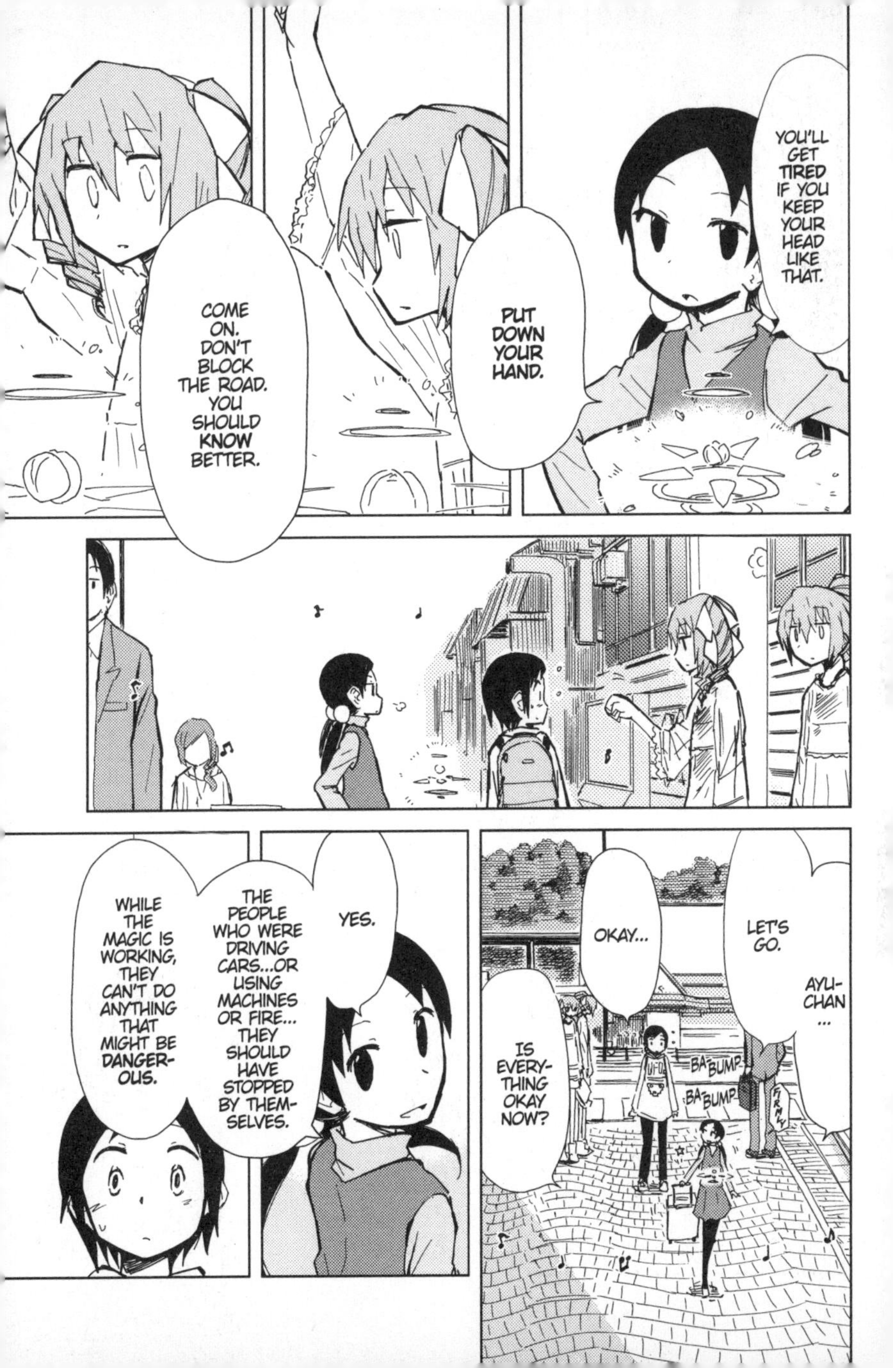
YOU'LL GET TIRED IF YOU KEEP YOUR HEAD LIKE THAT.
PUT DOWN YOUR HAND.
COME ON. DON'T BLOCK THE ROAD. YOU SHOULD KNOW BETTER.
LET'S GO.
AYU-CHAN ...
OKAY...
IS EVERYTHING OKAY NOW?
BA-BUMP
BA-BUMP
FIRMLY
YES.
THE PEOPLE WHO WERE DRIVING CARS...OR USING MACHINES OR FIRE... THEY SHOULD HAVE STOPPED BY THEMSELVES.
WHILE THE MAGIC IS WORKING, THEY CAN'T DO ANYTHING THAT MIGHT BE DANGEROUS.

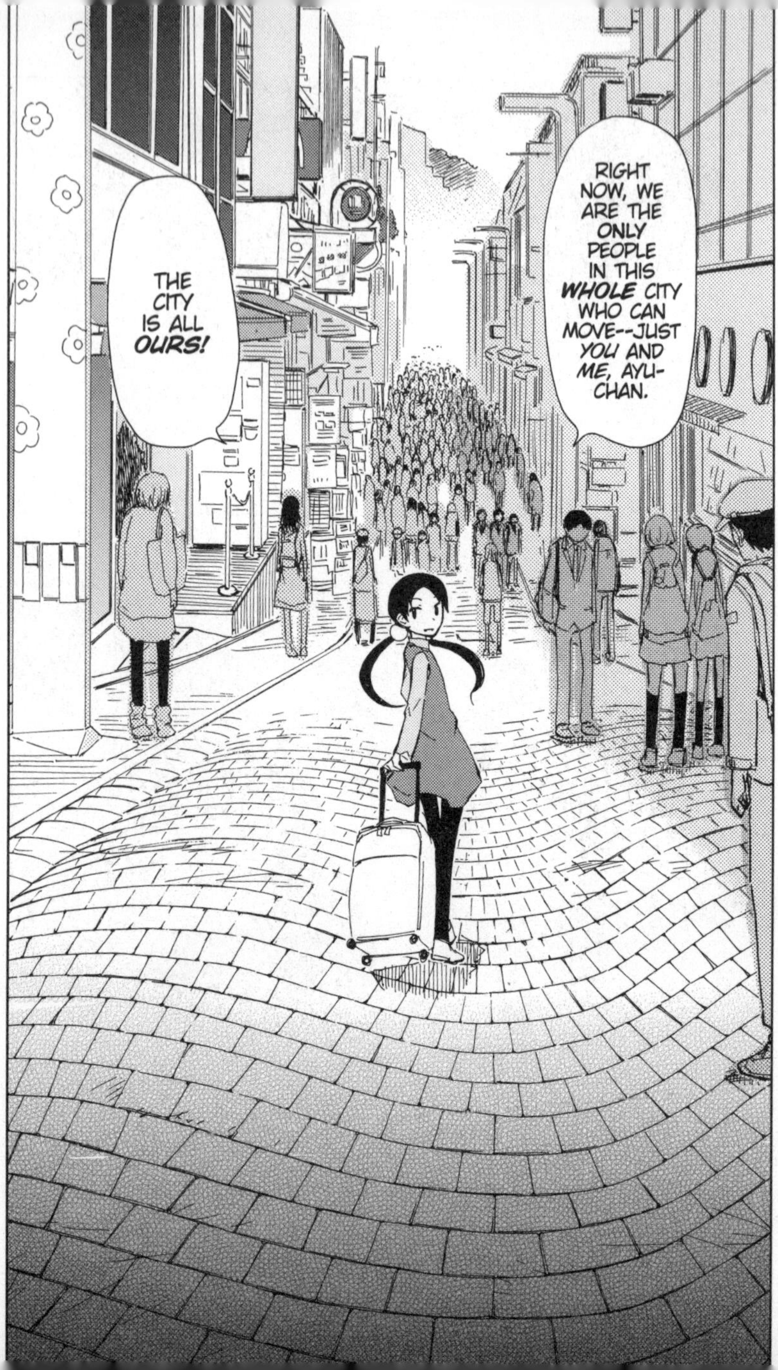
RIGHT NOW, WE ARE THE ONLY PEOPLE IN THIS *WHOLE* CITY WHO CAN MOVE--JUST *YOU* AND *ME*, AYU-CHAN.
THE CITY IS ALL ***OURS!***

Chapter 12
Here Come the King and Queen of Hearts

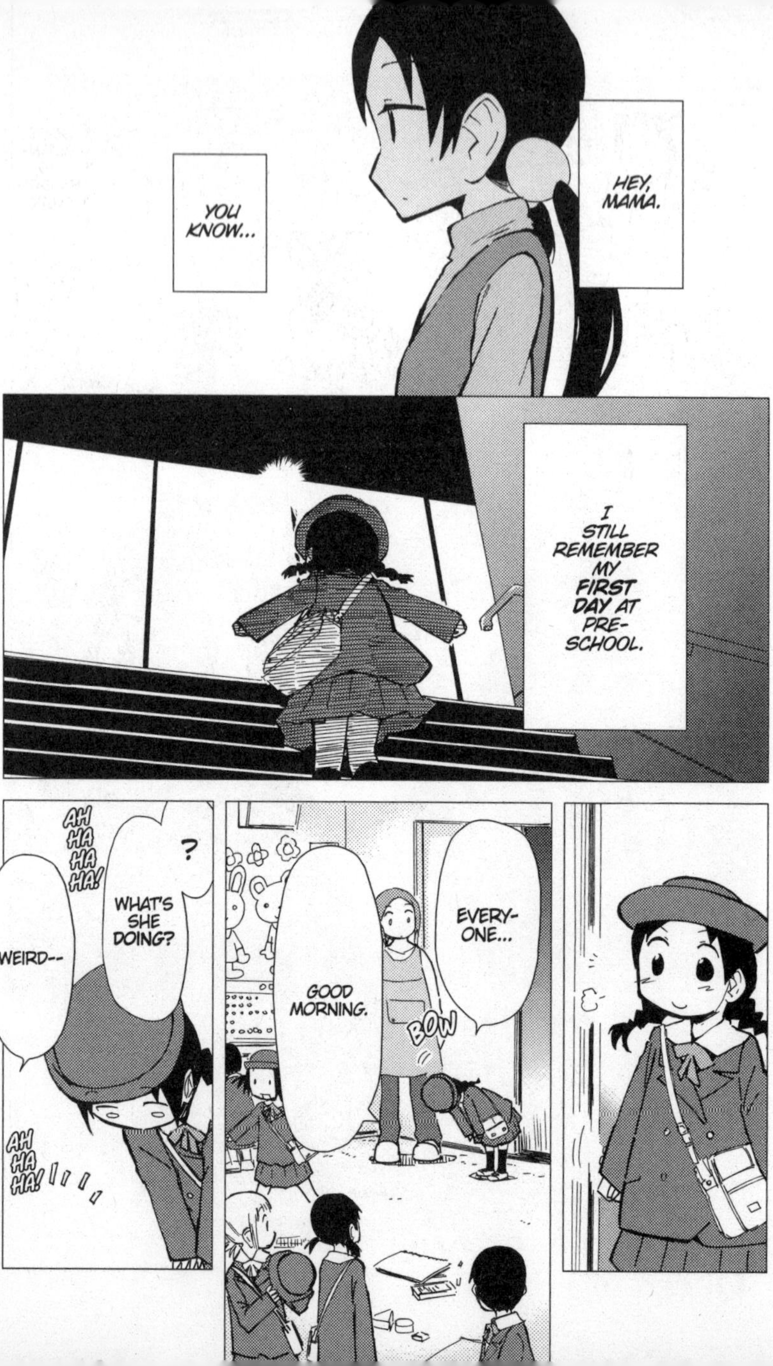
HEY, MAMA.
YOU KNOW...
I STILL REMEMBER MY FIRST DAY AT PRE-SCHOOL.
EVERY-ONE...
GOOD MORNING.
BOW
?
WHAT'S SHE DOING?
AH HA HA HA!
WEIRD--
AH HA HA!

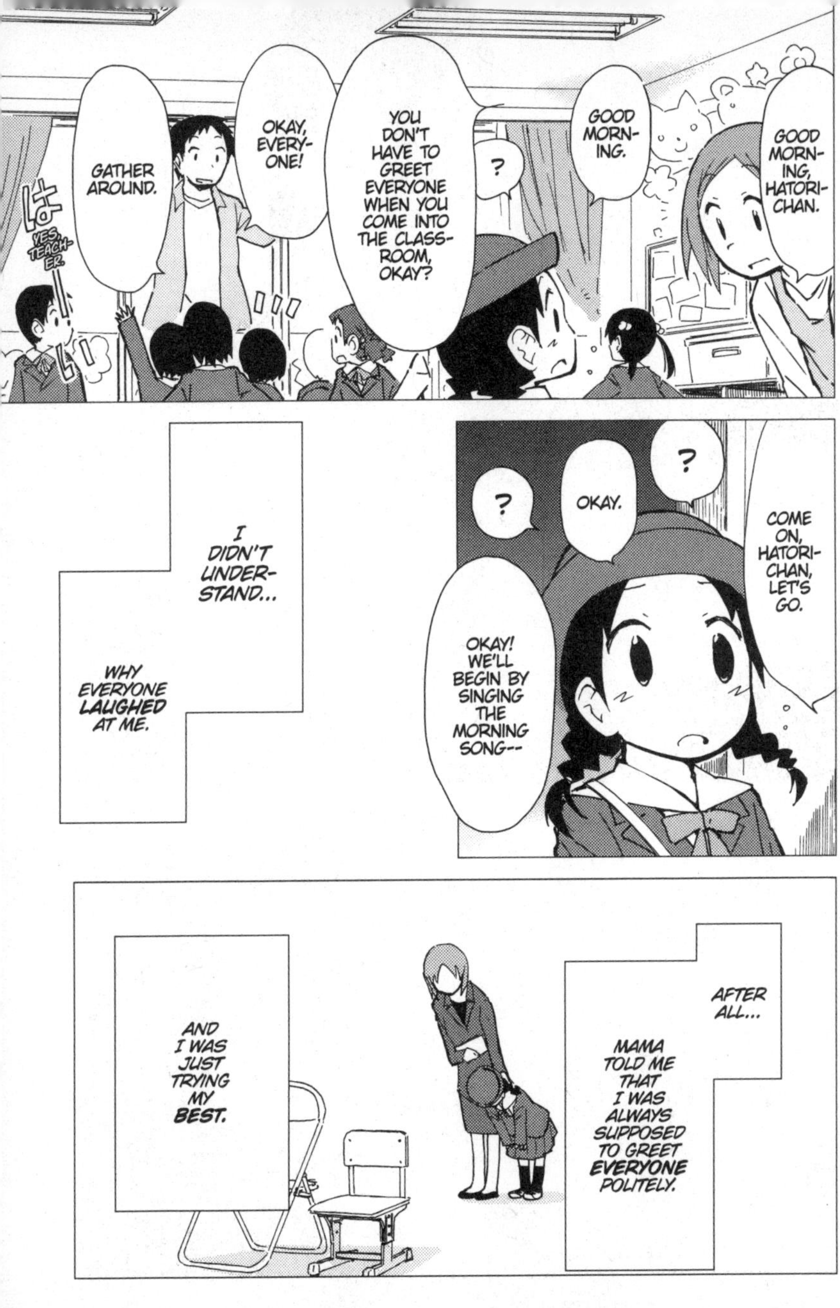
GOOD MORNING, HATORI-CHAN.
GOOD MORNING.
?
YOU DON'T HAVE TO GREET EVERYONE WHEN YOU COME INTO THE CLASSROOM, OKAY?
OKAY, EVERYONE!
GATHER AROUND.
YES, TEACHER.
COME ON, HATORI-CHAN, LET'S GO.
?
OKAY.
?
OKAY! WE'LL BEGIN BY SINGING THE MORNING SONG--
I DIDN'T UNDERSTAND...
WHY EVERYONE LAUGHED AT ME.
AFTER ALL...
MAMA TOLD ME THAT I WAS ALWAYS SUPPOSED TO GREET EVERYONE POLITELY.
AND I WAS JUST TRYING MY BEST.

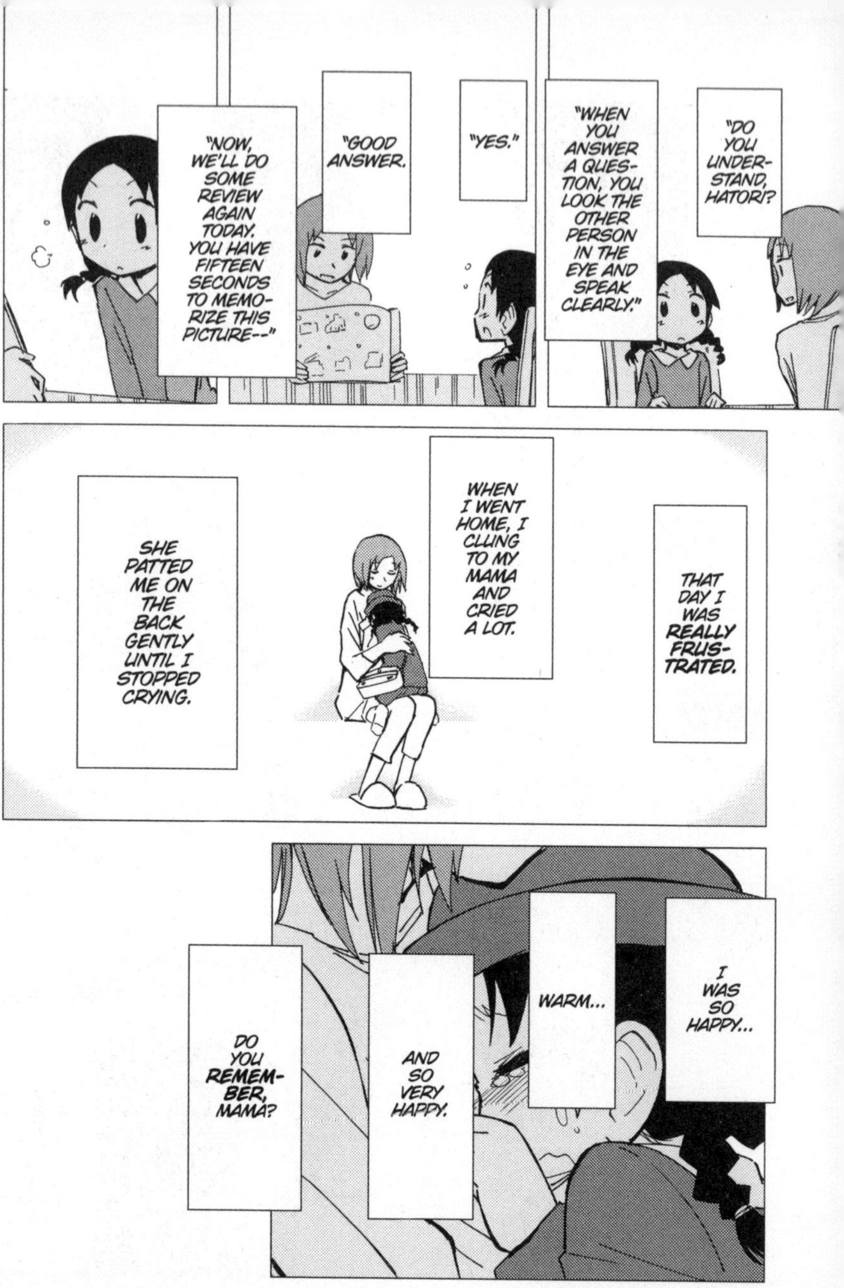
"DO YOU UNDER-STAND, HATORI?
"WHEN YOU ANSWER A QUES-TION, YOU LOOK THE OTHER PERSON IN THE EYE AND SPEAK CLEARLY."
"YES."
"GOOD ANSWER.
"NOW, WE'LL DO SOME REVIEW AGAIN TODAY. YOU HAVE FIFTEEN SECONDS TO MEMO-RIZE THIS PICTURE--"
THAT DAY I WAS REALLY FRUS-TRATED.
WHEN I WENT HOME, I CLUNG TO MY MAMA AND CRIED A LOT.
SHE PATTED ME ON THE BACK GENTLY UNTIL I STOPPED CRYING.
I WAS SO HAPPY...
WARM...
AND SO VERY HAPPY.
DO YOU REMEM-BER, MAMA?

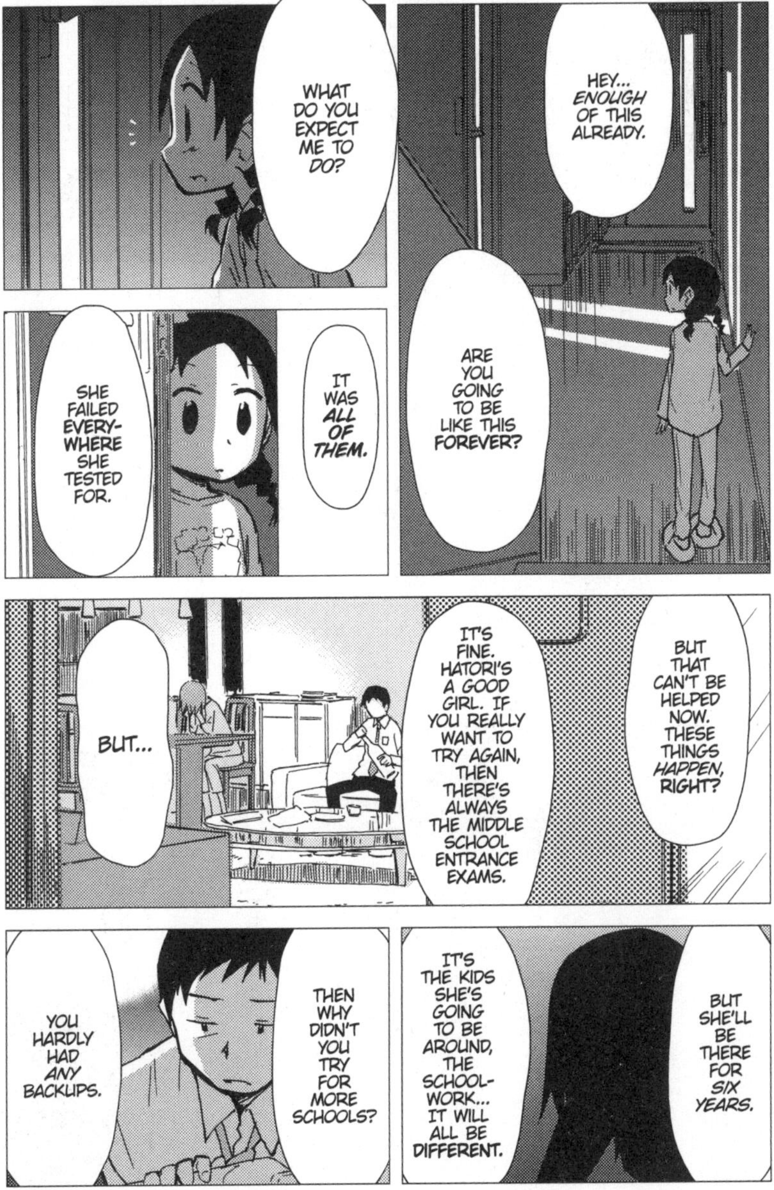
HEY... ENOUGH OF THIS ALREADY.
ARE YOU GOING TO BE LIKE THIS FOREVER?
WHAT DO YOU EXPECT ME TO DO?
IT WAS ALL OF THEM.
SHE FAILED EVERYWHERE SHE TESTED FOR.
BUT THAT CAN'T BE HELPED NOW. THESE THINGS HAPPEN, RIGHT?
IT'S FINE. HATORI'S A GOOD GIRL. IF YOU REALLY WANT TO TRY AGAIN, THEN THERE'S ALWAYS THE MIDDLE SCHOOL ENTRANCE EXAMS.
BUT...
BUT SHE'LL BE THERE FOR SIX YEARS.
IT'S THE KIDS SHE'S GOING TO BE AROUND, THE SCHOOLWORK... IT WILL ALL BE DIFFERENT.
THEN WHY DIDN'T YOU TRY FOR MORE SCHOOLS?
YOU HARDLY HAD ANY BACKUPS.

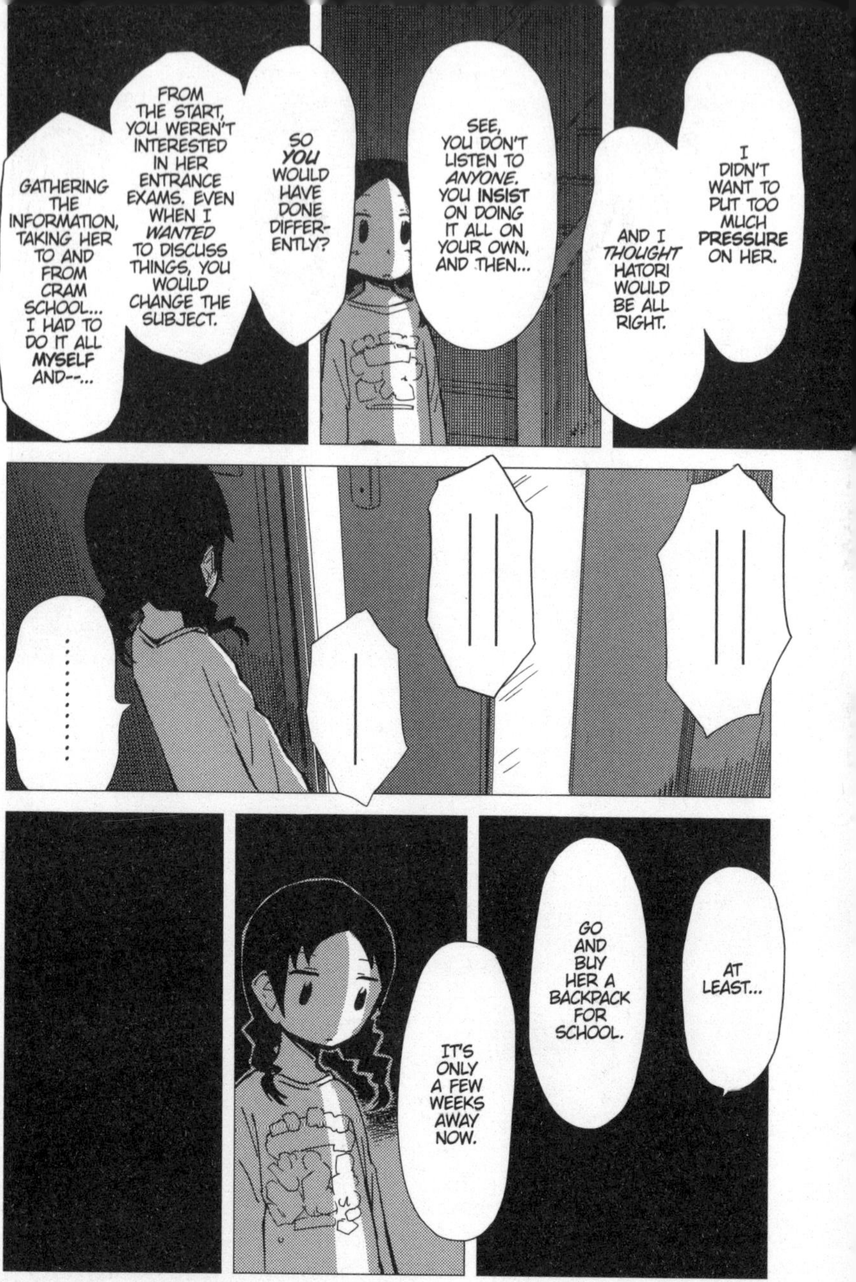
I DIDN'T WANT TO PUT TOO MUCH PRESSURE ON HER.
AND I THOUGHT HATORI WOULD BE ALL RIGHT.
SEE, YOU DON'T LISTEN TO ANYONE. YOU INSIST ON DOING IT ALL ON YOUR OWN, AND THEN...
SO YOU WOULD HAVE DONE DIFFER-ENTLY?
FROM THE START, YOU WEREN'T INTERESTED IN HER ENTRANCE EXAMS. EVEN WHEN I WANTED TO DISCUSS THINGS, YOU WOULD CHANGE THE SUBJECT.
GATHERING THE INFORMATION, TAKING HER TO AND FROM CRAM SCHOOL... I HAD TO DO IT ALL MYSELF AND--...
......
AT LEAST...
GO AND BUY HER A BACKPACK FOR SCHOOL.
IT'S ONLY A FEW WEEKS AWAY NOW.

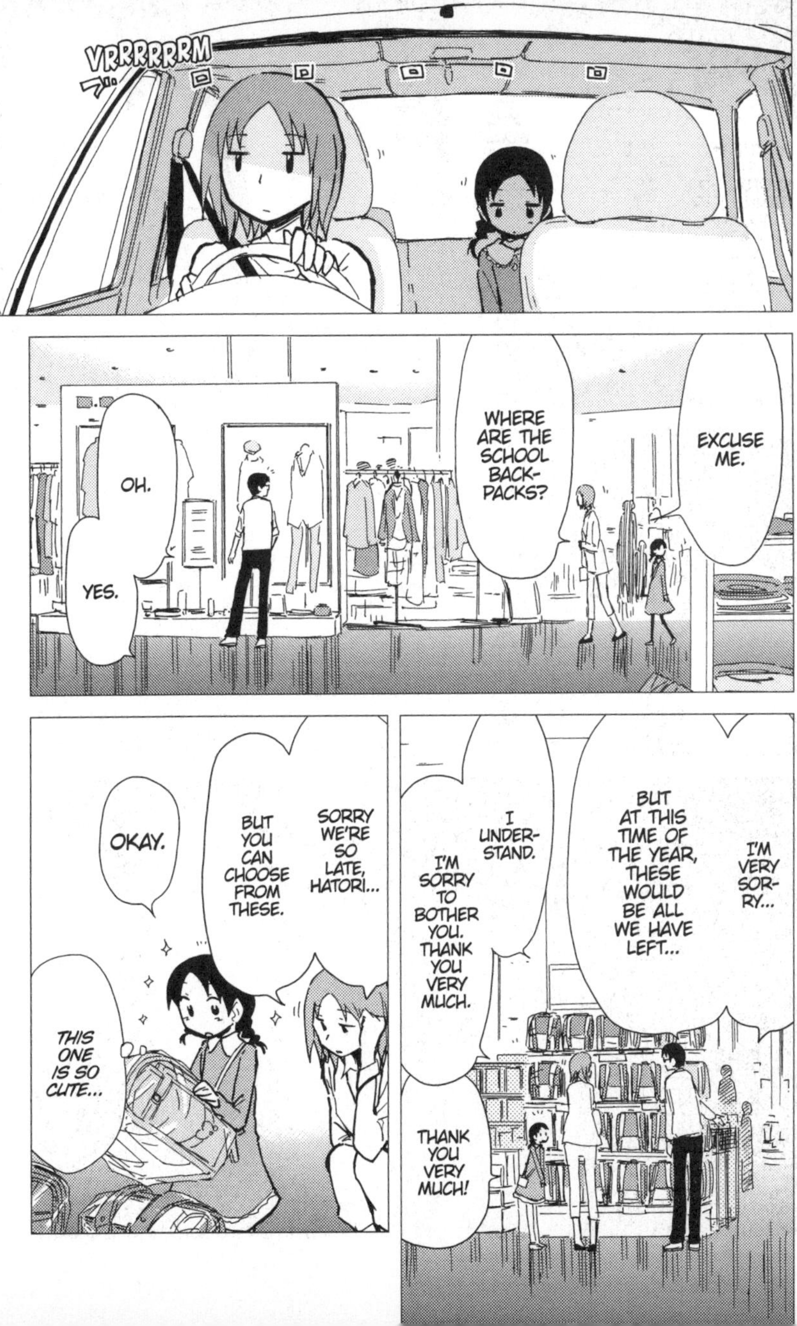
VRRRRRRM
EXCUSE ME.
WHERE ARE THE SCHOOL BACK-PACKS?
OH.
YES.
I'M VERY SOR-RY...
BUT AT THIS TIME OF THE YEAR, THESE WOULD BE ALL WE HAVE LEFT...
I UNDER-STAND.
I'M SORRY TO BOTHER YOU. THANK YOU VERY MUCH.
THANK YOU VERY MUCH!
SORRY WE'RE SO LATE, HATORI...
BUT YOU CAN CHOOSE FROM THESE.
OKAY.
THIS ONE IS SO CUTE...

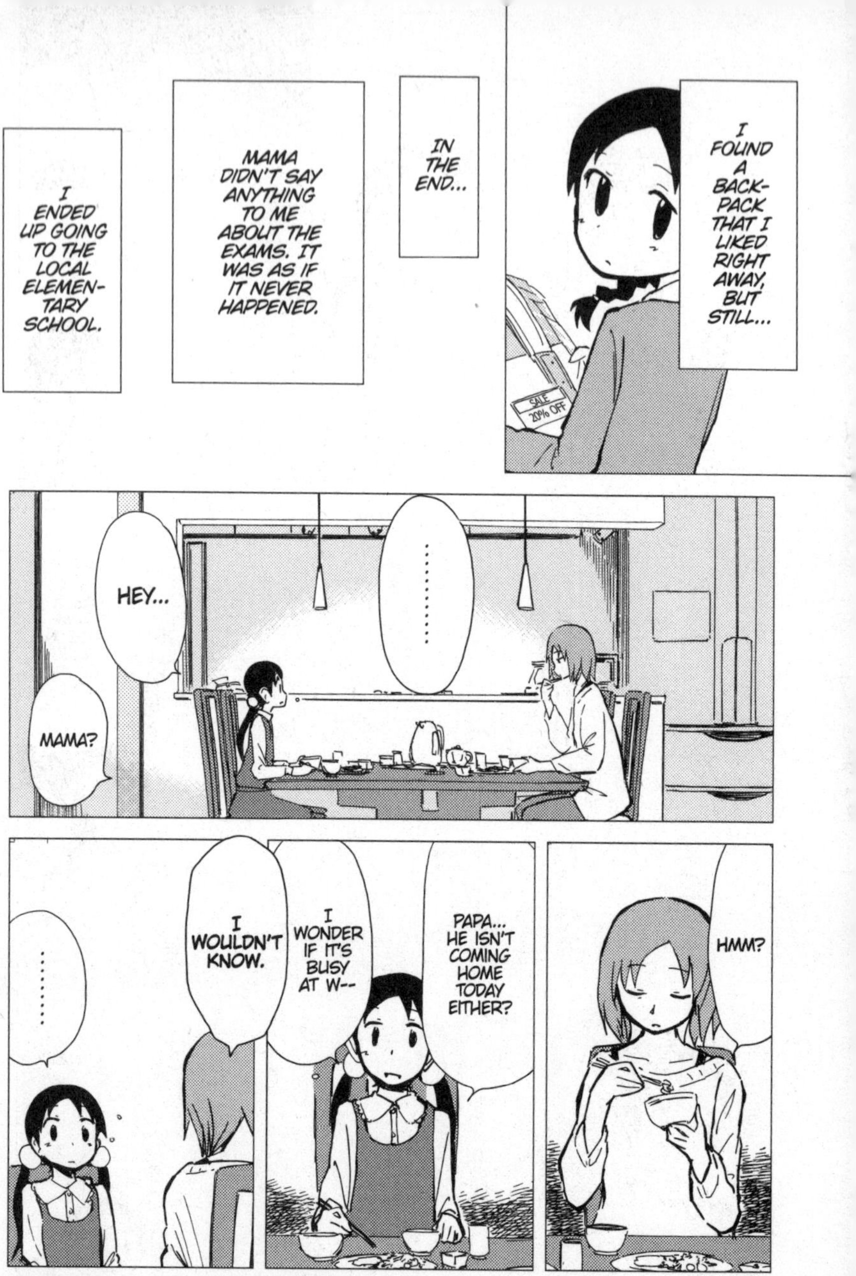
I FOUND A BACKPACK THAT I LIKED RIGHT AWAY, BUT STILL...
SALE 20% OFF
IN THE END...
MAMA DIDN'T SAY ANYTHING TO ME ABOUT THE EXAMS. IT WAS AS IF IT NEVER HAPPENED.
I ENDED UP GOING TO THE LOCAL ELEMENTARY SCHOOL.
HEY...
MAMA?
....
HMM?
PAPA... HE ISN'T COMING HOME TODAY EITHER?
I WONDER IF IT'S BUSY AT W--
I WOULDN'T KNOW.
....

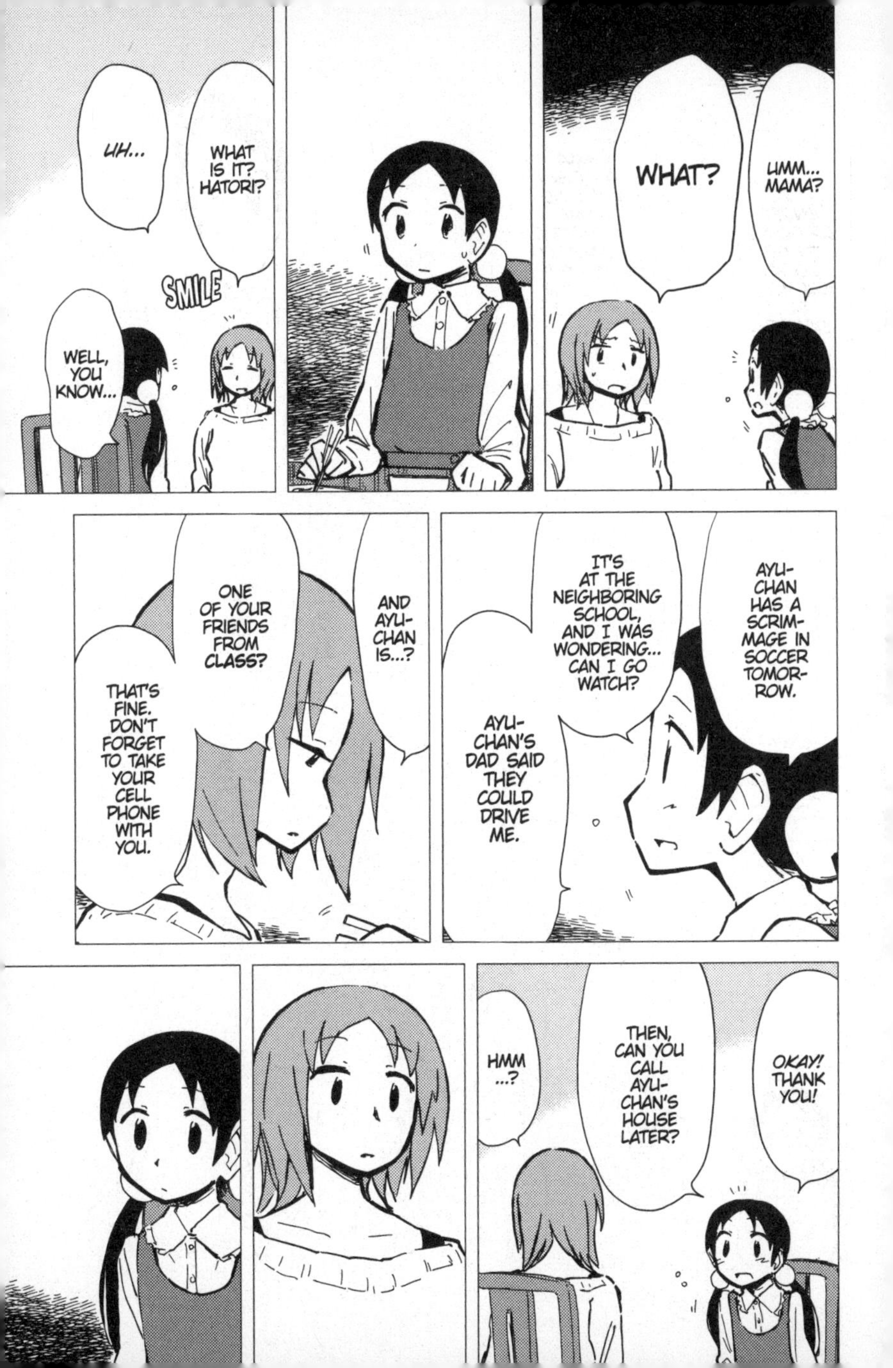

UMM... MAMA?
WHAT?
WHAT IS IT? HATORI?
UH...
SMILE
WELL, YOU KNOW...
AYU-CHAN HAS A SCRIMMAGE IN SOCCER TOMORROW.
IT'S AT THE NEIGHBORING SCHOOL, AND I WAS WONDERING... CAN I GO WATCH?
AYU-CHAN'S DAD SAID THEY COULD DRIVE ME.
AND AYU-CHAN IS...?
ONE OF YOUR FRIENDS FROM CLASS?
THAT'S FINE. DON'T FORGET TO TAKE YOUR CELL PHONE WITH YOU.
OKAY! THANK YOU!
THEN, CAN YOU CALL AYU-CHAN'S HOUSE LATER?
HMM ...?

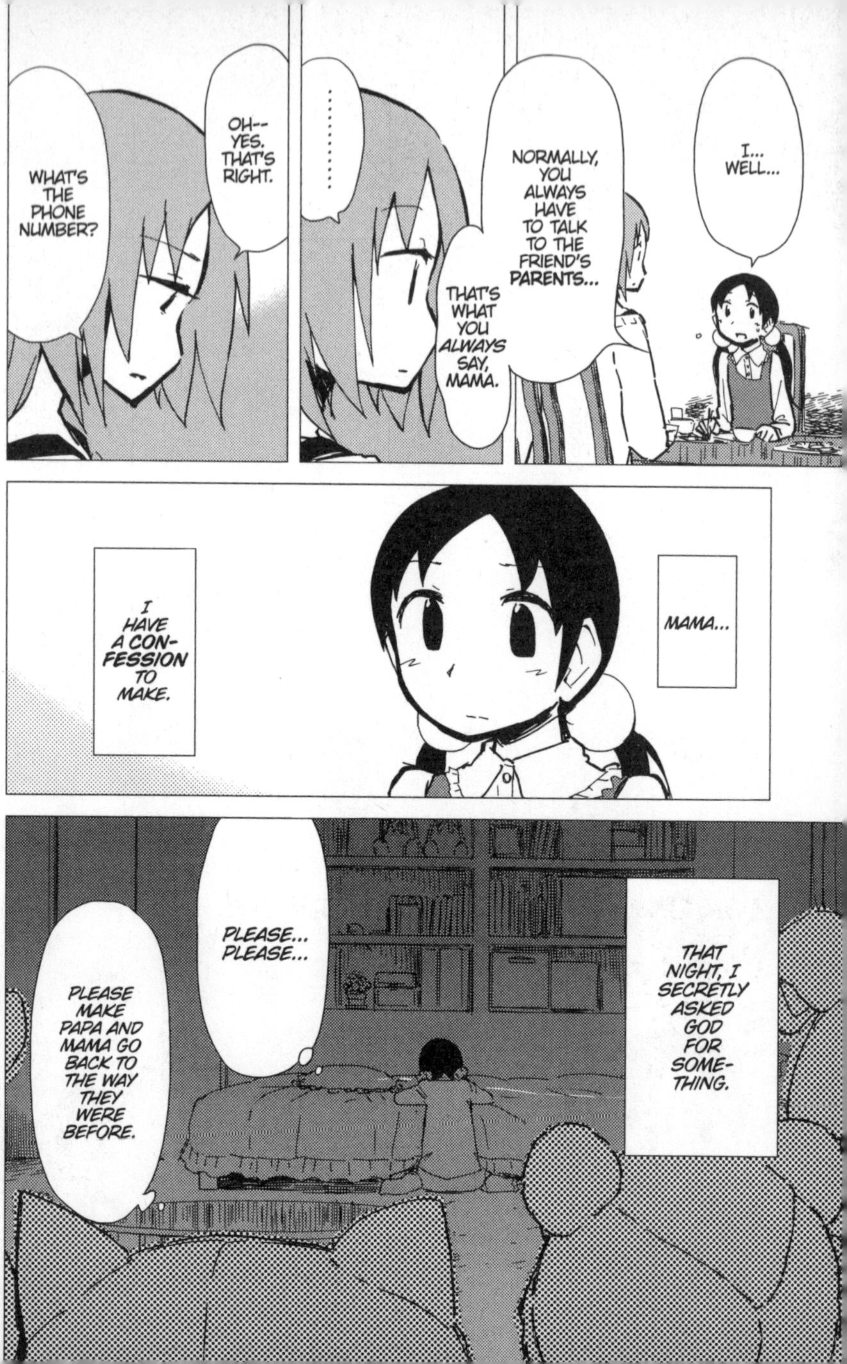

I... WELL...
NORMALLY, YOU ALWAYS HAVE TO TALK TO THE FRIEND'S PARENTS...
......
THAT'S WHAT YOU ALWAYS SAY, MAMA.
OH-- YES. THAT'S RIGHT.
WHAT'S THE PHONE NUMBER?
MAMA...
I HAVE A CONFESSION TO MAKE.
THAT NIGHT, I SECRETLY ASKED GOD FOR SOMETHING.
PLEASE... PLEASE...
PLEASE MAKE PAPA AND MAMA GO BACK TO THE WAY THEY WERE BEFORE.

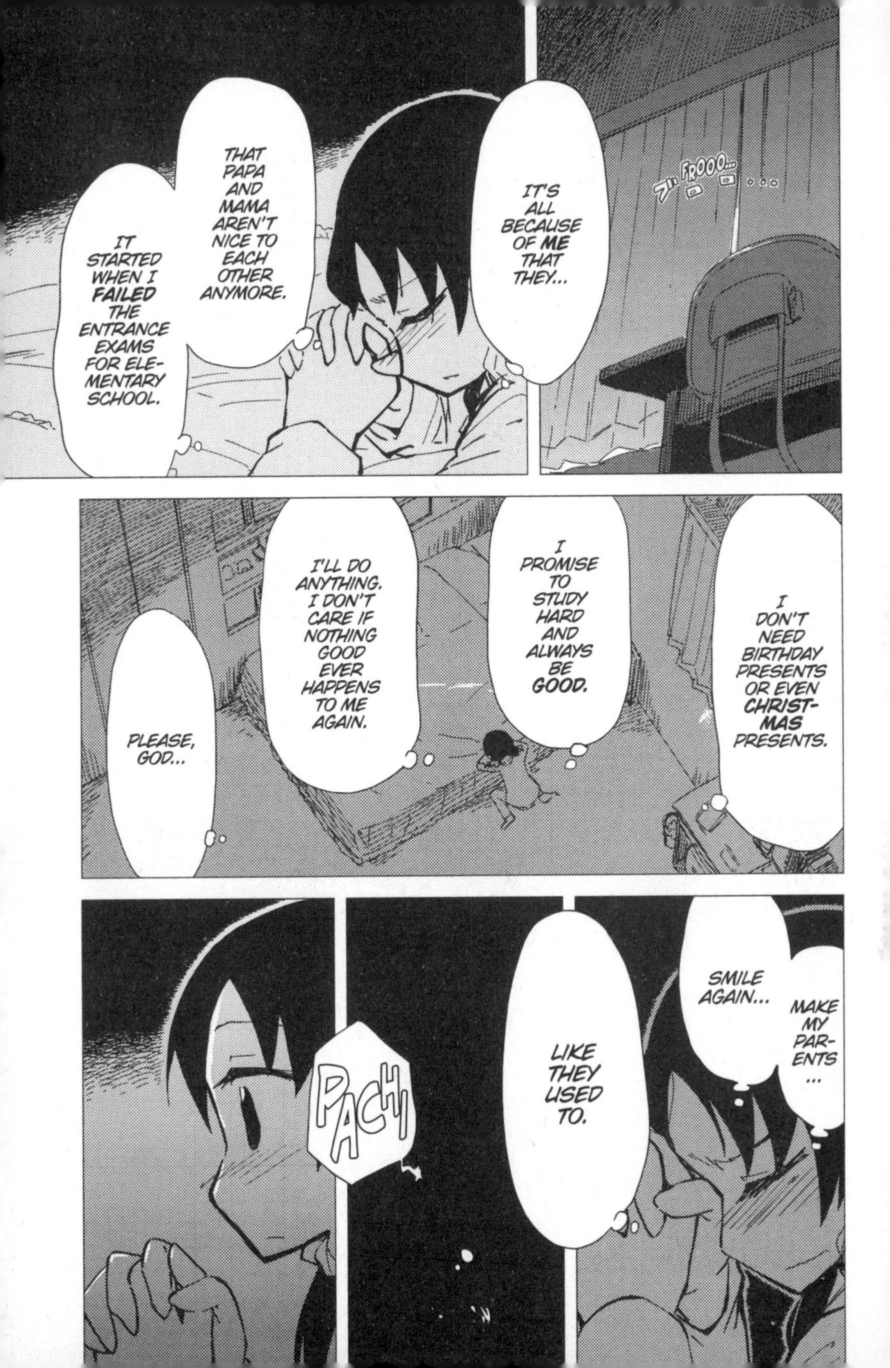
FROOO...
IT'S ALL BECAUSE OF ME THAT THEY...
THAT PAPA AND MAMA AREN'T NICE TO EACH OTHER ANYMORE.
IT STARTED WHEN I FAILED THE ENTRANCE EXAMS FOR ELEMENTARY SCHOOL.
I DON'T NEED BIRTHDAY PRESENTS OR EVEN CHRISTMAS PRESENTS.
I PROMISE TO STUDY HARD AND ALWAYS BE GOOD.
I'LL DO ANYTHING. I DON'T CARE IF NOTHING GOOD EVER HAPPENS TO ME AGAIN.
PLEASE, GOD...
MAKE MY PARENTS...
SMILE AGAIN...
LIKE THEY USED TO.
PACHI

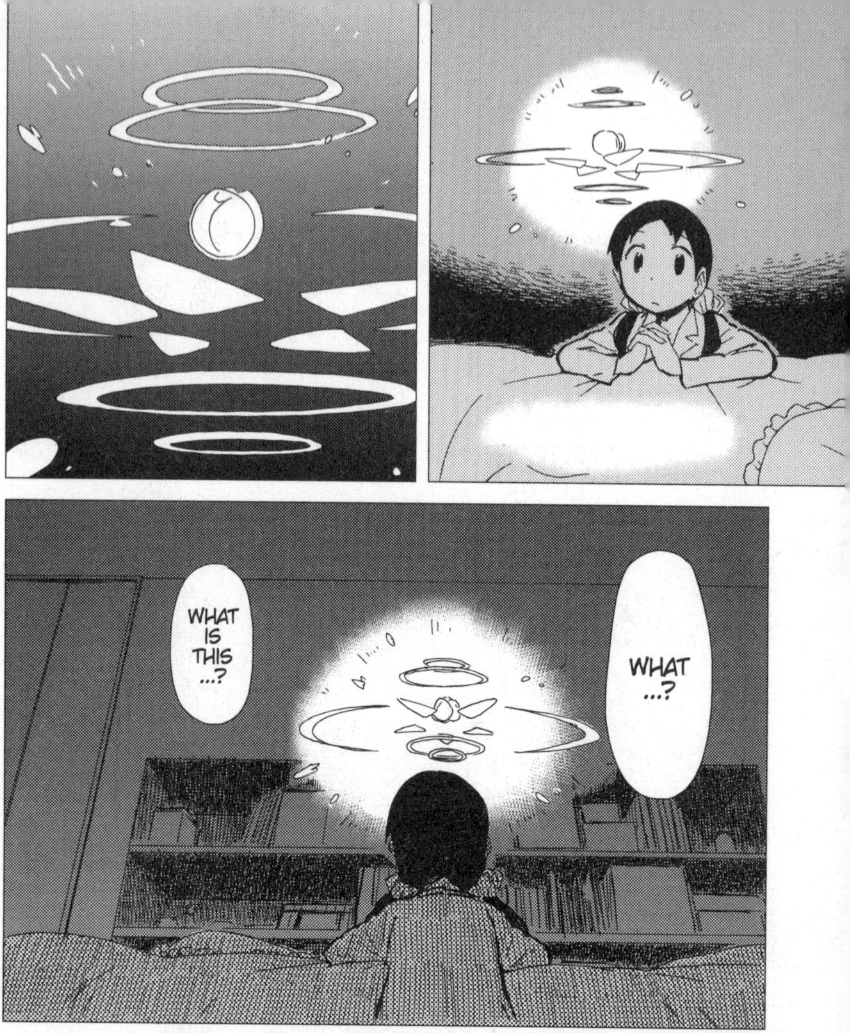
WHAT ...?
WHAT IS THIS ...?

AND THEN IT CAME TRUE. JUST LIKE THAT.

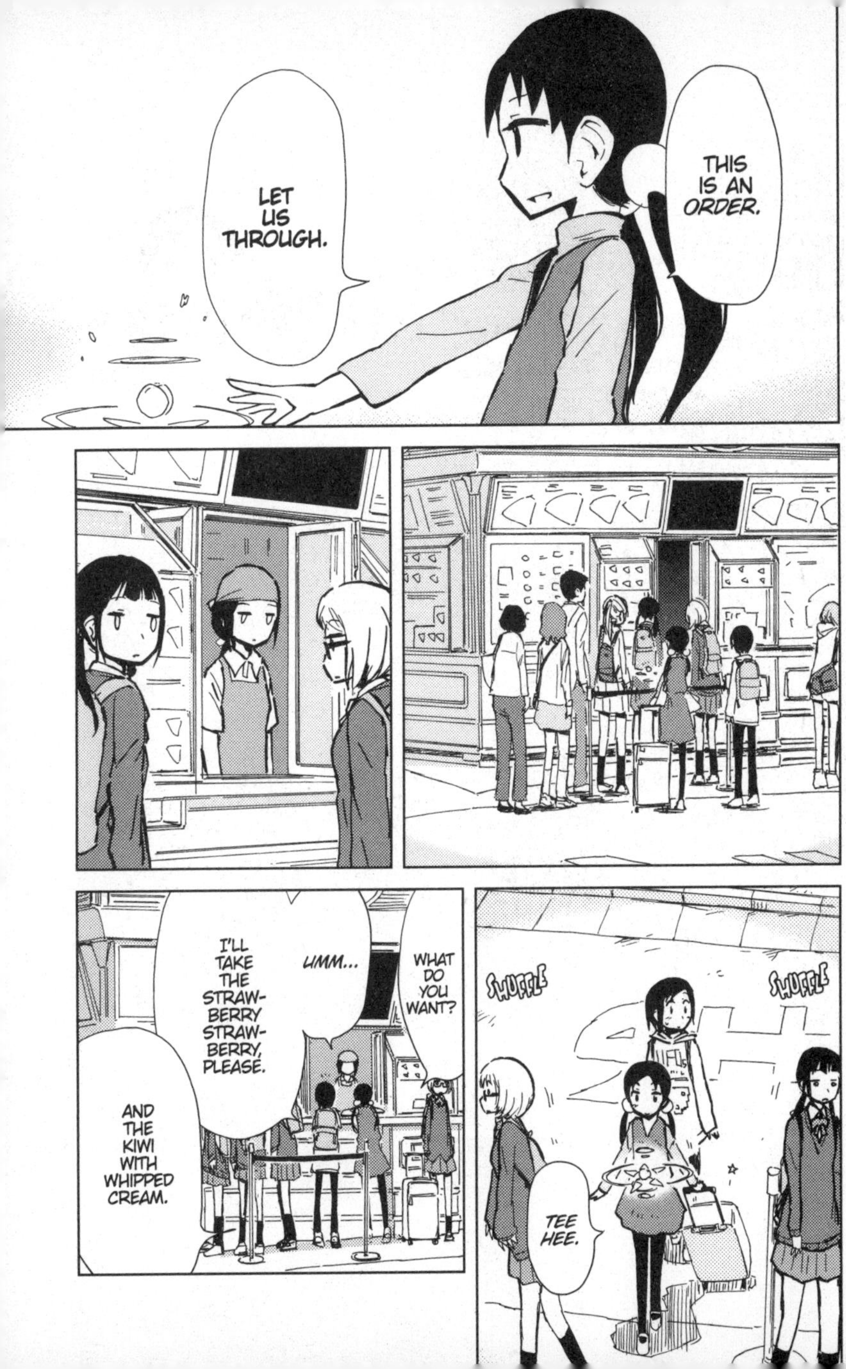
THIS IS AN ORDER.
LET US THROUGH.
SHUFFLE
SHUFFLE
TEE HEE.
WHAT DO YOU WANT?
UMM...
I'LL TAKE THE STRAWBERRY STRAWBERRY, PLEASE.
AND THE KIWI WITH WHIPPED CREAM.

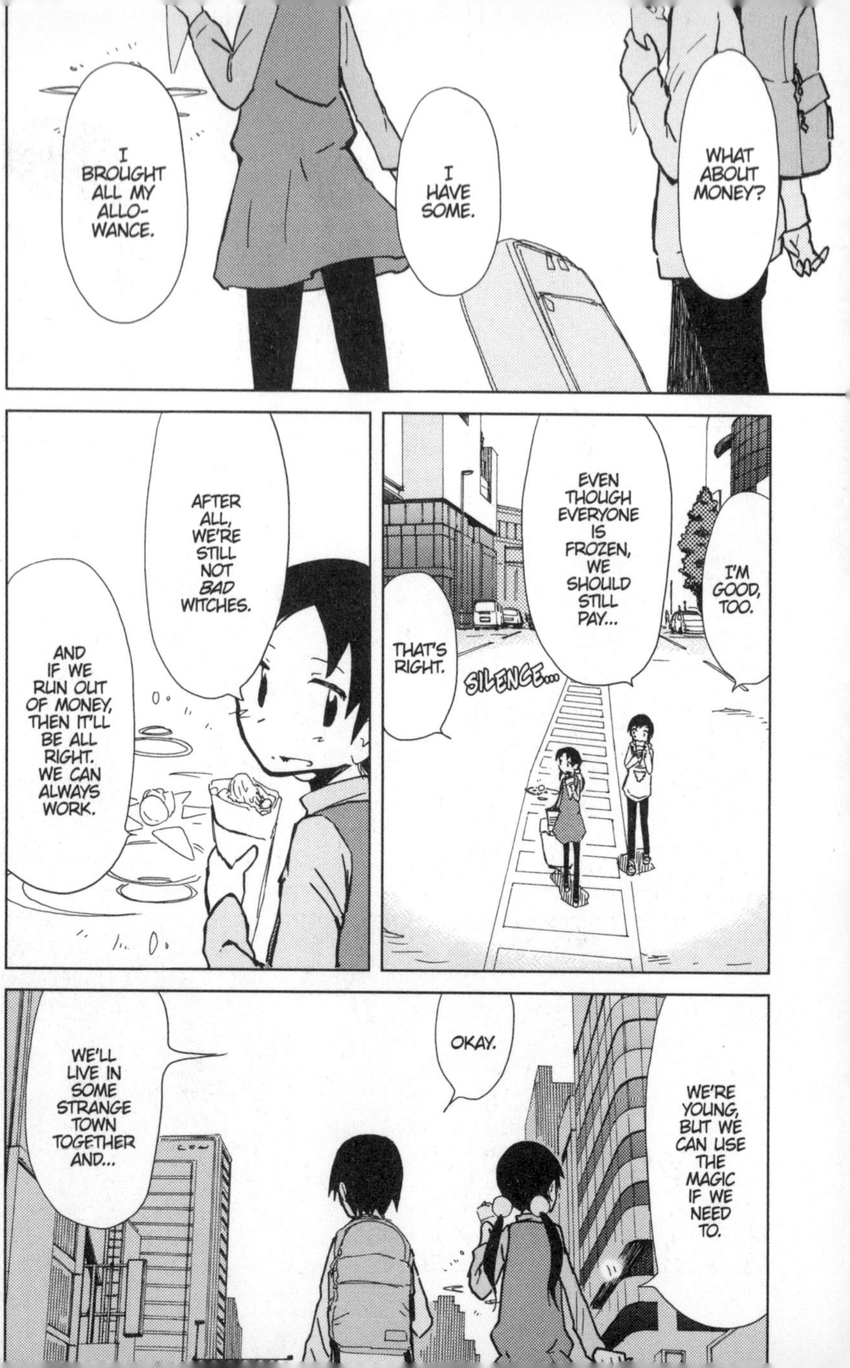
WHAT ABOUT MONEY?
I HAVE SOME.
I BROUGHT ALL MY ALLO-WANCE.
I'M GOOD, TOO.
EVEN THOUGH EVERYONE IS FROZEN, WE SHOULD STILL PAY...
THAT'S RIGHT.
SILENCE...
AFTER ALL, WE'RE STILL NOT BAD WITCHES.
AND IF WE RUN OUT OF MONEY, THEN IT'LL BE ALL RIGHT. WE CAN ALWAYS WORK.
WE'RE YOUNG, BUT WE CAN USE THE MAGIC IF WE NEED TO.
OKAY.
WE'LL LIVE IN SOME STRANGE TOWN TOGETHER AND...

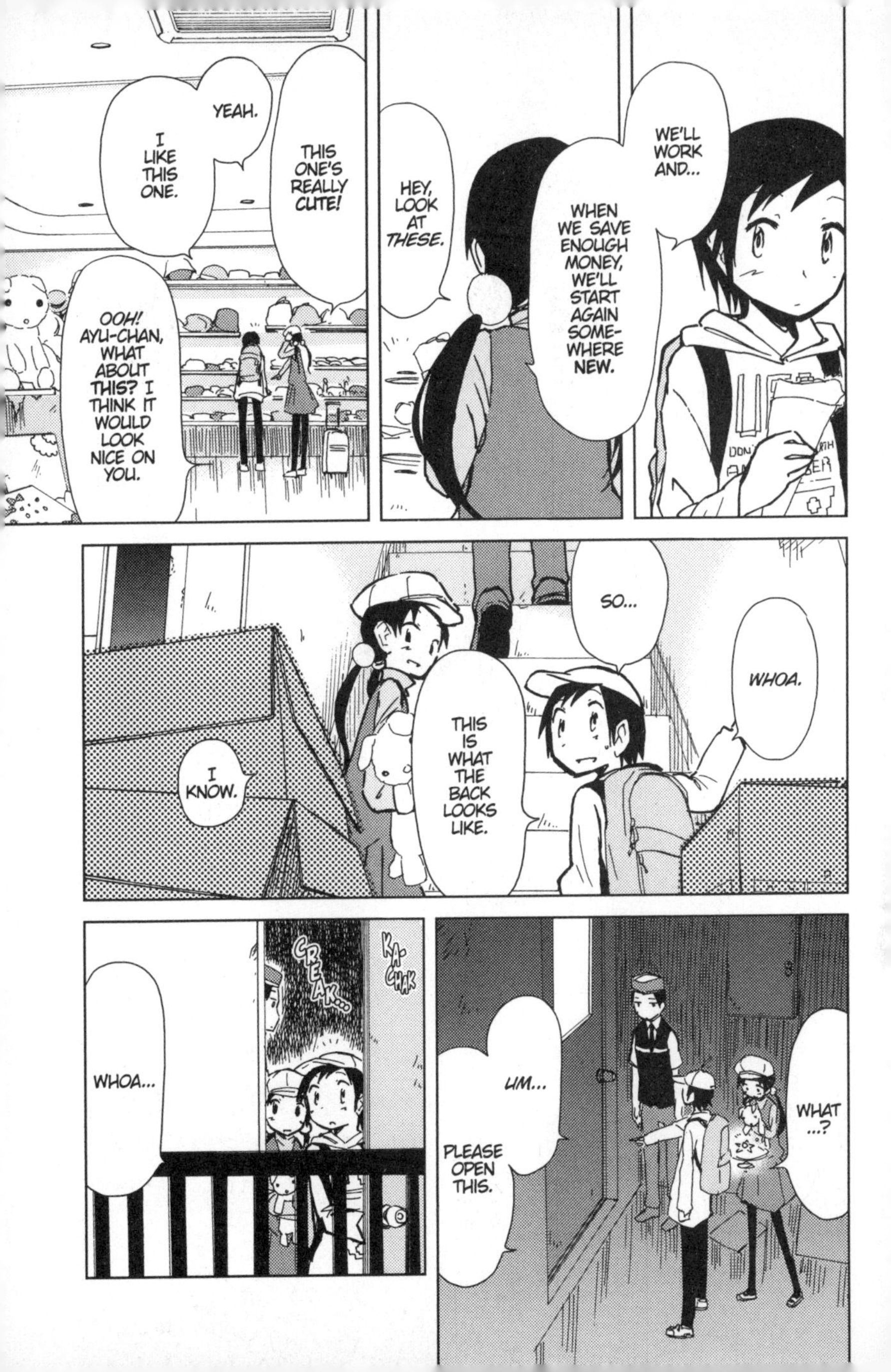
WE'LL WORK AND...
WHEN WE SAVE ENOUGH MONEY, WE'LL START AGAIN SOMEWHERE NEW.
HEY, LOOK AT THESE.
THIS ONE'S REALLY CUTE!
YEAH.
I LIKE THIS ONE.
OOH! AYU-CHAN, WHAT ABOUT THIS? I THINK IT WOULD LOOK NICE ON YOU.
SO...
WHOA.
THIS IS WHAT THE BACK LOOKS LIKE.
I KNOW.
WHAT ...?
UM...
PLEASE OPEN THIS.
KA-CHAK
CREAK...
WHOA...

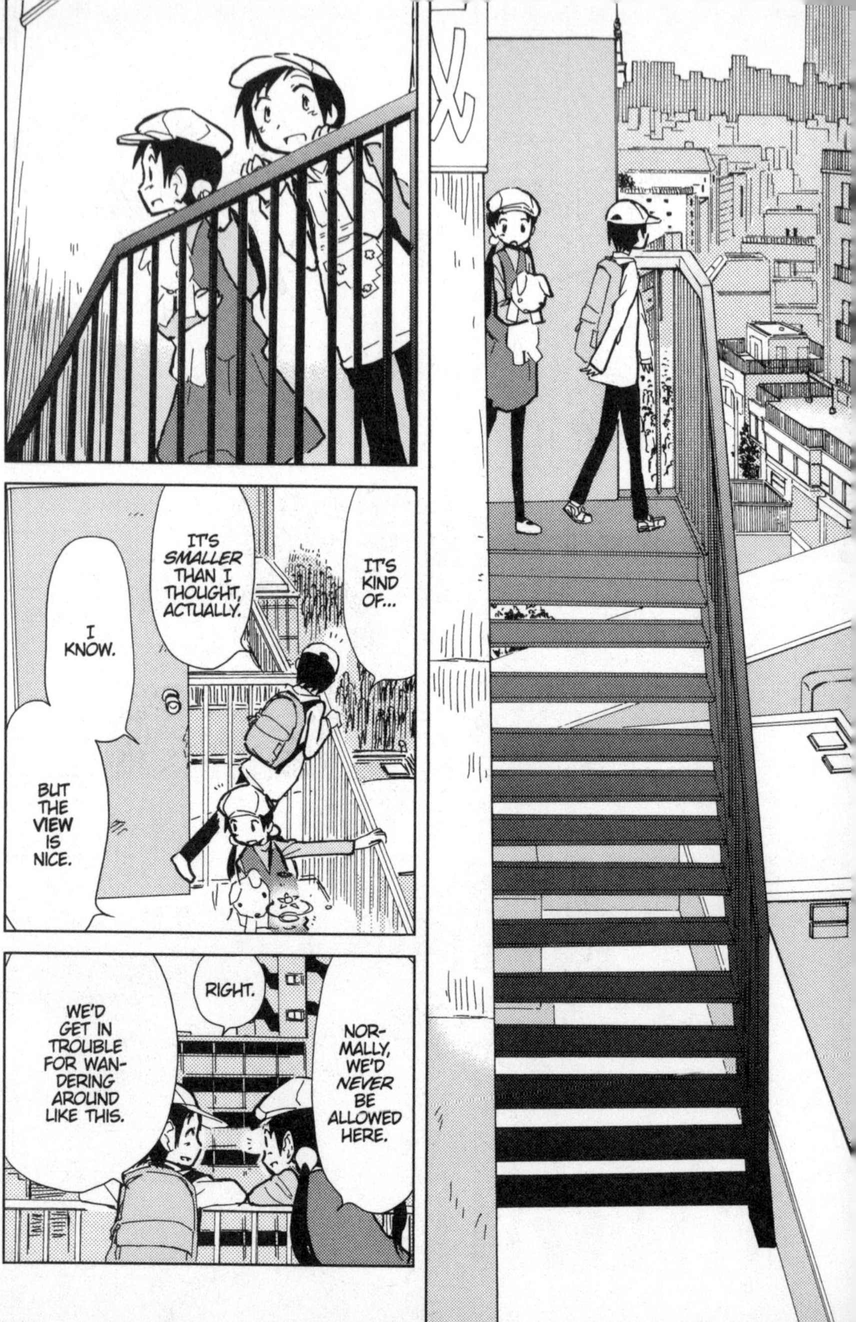
IT'S KIND OF...
IT'S *SMALLER* THAN I THOUGHT, ACTUALLY.
I KNOW.
BUT THE VIEW IS NICE.
NOR-MALLY, WE'D *NEVER* BE ALLOWED HERE.
RIGHT.
WE'D GET IN TROUBLE FOR WAN-DERING AROUND LIKE THIS.

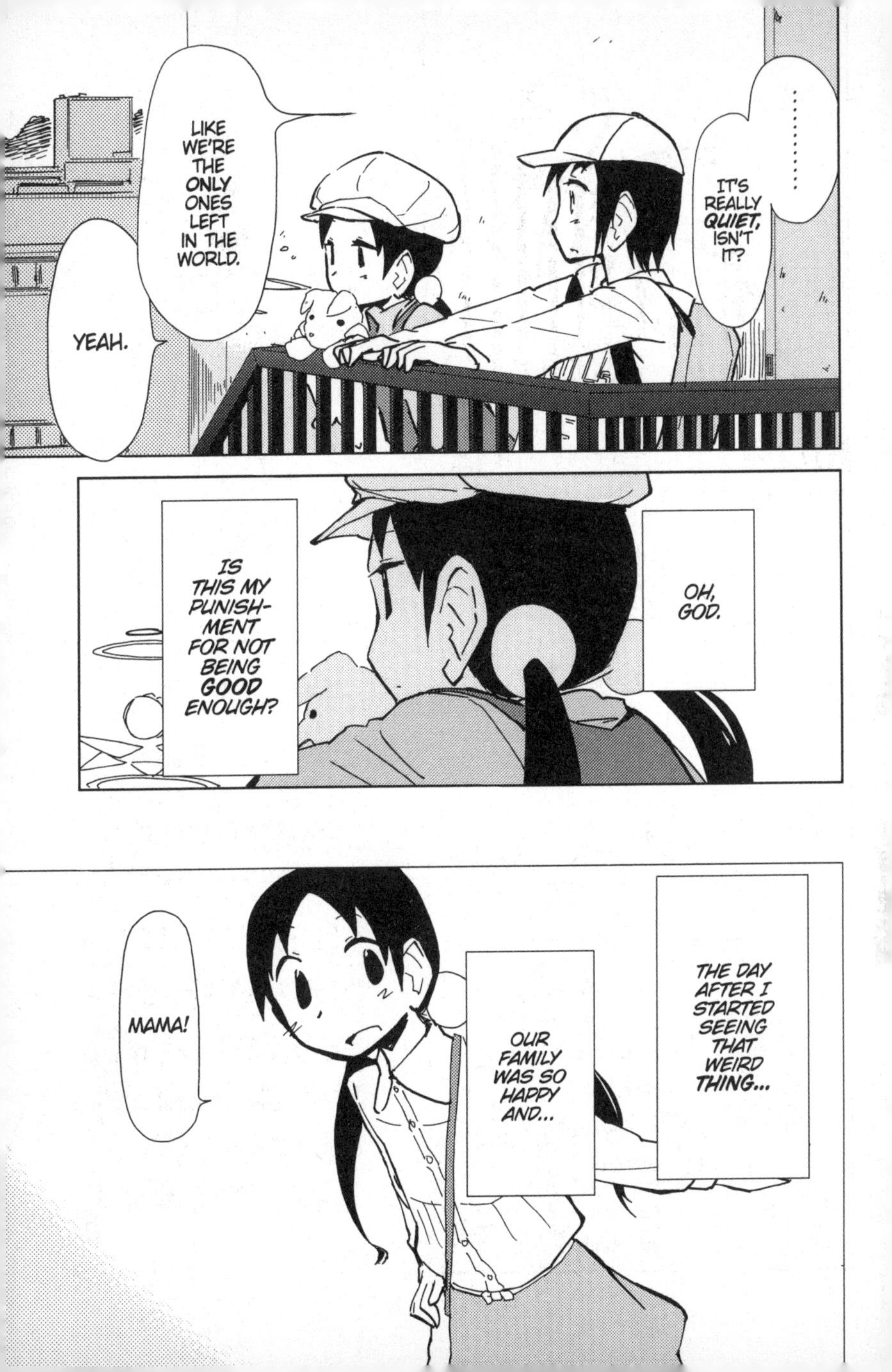
......
IT'S REALLY QUIET, ISN'T IT?
LIKE WE'RE THE ONLY ONES LEFT IN THE WORLD.
YEAH.
OH, GOD.
IS THIS MY PUNISHMENT FOR NOT BEING GOOD ENOUGH?
THE DAY AFTER I STARTED SEEING THAT WEIRD THING...
OUR FAMILY WAS SO HAPPY AND...
MAMA!

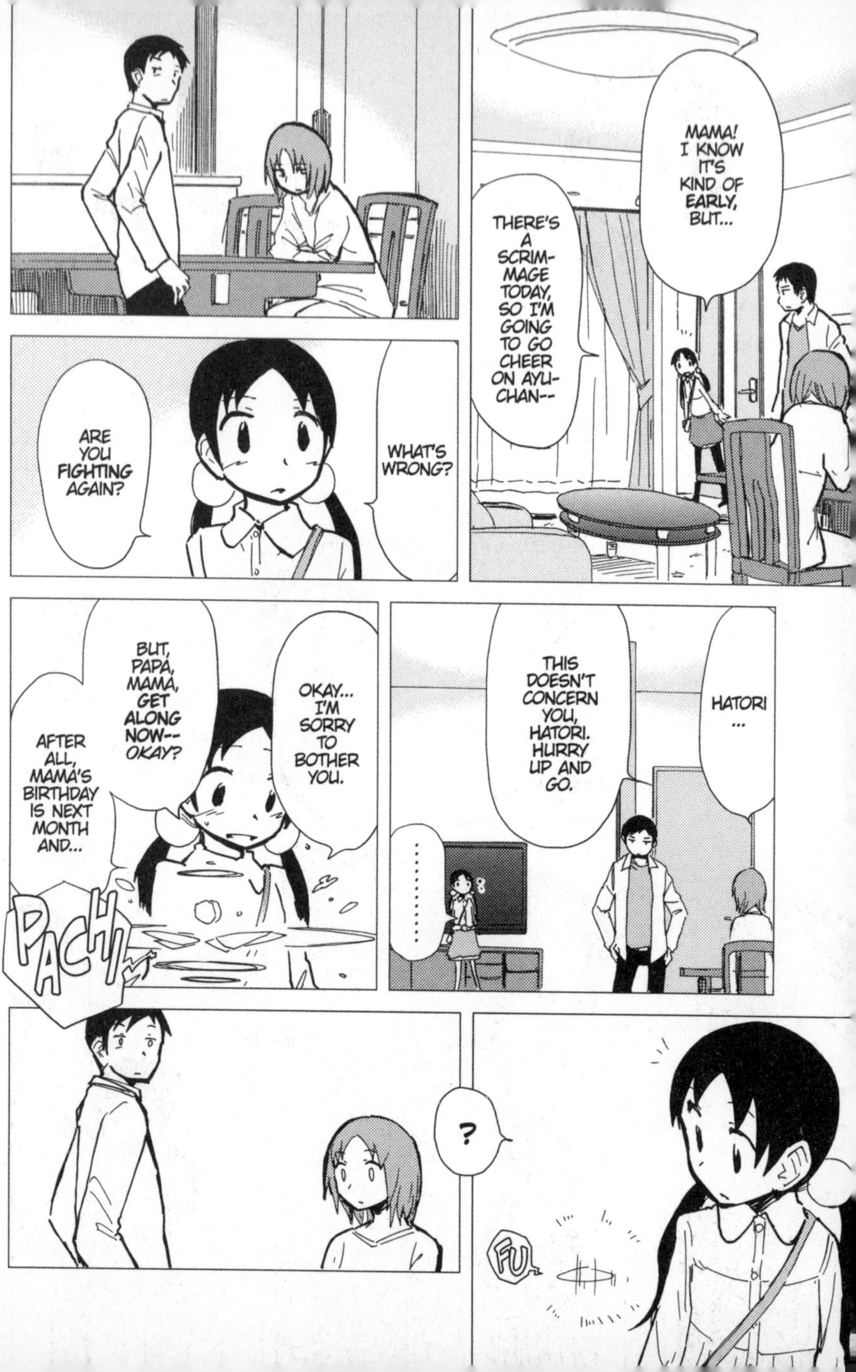
MAMA! I KNOW IT'S KIND OF EARLY, BUT...
THERE'S A SCRIM-MAGE TODAY, SO I'M GOING TO GO CHEER ON AYU-CHAN--
WHAT'S WRONG?
ARE YOU FIGHTING AGAIN?
HATORI...
THIS DOESN'T CONCERN YOU, HATORI. HURRY UP AND GO.
......
OKAY... I'M SORRY TO BOTHER YOU.
BUT, PAPA, MAMA, GET ALONG NOW--OKAY?
AFTER ALL, MAMA'S BIRTHDAY IS NEXT MONTH AND...
PACHI
FU
?

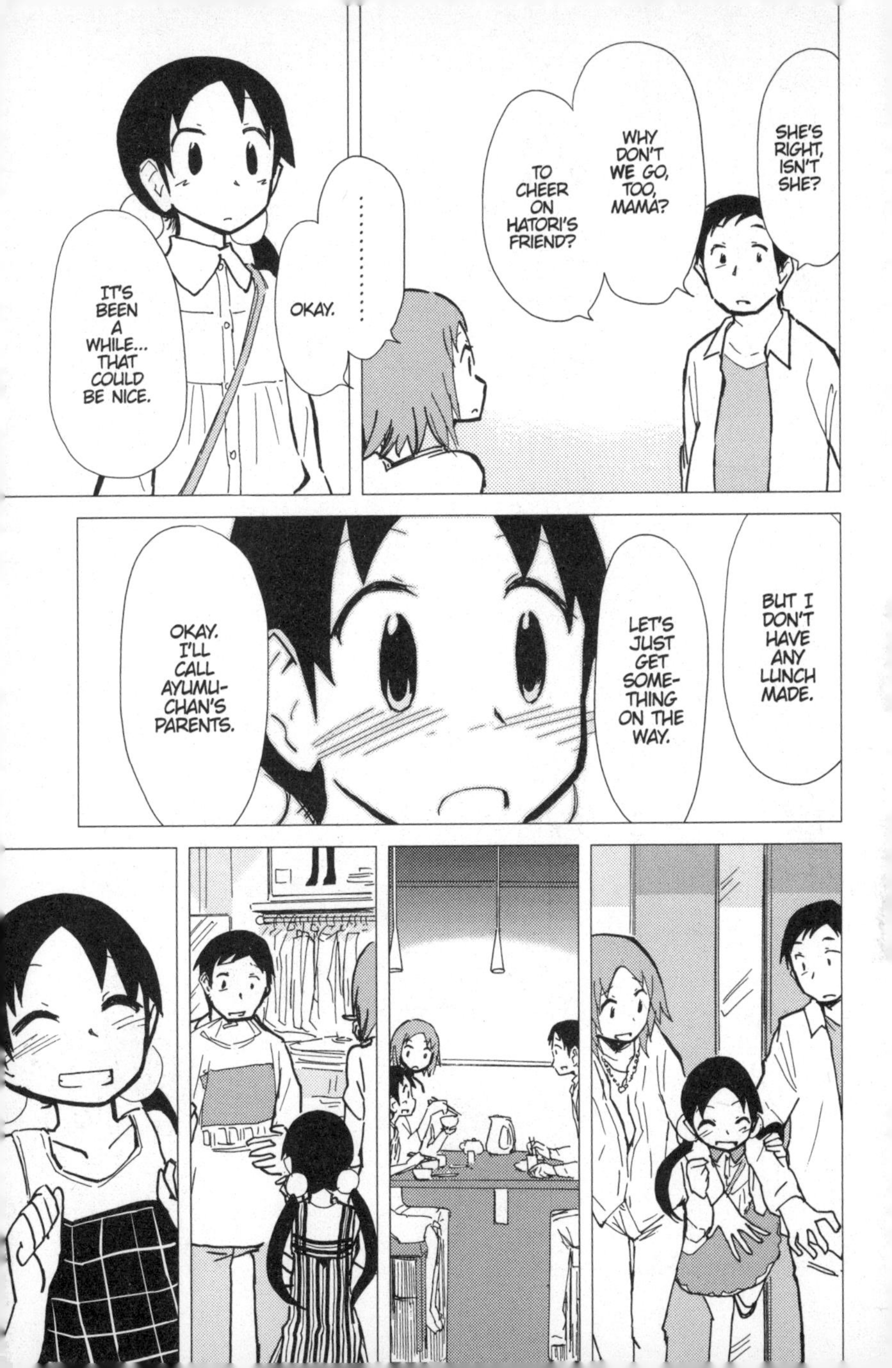
SHE'S RIGHT, ISN'T SHE?
WHY DON'T WE GO, TOO, MAMA?
TO CHEER ON HATORI'S FRIEND?
......
OKAY.
IT'S BEEN A WHILE... THAT COULD BE NICE.
BUT I DON'T HAVE ANY LUNCH MADE.
LET'S JUST GET SOME-THING ON THE WAY.
OKAY. I'LL CALL AYUMU-CHAN'S PARENTS.

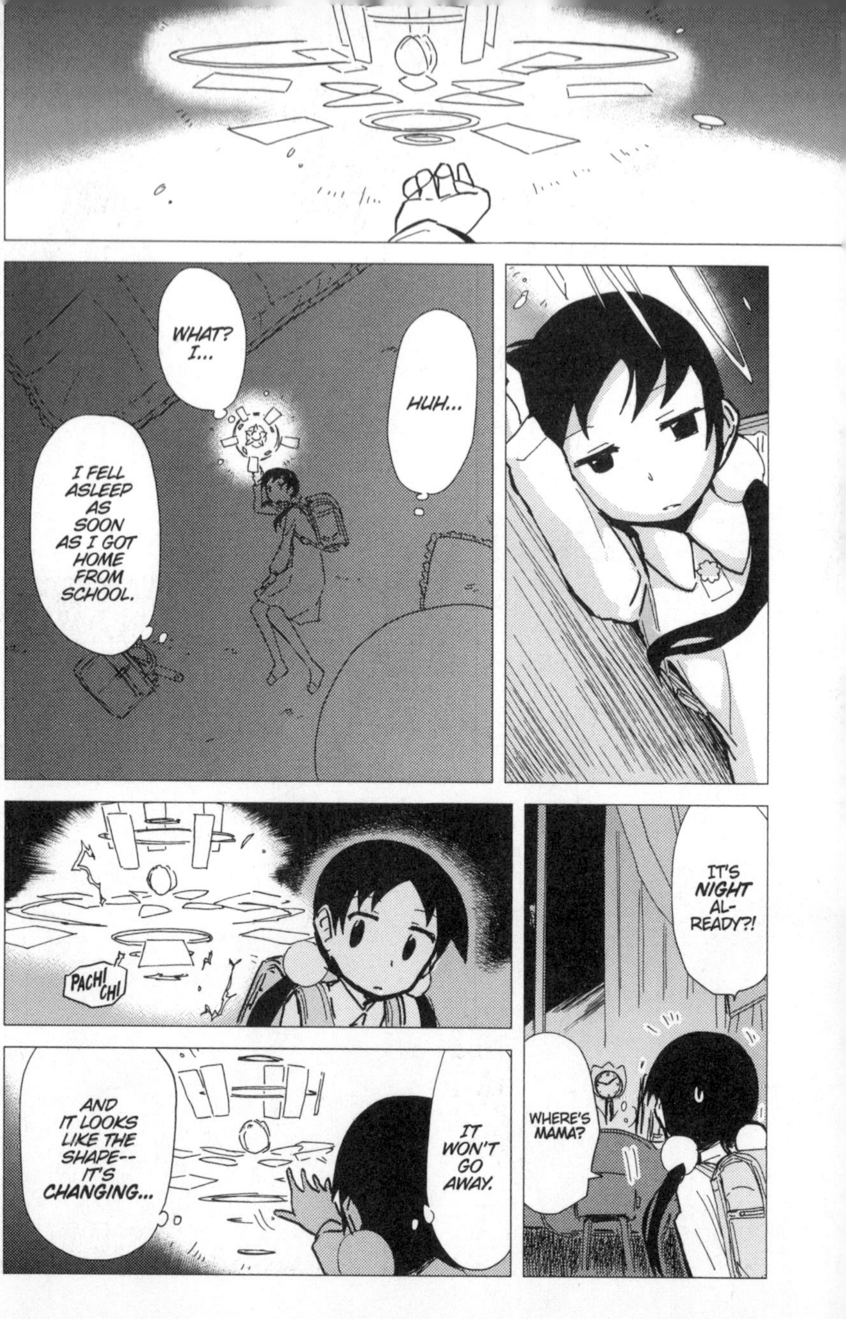
HUH...
WHAT? I...
I FELL ASLEEP AS SOON AS I GOT HOME FROM SCHOOL.
IT'S NIGHT AL-READY?!
WHERE'S MAMA?
PACHI CHI
IT WON'T GO AWAY.
AND IT LOOKS LIKE THE SHAPE-- IT'S CHANGING...

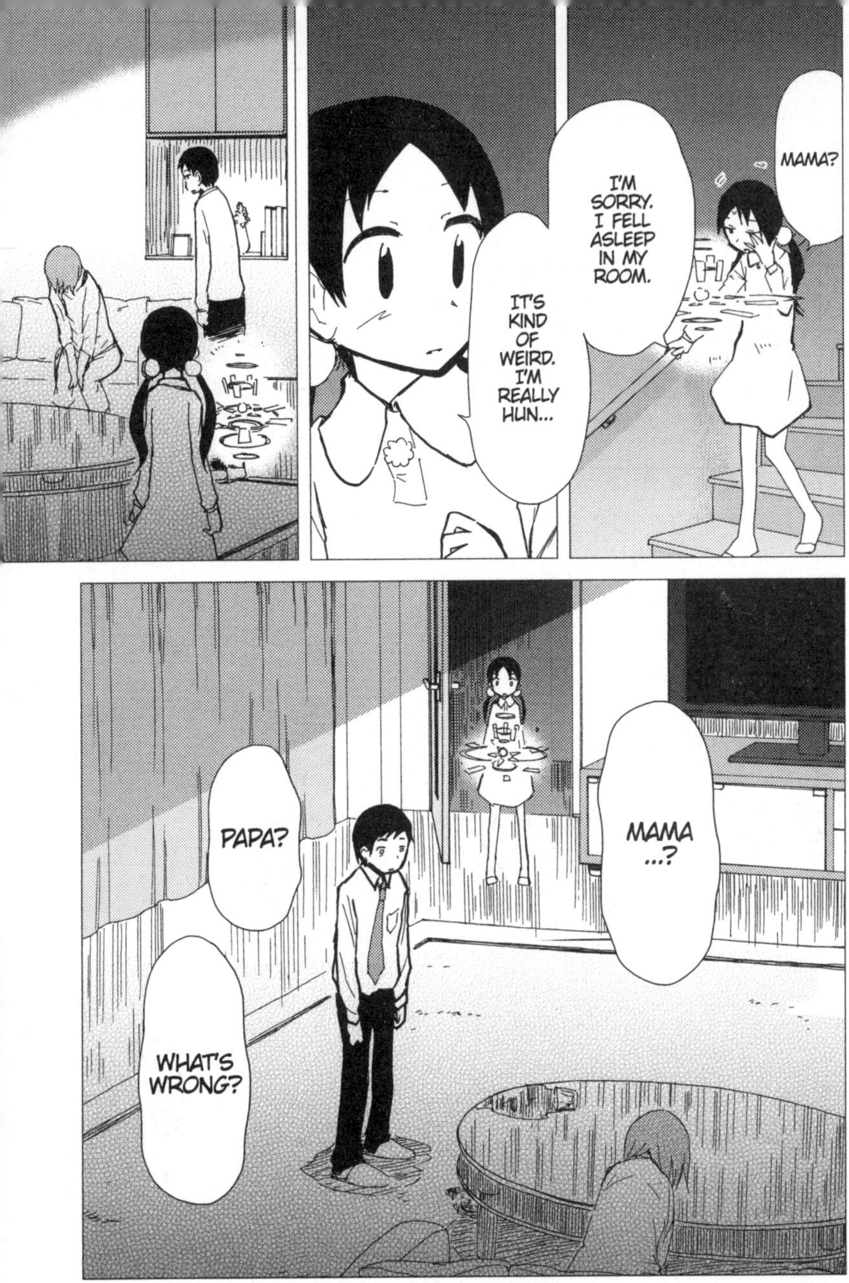
MAMA?
I'M SORRY. I FELL ASLEEP IN MY ROOM.
IT'S KIND OF WEIRD. I'M REALLY HUN...
MAMA ...?
PAPA?
WHAT'S WRONG?

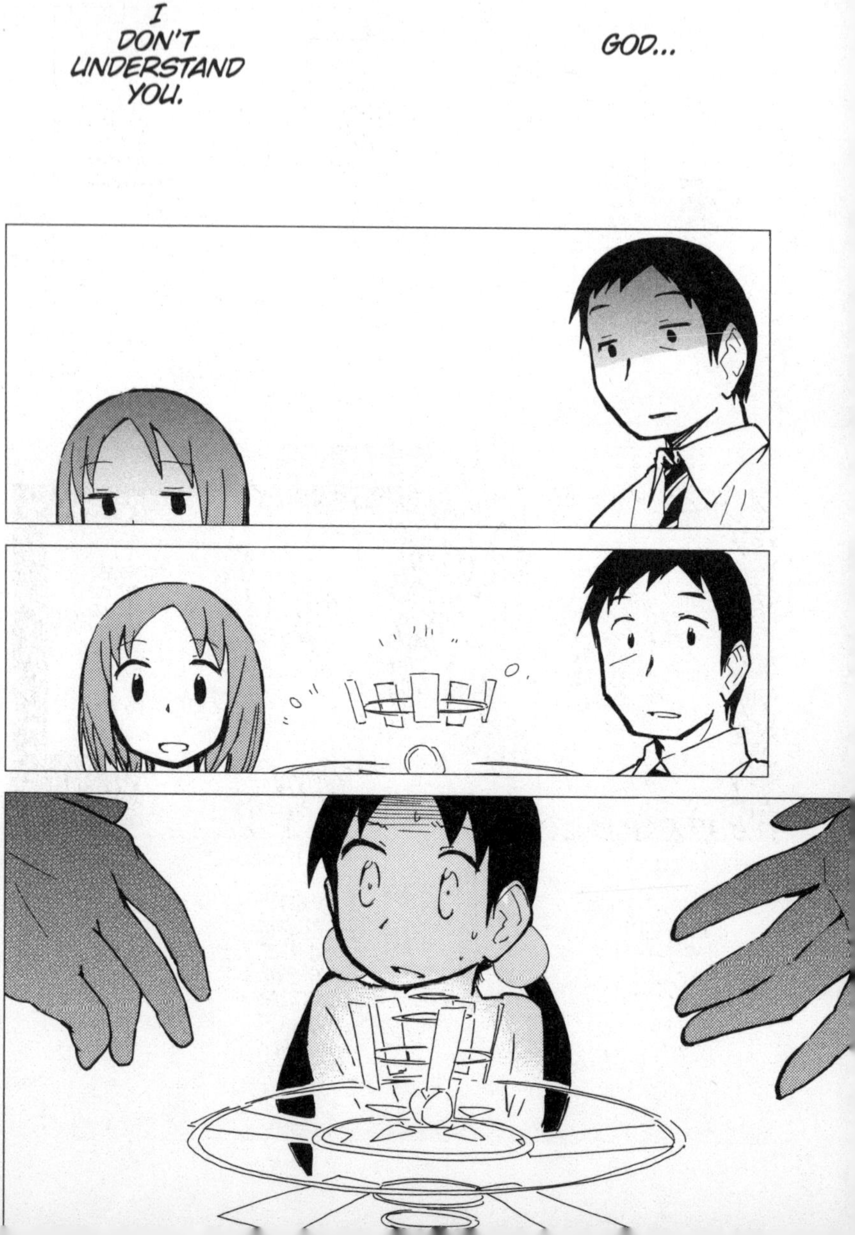
GOD...
I DON'T UNDERSTAND YOU.

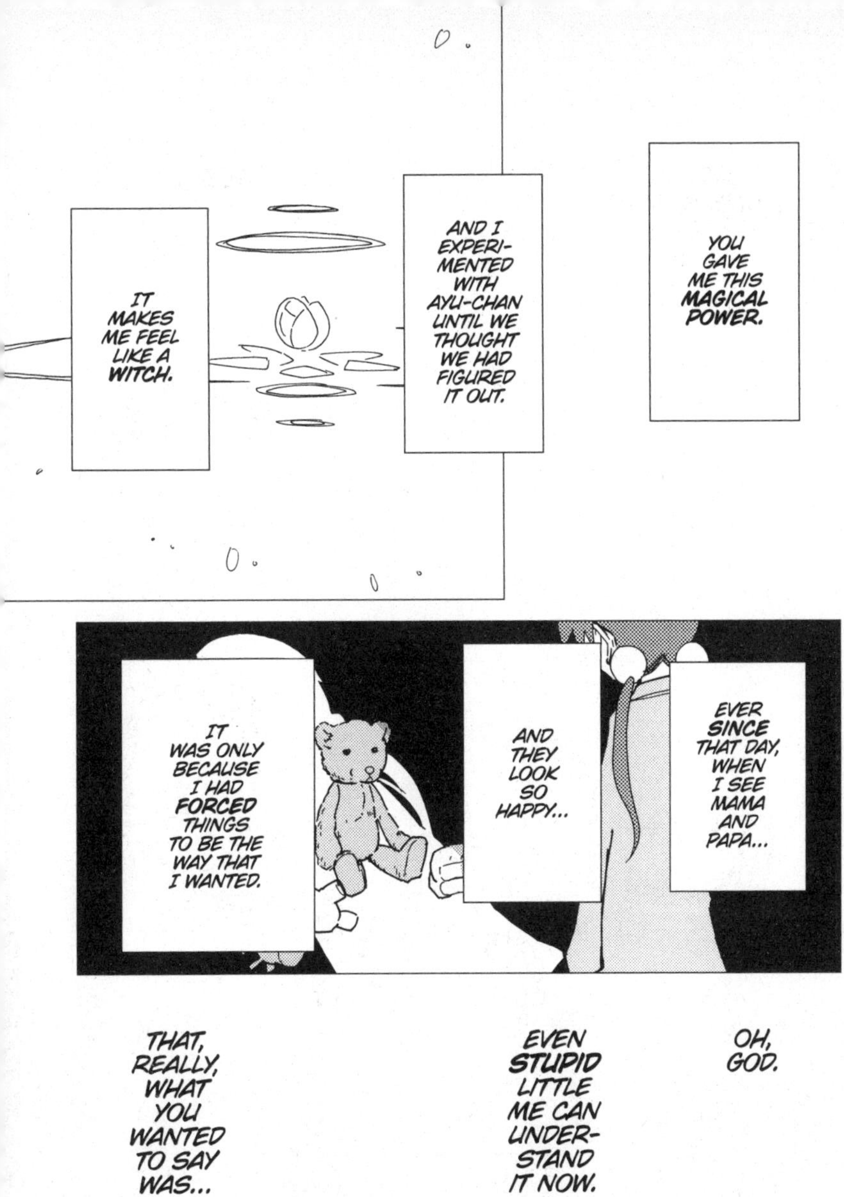
YOU GAVE ME THIS MAGICAL POWER.
AND I EXPERIMENTED WITH AYU-CHAN UNTIL WE THOUGHT WE HAD FIGURED IT OUT.
IT MAKES ME FEEL LIKE A WITCH.
EVER SINCE THAT DAY, WHEN I SEE MAMA AND PAPA...
AND THEY LOOK SO HAPPY...
IT WAS ONLY BECAUSE I HAD FORCED THINGS TO BE THE WAY THAT I WANTED.
OH, GOD.
EVEN STUPID LITTLE ME CAN UNDERSTAND IT NOW.
THAT, REALLY, WHAT YOU WANTED TO SAY WAS...

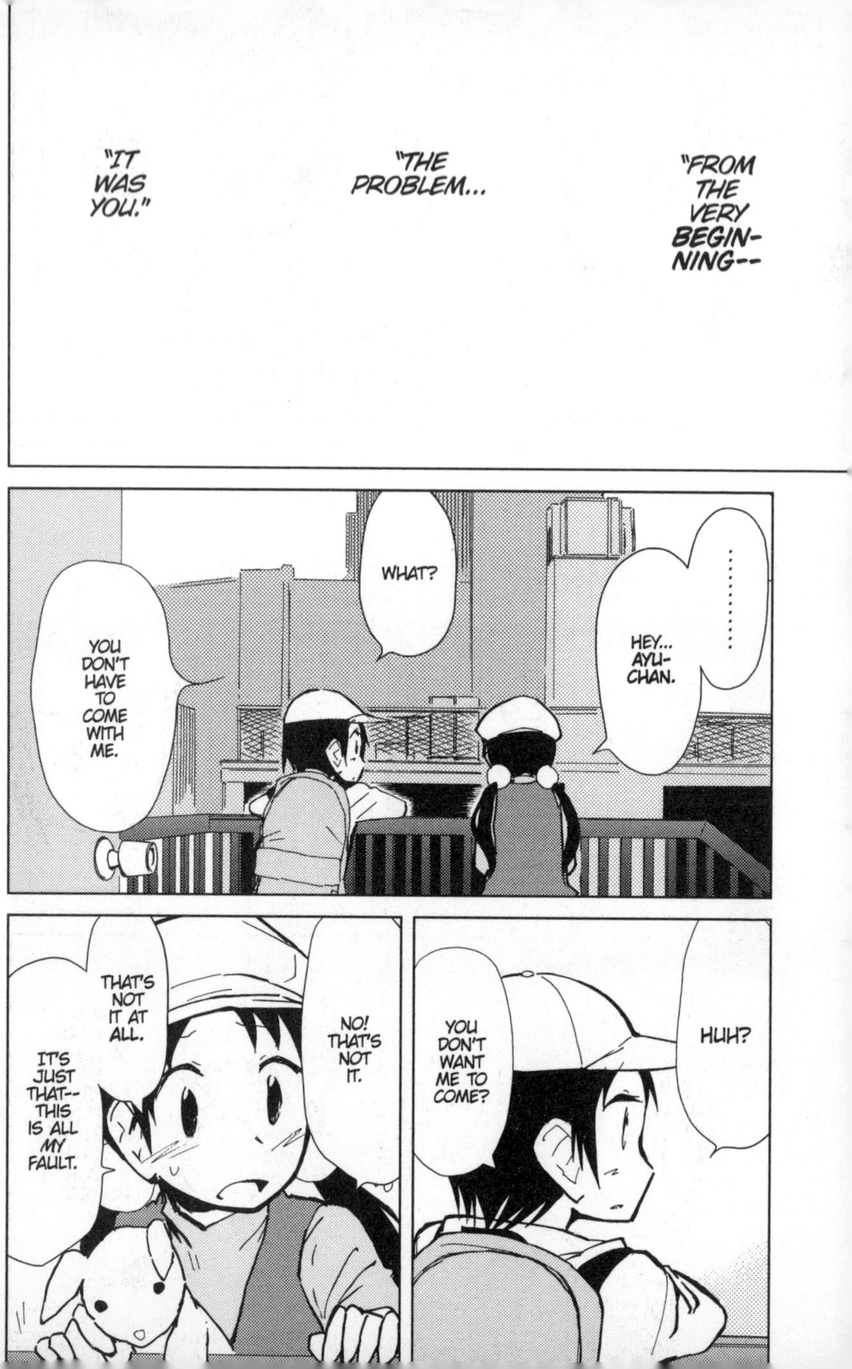
"FROM THE VERY BEGINNING--
"THE PROBLEM...
"IT WAS YOU."
......
HEY... AYU-CHAN.
WHAT?
YOU DON'T HAVE TO COME WITH ME.
HUH?
YOU DON'T WANT ME TO COME?
NO! THAT'S NOT IT.
THAT'S NOT IT AT ALL.
IT'S JUST THAT-- THIS IS ALL MY FAULT.

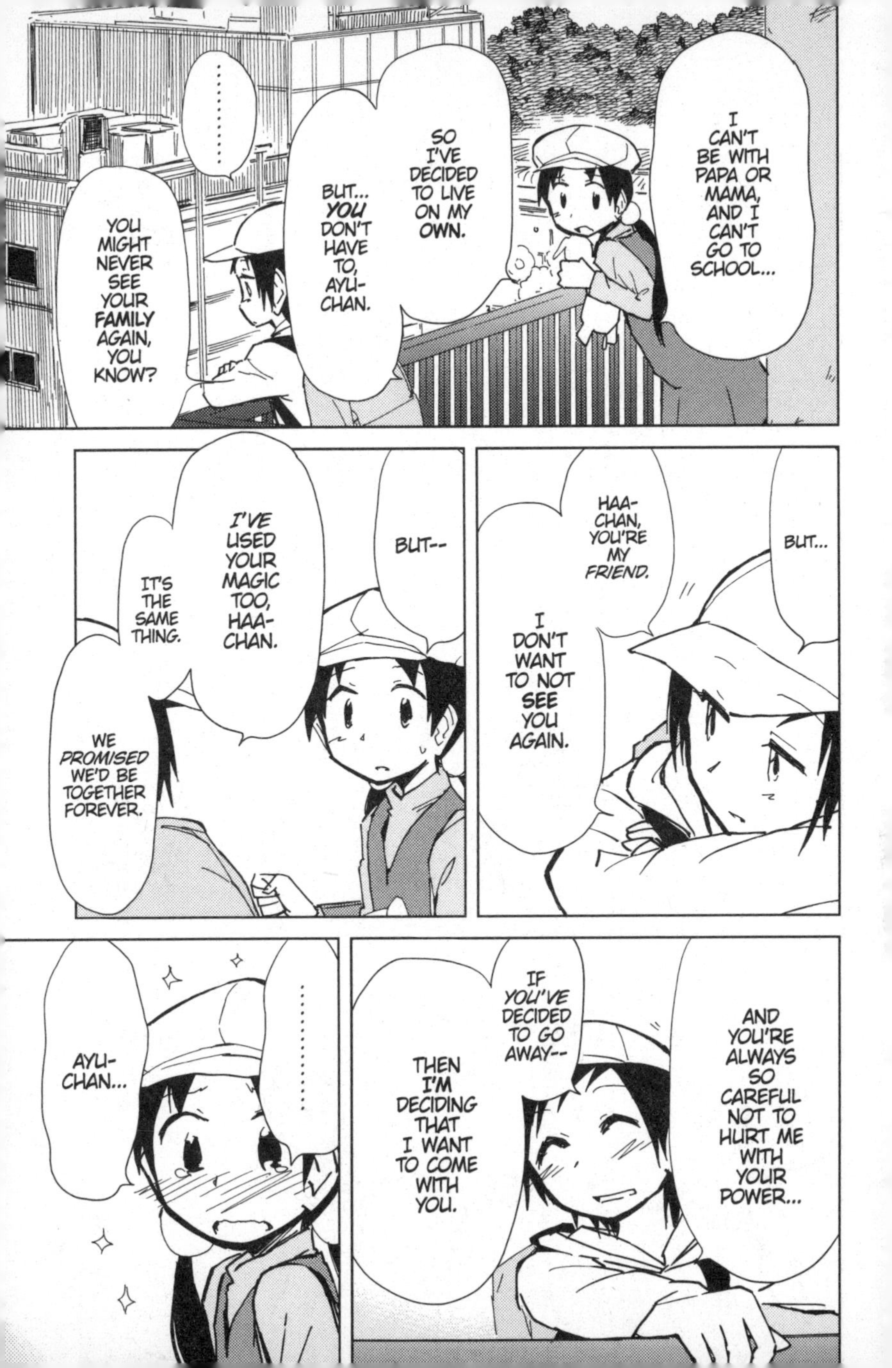
I CAN'T BE WITH PAPA OR MAMA, AND I CAN'T GO TO SCHOOL...
SO I'VE DECIDED TO LIVE ON MY **OWN.**
BUT... ***YOU*** DON'T HAVE TO, AYU-CHAN.
......
YOU MIGHT NEVER SEE YOUR **FAMILY** AGAIN, YOU KNOW?
BUT...
HAA-CHAN, YOU'RE MY *FRIEND.*
I DON'T WANT TO NOT **SEE** YOU AGAIN.
BUT--
I'VE USED YOUR MAGIC TOO, HAA-CHAN.
IT'S THE SAME THING.
WE *PROMISED* WE'D BE TOGETHER FOREVER.
AND YOU'RE ALWAYS SO CAREFUL NOT TO HURT ME WITH YOUR POWER...
IF *YOU'VE* DECIDED TO GO AWAY--
THEN *I'M* DECIDING THAT I WANT TO COME WITH YOU.
......
AYU-CHAN...

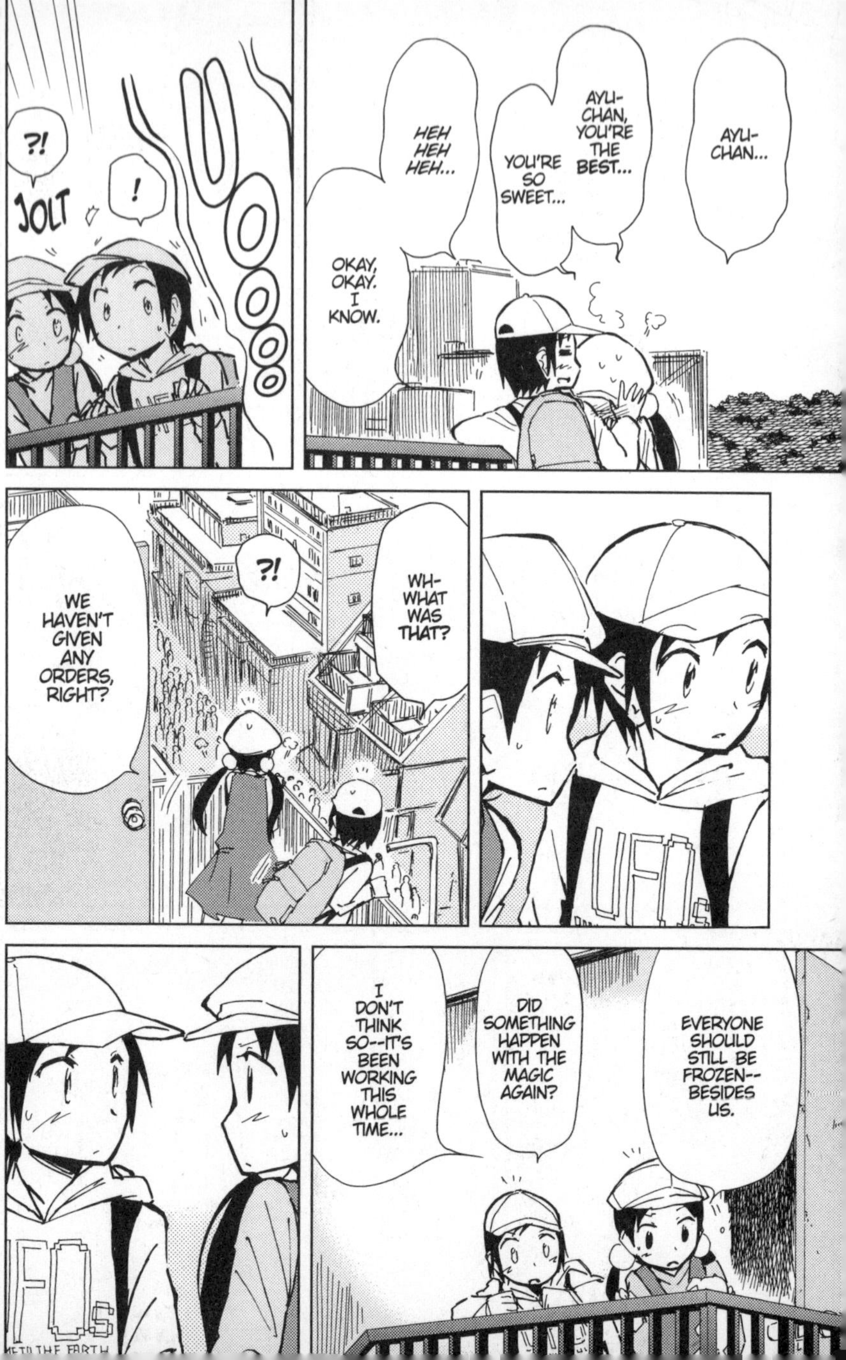
AYU-CHAN...
AYU-CHAN, YOU'RE THE BEST...
YOU'RE SO SWEET...
HEH HEH HEH...
OKAY, OKAY. I KNOW.
?!
!
JOLT
WH-WHAT WAS THAT?
?!
WE HAVEN'T GIVEN ANY ORDERS, RIGHT?
EVERYONE SHOULD STILL BE FROZEN--BESIDES US.
DID SOMETHING HAPPEN WITH THE MAGIC AGAIN?
I DON'T THINK SO--IT'S BEEN WORKING THIS WHOLE TIME...

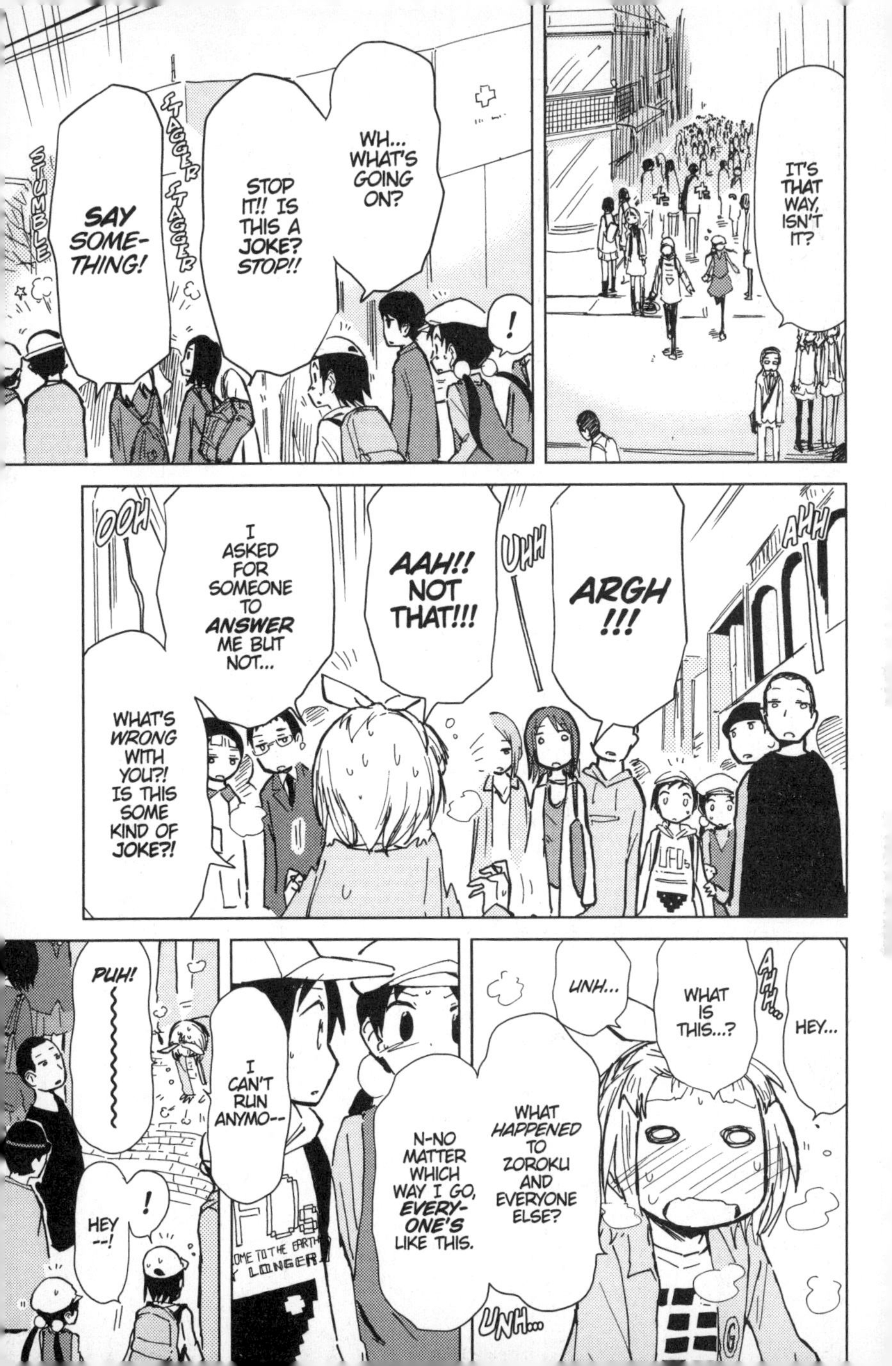
IT'S THAT WAY, ISN'T IT?
WH... WHAT'S GOING ON?
!
STOP IT!! IS THIS A JOKE? STOP!!
STAGGER STAGGER
SAY SOME-THING!
STUMBLE
AHH
ARGH!!!
UHH
AAH!! NOT THAT!!!
I ASKED FOR SOMEONE TO ANSWER ME BUT NOT...
OOH
WHAT'S WRONG WITH YOU?! IS THIS SOME KIND OF JOKE?!
HEY...
AHH...
WHAT IS THIS...?
UNH...
WHAT HAPPENED TO ZOROKU AND EVERYONE ELSE?
UNH...
N-NO MATTER WHICH WAY I GO, EVERY-ONE'S LIKE THIS.
I CAN'T RUN ANYMO--
PUH!
!
HEY--!

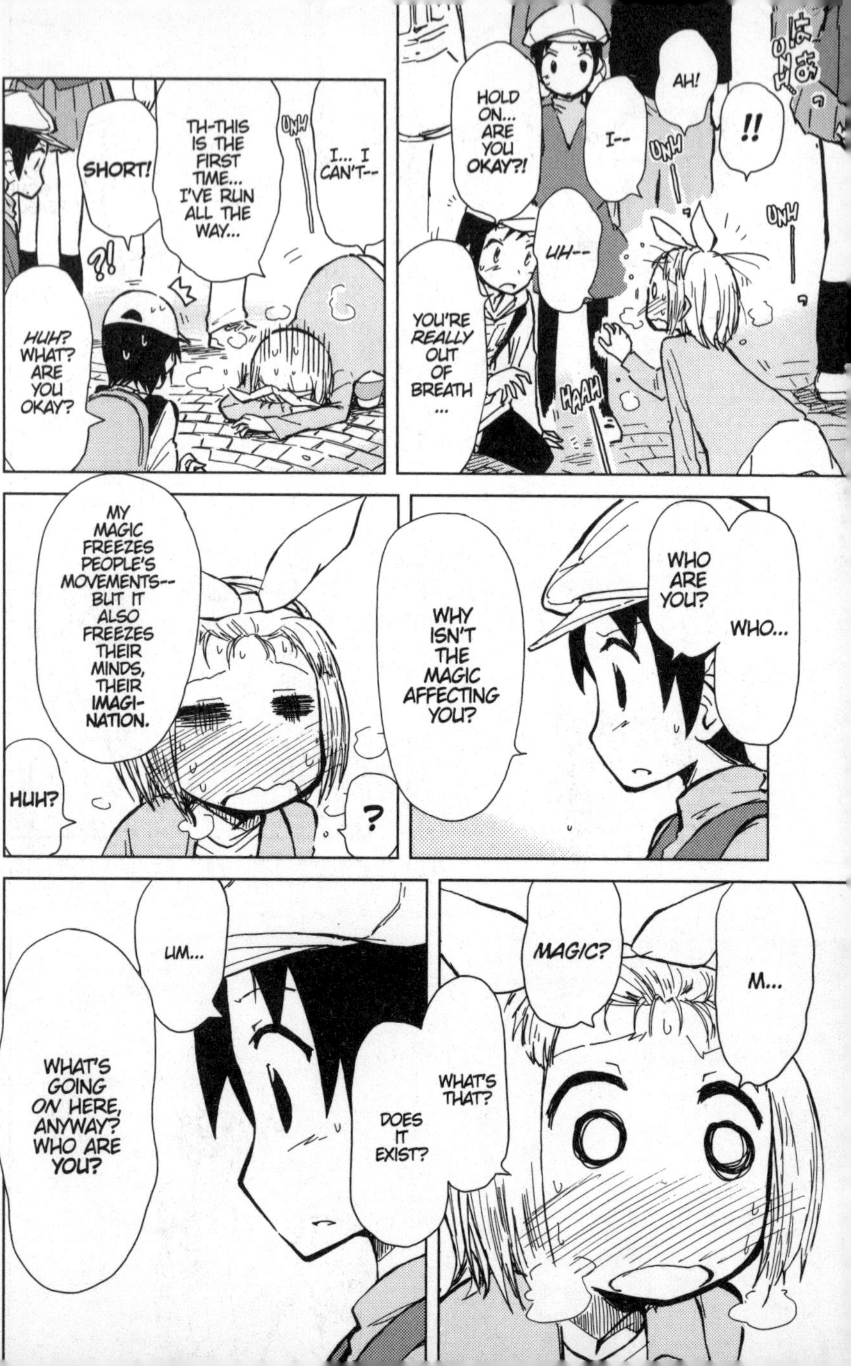
は!はあっ
UNH...
!!
AH!
UNH
I--
HOLD ON... ARE YOU OKAY?!
UH--
UNH
HAAH
YOU'RE *REALLY* OUT OF BREATH...
I... I CAN'T--
UNH
TH-THIS IS THE FIRST TIME... I'VE RUN ALL THE WAY...
SHORT!
?!
HUH? WHAT? ARE YOU OKAY?
WHO ARE YOU?
WHO...
WHY ISN'T THE MAGIC AFFECTING YOU?
?
MY MAGIC FREEZES PEOPLE'S MOVEMENTS-- BUT IT ALSO FREEZES THEIR MINDS, THEIR IMAGINATION.
HUH?
M...
MAGIC?
WHAT'S THAT?
DOES IT EXIST?
UM...
WHAT'S GOING ON HERE, ANYWAY? WHO ARE YOU?

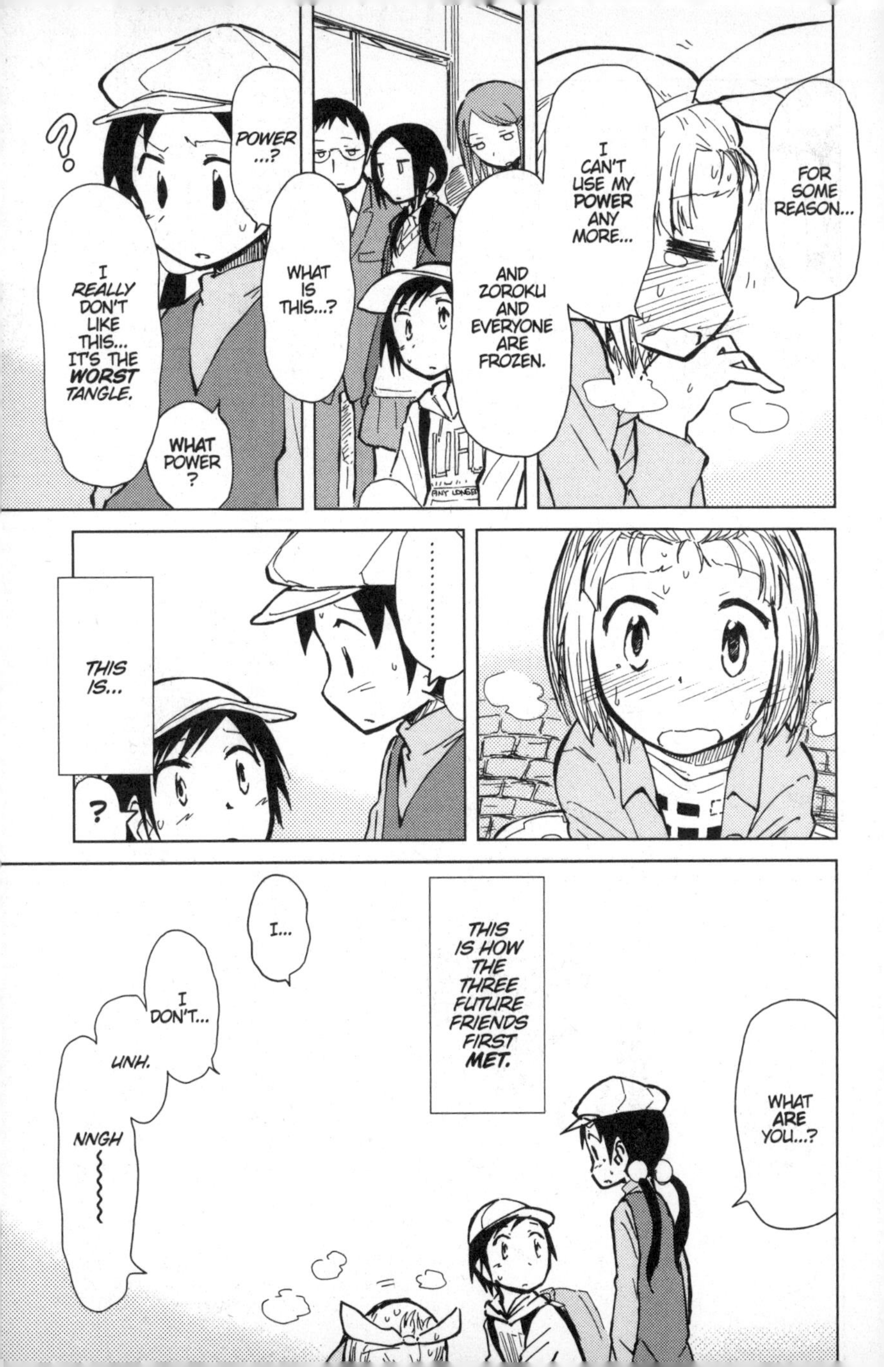
FOR SOME REASON...
I CAN'T USE MY POWER ANY MORE...
AND ZOROKU AND EVERYONE ARE FROZEN.
WHAT IS THIS...?
POWER ...?
I REALLY DON'T LIKE THIS... IT'S THE WORST TANGLE.
WHAT POWER ?
......
THIS IS...
?
WHAT ARE YOU...?
THIS IS HOW THE THREE FUTURE FRIENDS FIRST MET.
I...
I DON'T...
UNH.
NNGH ~~~

Alice & Zoroku

(3)

Editor
Kanta Inogai
(COMIC Ryu Editorial Department)

◆

Design and Formatting
AFTERGLOW

◆

Report Assistance
The People at Massa&Artists

◆

Illustration Assistants
Taro Nagami
Yuzuco Amanatsu

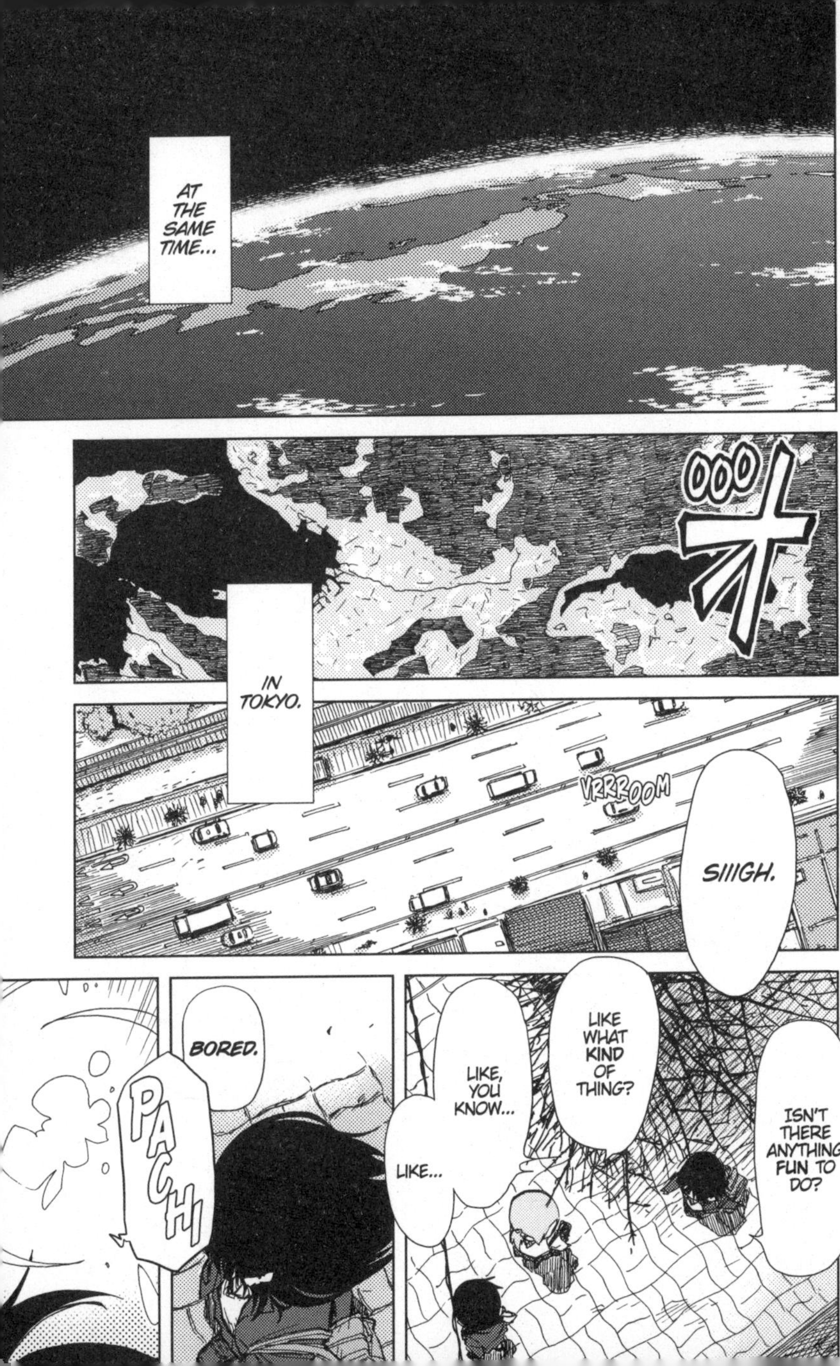
AT THE SAME TIME...
OOO
IN TOKYO.
VRRROOM
SIIIGH.
ISN'T THERE ANYTHING FUN TO DO?
LIKE WHAT KIND OF THING?
LIKE, YOU KNOW...
LIKE...
BORED.
PACHI

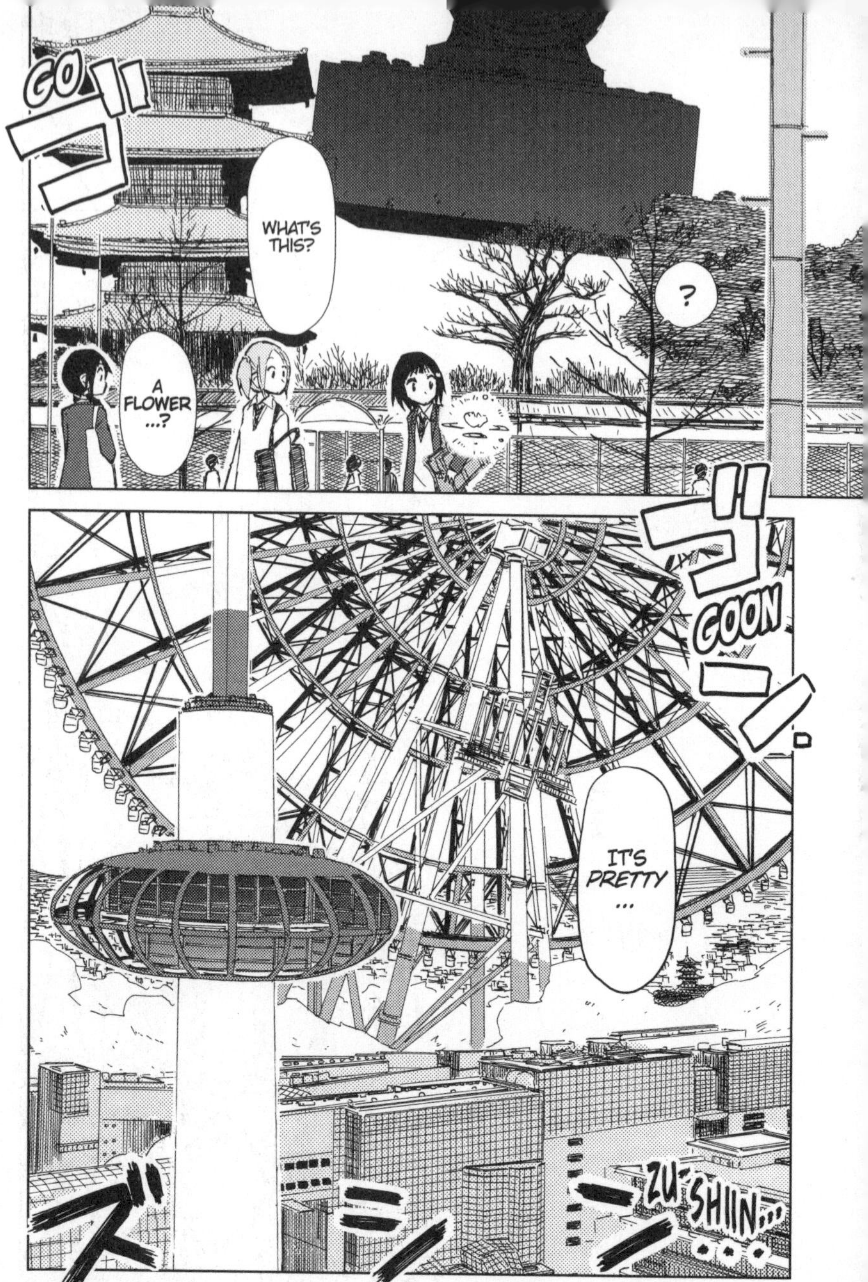
GO
?
WHAT'S THIS?
A FLOWER ...?
GOON
IT'S PRETTY ...
ZU SHIIN... ...

THE WORLD IN WHICH THE THREE WOULD SOMEDAY MEET AGAIN...

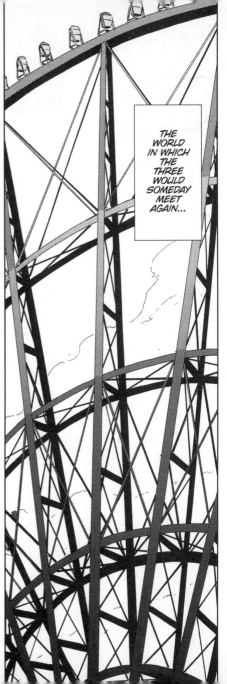

SLOWLY BEGAN TO BECOME... **WONDER-LAND.**

To be continued.........

Alice & Zoroku

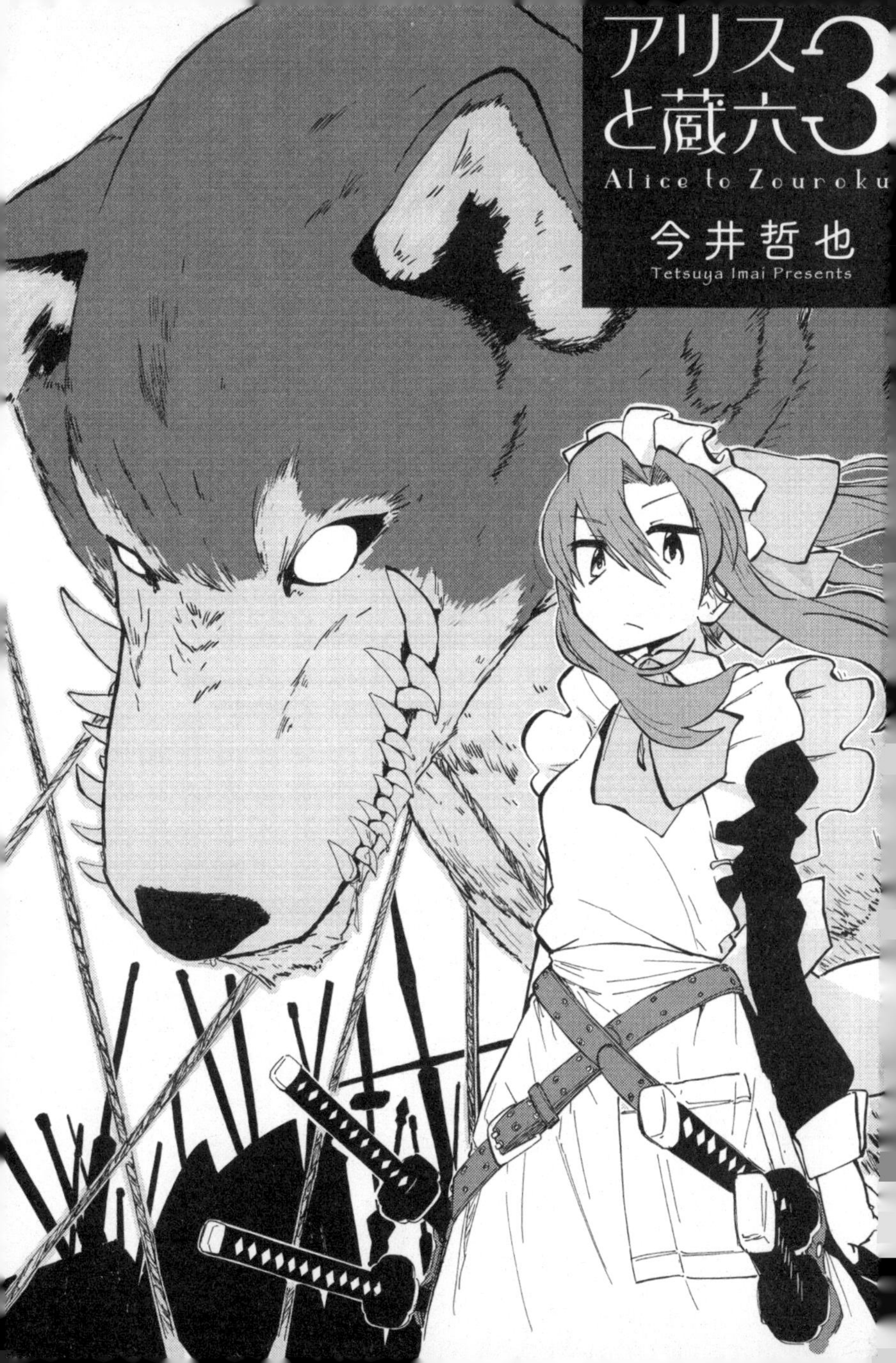
アリスと蔵六3
Alice to Zouroku
今井哲也
Tetsuya Imai Presents

SEVEN SEAS ENTERTAINMENT

3 9077 08446 8951

Alice & Zoroku

story and art by TETSUYA IMAI

VOLUME 3

TRANSLATION
Beni Axia Conrad

ADAPTATION
Maggie Cooper

LETTERING
Ludwig Sacramento

COVER DESIGN
Nicky Lim

PROOFREADER
Janet Houck
Tim Roddy

PRO

PRO

PUBLISHER
Jason DeAngelis

ALICE TO ZOROKU VOLUME 3
© TETSUYA IMAI 2014
Originally published in Japan in 2014 by TOKUMA SHOTEN PUBLISHING
CO., LTD., Tokyo. English translation rights arranged with TOKUMA SHOTEN
PUBLISHING CO., LTD., Tokyo, through TOHAN CORPORATION, Tokyo.

Seven Seas books may be purchased in bulk for promotional, educational, or

First Printing: January 2018

10 9 8 7 6 5 4 3 2 1

FOLLOW US ONLINE: *www.gomanga.com*

READING DIRECTIONS

This book reads from *right to left*, Japanese style.
If this is your first time reading manga, you start
reading from the top right panel on each page and
take it from there. If you get lost, just follow the
numbered diagram here. It may seem backwards at
first, but you'll get the hang of it! Have fun!!

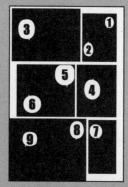